A Soup for Every Day

365 OF OUR FAVOURITE RECIPES

January

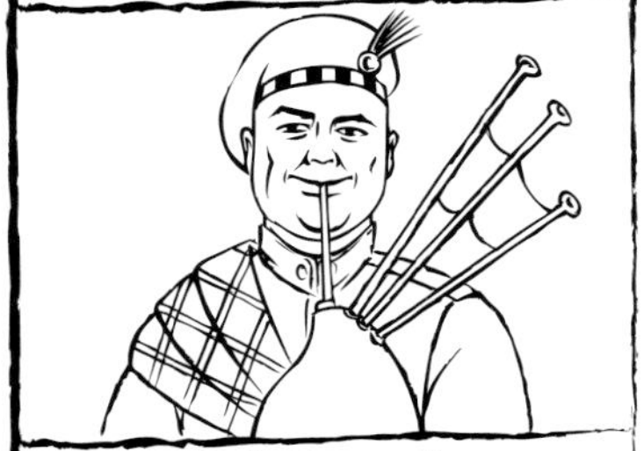

Rob Burnett
our great leader

February

Sophie Hussey
one of our chefs

March

Andrew Ovens
our creative thinker

April

Michelle Harriman
our design guru

May

Jeremy Hudson
our figures man

June

Nick Munby
guardian of our good name

July

Tim Thompson
our soup maker

August

Nicola Diogenous
our recipe queen

September

Vicki Mitchell
our Soup of the Month creator

October

Kendal Connon
new recipe perfector

November

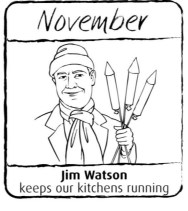

Jim Watson
keeps our kitchens running

December

Nigel Parrott
our marketing marvel

NEW COVENT GARDEN FOOD Co

A Soup for Every Day

365 OF OUR FAVOURITE RECIPES

BOXTREE

First published 2010 by Boxtree, an imprint of Pan Macmillan,
a division of Macmillan Publishers Limited
Pan Macmillan, 20 New Wharf Road, London N1 9RR
Basingstoke and Oxford
Associated companies throughout the world
www.panmacmillan.com

ISBN 978-0-75222-743-6

3 5 7 9 8 6 4

A CIP catalogue record for this book is available from the British Library.

Printed and bound in China.

Introduction

A year in soup

There's something special about soup. It's so variable and versatile, and since it's not difficult or time-consuming to make most soups, they're an easy way to a nutritious and satisfying meal.

A soup can provide the perfect beginning to the poshest dinner party or a quick and healthy snack when you're feeling peckish. It's a great way to comfort kids who are feeling under the weather or to fuel a long day's hike in the woods.

You can make the most of soup with this new book. It's packed full of ideas to suit all sorts of occasions. Indeed, you could cook a different soup every day of the year without repeating yourself.

Here at New Covent Garden Food Company, we're passionate about soup, as you might expect. Ever since we put the first fresh soups on the nation's shelves we've never rested on our ladles. Our kitchen is always buzzing with new ideas, with inspiration coming from all sorts of places: from soups that granny used to make to recipes we've come across on trips to exotic places. And all our recipes use only the freshest, in-season ingredients.

We're always adding new recipes to our cartons, but we also put them into our popular soup books for you to try at home. We now have four bestsellers under our belt, prompting more and more good soup ideas from enthusiastic readers.

Now we have selected the very best recipes, as well as tested, improved and sometimes simplified them, to find one that is just right for every situation.

Soup throughout the year

Since every day has its own soup in this book, you can find one for a hot summer's evening or a freezing winter's day. One for Valentine's Day or one for Halloween. You can even cook your loved one his or her birthday soup.

Fresh in season

These days, we're used to ingredients from around the world, but for many of us there's nothing better than fresh produce from the garden or allotment – better still the garden of someone else who has done all the work.

Soups are a great way to use fresh ingredients when they come into season. Here you'll find recipes for making the best use of the courgettes that are all ready at the same time, how to be grateful if Dad turns up with a box full of carrots and what to do when Uncle Jim produces a pheasant he shot yesterday.

Soup for enjoying life

Not every English outdoor event takes place in the blazing sunshine. A flask of soup can be a great addition to a picnic, brilliant on the touchline as the offspring compete or just the thing to accompany a long walk.

A soup is perfect for any occasion. You can take it to work, or keep some in the freezer for supper when you get home late.

Soup for the crafty cook

Most soup recipes are pretty forgiving. Few of the quantities or timings are critical, so it's easy to vary recipes according to ingredients you have to hand. View these recipes as an inspiration rather than an instruction. Experiment and invent as you go along. We do.

Adding a garnish can lift a soup from good to spectacular. Here's another way to create your own style. A sprinkling of this or a spoonful of that can make all the difference. Almost anything can be used: flavoured oils; nuts and seeds; leftover cheeses from a dinner party; fried delights – pancetta cubes, finely sliced leeks or onions, shallow fried and piled in the middle; croutons and toasties; flavoured butters; or a torn-off piece of crusty bread.

New Year Root Vegetable

Fresh for...
January
1st

Ingredients

2 tablespoons olive oil
1 parsnip, diced
1 sweet potato, diced
2 small carrots, diced
1 small red onion, diced
1 leek, sliced
2 sticks celery, diced
445ml water
1 teaspoon ground cumin
half a fresh red chilli, sliced

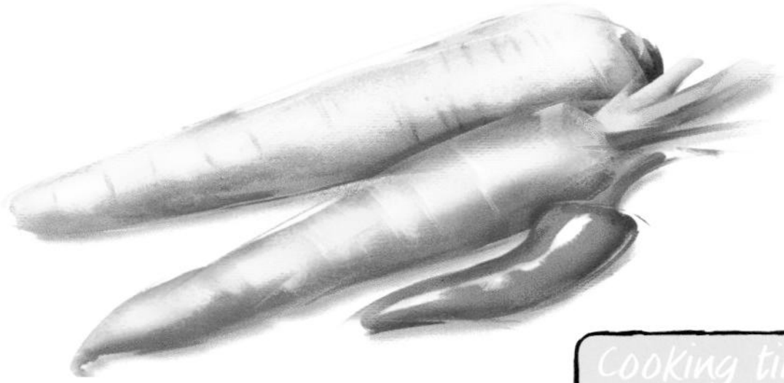

Cooking time: 45 minutes
Serves: 4

- Heat the olive oil in a saucepan, add the parsnip, sweet potato, carrots, red onion, leek and celery, then cook for 5 minutes until the vegetables have a little colour.
- Add the water, bring to the boil, then cover and cook for 20 minutes or until the vegetables are soft.
- Blend until smooth.
- Return to the pan, add the cumin and chilli, then season to taste.
- Simmer for a further 10 minutes and serve.

Fresh for...
January
2nd

Savoy Cabbage & Turnip

Ingredients

knob of butter
1 medium onion, diced
2 sticks celery, diced
1 potato, diced
1 small turnip, diced
260ml vegetable stock
25g Stilton cheese
pinch of white pepper
quarter of a savoy cabbage, finely shredded
50ml double cream

Cooking time	Serves
45 minutes	4

+ 1 HOUR SOAKING TIME

- Melt the butter in a large saucepan, then add the onion and celery and fry for 10 minutes, until softened.
- Add the potato, three-quarters of the turnip and the vegetable stock. Bring to the boil and then simmer gently for 20 minutes.
- Stir in the Stilton, then season to taste with salt and white pepper. Blend until smooth.
- Return to the heat, add the savoy cabbage and remaining turnip, then simmer gently for 15 minutes.
- Stir in the cream, heat gently for a further 10 minutes, then serve.

Carrot & Cumin

Fresh for...
January
3rd

Ingredients

50g butter
600g carrots, sliced
1 medium onion, finely diced
1 clove garlic, sliced
1 tablespoon sweet paprika
1 tablespoon ground cumin
900ml boiling water
100ml milk
2 teaspoons lemon juice
1 tablespoon chives, chopped

Cooking time: 35 minutes

Serves

- Melt the butter in a saucepan, then add the carrots, onion, garlic, paprika and cumin.
- Stir, then cover and cook on a gentle heat for 20 minutes, stirring occasionally.
- Add the boiling water, bring back to the boil, then cover and simmer for a further 10 minutes until the carrots are tender.
- Blend until completely smooth, then add the milk and lemon juice.
- Reheat gently, season to taste and serve topped with chopped chives.

Fresh for...
January
4th

Chicken Miso Broth

Ingredients

400ml chicken stock (made from concentrate or cube)
2 sachets instant miso soup
500ml boiling water
2 teaspoons Thai fish sauce
150g cooked chicken breast, sliced
150g pak choi, roughly chopped
150g pack cooked medium egg or udon noodles
4 spring onions, finely sliced into strips
soy sauce

Cooking time	Serves
10 minutes	4

- Place stock, miso sachet contents, boiling water and fish sauce in a large saucepan, bring to the boil, then reduce to a simmer.
- Add the chicken and pak choi, then cook for 2–3 minutes.
- Stir in the noodles, then continue to simmer for a further minute or so to heat the noodles.
- Serve in large flat bowls, sprinkled with spring onion and soy sauce to taste.

Roasted Tomato with Basil Purée

Fresh for...
January
5th

Ingredients

For the soup:
1.8kg ripe tomatoes
200ml extra virgin olive oil
6 large garlic cloves, crushed
4 bay leaves
4 sprigs of fresh thyme
4 sprigs of fresh rosemary
4 medium onions, finely sliced
4 sticks celery, sliced
1 medium head of fennel, sliced
half a fresh red chilli, deseeded, or to taste
2 teaspoons tomato purée
2 teaspoons sugar
1 lemon, juice of

For the basil purée:
60g fresh basil leaves
half a teaspoon of salt
4 tablespoons extra virgin olive oil
2 teaspoons balsamic vinegar

For the ciabatta croutons:
4 medium slices of ciabatta bread
1 tablespoon extra virgin olive oil
1 dessertspoon olive paste

To garnish:
a little good olive oil
6 small sprigs of fresh flat-leaf parsley or thyme

Cooking time	Serves
55 minutes	6

- Preheat the grill. Cut the tomatoes in half, then place cut side up on a baking sheet. Grill until soft and beginning to darken at the edges. Remove from the grill, then preheat the oven to 190°C/375°F/gas mark 5.
- Heat the oil in a saucepan, add the garlic and herbs, then add all the other vegetables. Cook gently for a few minutes, stirring occasionally, until the vegetables begin to soften, then transfer to a roasting tin and roast in the oven for 30 minutes until soft.
- Remove from the oven, then blend until smooth with the tomatoes, tomato purée, sugar and lemon juice. Add water if necessary to make a smooth pouring consistency. Pass through a sieve, then season to taste.
- For the basil purée: pound the basil leaves with the salt in a pestle and mortar until smooth. Add the olive oil and balsamic vinegar, then stir well.
- For the croutons: cut the ciabatta into 2cm cubes, then toss with olive oil and olive paste in a bowl. Arrange on a baking tray in a single layer, then bake in the oven for 8–10 minutes.
- Reheat the soup, then ladle into soup bowls, add a heaped teaspoon of basil purée on top and a few ciabatta croutons. Garnish with the oil and sprigs of herbs.

Fresh for...

January

6th

Cream of Artichoke

Ingredients

500ml water
1 tablespoon white wine vinegar
4 (300g) globe artichokes
850ml chicken stock
1 small onion, finely chopped
2 tablespoons fresh lemon juice
1 teaspoon fresh thyme, chopped
105ml single cream

Cooking time	Serves
50 minutes	

- Fill a large bowl with the water, then add the white wine vinegar.
- Trim the artichoke stems flush with the bottom of the artichoke so they sit flat. Slice off the top quarter of the artichoke then remove tips of the leaves, with a sharp knife. Remove the outer leaves then cut the artichokes into quarters.
- Place the artichoke quarters in the bowl of prepared water to prevent discoloration.
- With a small knife, remove the fuzzy centres, leaving the artichoke hearts intact.
- Add the stock, prepared artichokes, onion, lemon juice and thyme to a large pan, bring to the boil, then cover and simmer for 30 minutes or until the artichokes are tender.
- Drain the artichokes from the mixture and reserve the cooking liquor.
- Scrape the flesh from the base of each leaf and add to the artichoke hearts.
- Blend the artichokes and cooking liquor until smooth.
- Return to the pan, add the cream, then season to taste. Heat gently for 3 minutes, then serve. Tastes delicious served chilled.

Rich Miso Soup with Garlic

Fresh for...
January
7th

Ingredients

2 tablespoons extra virgin olive oil
4 medium onions, finely chopped
2 large garlic cloves, crushed
350g potatoes, peeled and chopped
2 medium carrots, chopped
1 teaspoon ground cumin
1 tablespoon tamari or soy sauce
1.2 litres stock (as below or made with vegetable stock cube or concentrate with 7 additional garlic cloves and 1–2 tablespoons tamari or soy sauce)
1 generous dessertspoon brown miso (available from specialist shops)

For the stock:
2 tablespoons extra virgin olive oil
4 medium onions, sliced
9 garlic cloves, peeled
3 medium carrots, chopped
2 sprigs of fresh thyme
1 teaspoon ground cumin
4 teaspoons tamari or soy sauce
1.75 litres water

Cooking time	Serves
2:15 hours & minutes	6

- For the stock: heat the oil in a saucepan, then add the onion, garlic cloves and carrots. Cover and simmer gently for 5 minutes, without browning.
- Add all the remaining stock ingredients, then cover and bring to the boil. Simmer gently for 1–1½ hours. Strain, then make up to 1.2 litres if necessary.
- For the soup: heat the oil in a saucepan, then add the onion and garlic. Cover and simmer gently for 5 minutes, without browning.
- Add the potatoes, carrots, ground cumin and tamari, then simmer gently for 5 minutes.
- Add the stock, cover, then bring to the boil. Simmer gently for about 30 minutes until the vegetables are tender.
- Cool a little then add the miso.
- Blend until smooth. Return to a clean saucepan, then reheat gently and serve.

Fresh for...
January
8th

Moroccan Chicken

Ingredients

2 tablespoons sunflower oil
2 tablespoons extra virgin olive oil
pinch of salt
600g chicken legs, jointed and skinned
2 small onions, roughly chopped
1 leek, cut into 1cm slices
2 medium carrots, roughly chopped
3 sticks celery, cut into 1cm slices
2 large garlic cloves, crushed
2 tablespoons honey
4 tablespoons raisins
3–4 teaspoons hot curry powder, to taste
1 teaspoon ground cumin
half a teaspoon of ground allspice
50g long-grain rice
1 large unwaxed lemon, thinly sliced
1 litre chicken stock

To garnish:
150ml Greek yoghurt
2 tablespoons fresh coriander, chopped

Cooking time: 40 minutes
Serves: 6

- Heat the oils together in a saucepan with a pinch of salt, then lightly brown the chicken pieces on both sides. Remove the chicken and reserve until later.
- In the same saucepan, cook the onion gently until soft, without browning.
- Add the leeks, carrots, celery and garlic, then cook for 2 minutes.
- Stir in the honey, raisins, curry, cumin and allspice over the heat for 1 minute.
- Return the chicken pieces to the pan, add the rice and lemon, then stir to coat in the spices.
- Add the stock, stir well, then bring to the boil. Cover, then simmer gently for 20–25 minutes until the chicken is cooked, stirring occasionally.
- Remove the chicken meat from the bones, then return to the pan. Season to taste, then serve garnished with a swirl of yoghurt and a sprinkling of fresh coriander.

Fresh for...
January
9th

Duck Noodle Soup*

Ingredients

2.25 litres well-flavoured duck stock (see below) with fat skimmed off
3 tablespoons soy sauce
2 and a half tablespoons of rice wine or dry sherry
2 tablespoons rice or cider vinegar
2 tablespoons Demerara sugar
1 star anise
3 cloves
10cm cinnamon stick
2.5cm piece fresh root ginger, cut into fine matchsticks
2 carrots, cut into fine matchsticks
1 red chilli, deseeded then cut into thin rings
8 spring onions, shredded
1 and a half layers of Chinese egg thread noodles
scraps of duck from the carcass
175g bean curd, cubed

For the stock:
1 duck carcass and, if available, giblets (not liver) and skin
1 onion, quartered
1 carrot, sliced
2 celery sticks, sliced
1 bay leaf
3 sprigs of parsley
2 sprigs of thyme
6 black peppercorns

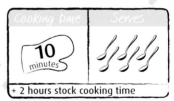

Cooking time	Serves
10 minutes	4

+ 2 hours stock cooking time

- For the stock: put all the stock ingredients in a saucepan then cover generously with water. Bring to the boil, then simmer gently for 2–3 hours, occasionally skimming off any scum that rises to the top. Add more boiling water if necessary. Strain, then cool. If you have time, chill overnight in the fridge and lift off the congealed fat from the surface the next day. Otherwise skim off as much fat as you can.
- For the soup: add the stock to a saucepan with the soy sauce, rice wine, vinegar, sugar, star anise, cloves, cinnamon and ginger.
- Cover, then bring gently to the boil, add the carrots and simmer for 2 minutes. Add the chilli, spring onions and noodles. Simmer for a further 2 minutes until the noodles are cooked and then gently stir in the scraps of duck and the bean curd.
- Heat through for 1 minute, season to taste, then serve.

* From Sophie Grigson's Meat Course, 1995.

Fresh for...
January
10th

Moroccan Chickpea & Spinach

Ingredients

2 tablespoons extra virgin olive oil
3 medium onions, finely chopped
2 garlic cloves, crushed
1 and a half teaspoons of ground cinnamon
1 teaspoon chilli powder (or to taste)
2 tablespoons tomato purée
150g dried apricots, chopped
half a lemon, finely grated rind of
4 teaspoons lemon juice
1.5 litres vegetable stock
250g chickpeas
200g fresh spinach, shredded

To garnish:
150ml natural yoghurt

Cooking time: 35 minutes

Serves

- Heat the oil in a saucepan, add the onions, then cover and cook gently for 5 minutes, without browning.
- Add the garlic and spices then cook, stirring, for 1 minute.
- Add the tomato purée, then cook for 3 minutes.
- Add the apricots, lemon rind and juice, stock and chickpeas.
- Cover and simmer for 20 minutes, until the chickpeas are tender.
- Blend until smooth.
- Return to a clean saucepan, then stir in the spinach. Cover and simmer for 5 minutes until the spinach has wilted.
- Season to taste, then serve garnished with a swirl of yoghurt.

Jerusalem Artichoke & Spinach with Parmesan croutons

Fresh for...
January
11th

Ingredients

25g butter
1 small onion, finely chopped
350g Jerusalem artichokes, finely sliced
570ml chicken stock
freshly grated nutmeg
175g young spinach leaves, washed and stalks removed
275ml milk
2 tablespoons double cream (optional)

For the Parmesan croutons:
3 tablespoons sunflower oil
3 slices fresh white bread, crusts removed
3 tablespoons freshly grated Parmesan cheese

Cooking time: 40 minutes
Serves

- Heat the butter in a saucepan, add the onion, then cover and cook gently until soft, without browning.
- Add the artichokes, then cook for 10 minutes, stirring occasionally.
- Add the stock, then season with salt, pepper and nutmeg. Cover, bring to the boil, then simmer gently for 20 minutes until the artichokes are tender.
- Meanwhile, make the Parmesan croutons. Cut the bread into 1cm cubes. Heat the oil in a frying pan until very hot, then fry the bread until crisp and golden. Put the Parmesan onto a sheet of greaseproof paper and then quickly toss the croutons in the Parmesan, ensuring they remain separate and do not become too clogged with cheese.
- Stir the spinach leaves into the soup and blend until smooth. Add the milk and cream, if using, season to taste, then reheat.
- Serve with the Parmesan croutons. Tastes delicious served chilled too.

Fresh for...
January
12th

Salsify with Mustard Seed

Ingredients

50g butter
1 large onion, finely chopped
1 tablespoon black mustard seeds
1 tablespoon white mustard seeds
1kg salsify, scraped and chopped
1.5 litres vegetable stock
1 lemon, juice of

To garnish:
150ml crème fraîche

Cooking time	Serves
40 minutes	

- Melt the butter in a saucepan, add the onion, then cover and cook gently for 5 minutes, without browning.
- Add the mustard seeds, then cook for 1 minute until they begin to pop.
- Add the salsify, then cook for 3 minutes, stirring occasionally.
- Add the vegetable stock, then cover, bring to the boil and simmer for 20 minutes until the vegetables are tender. Season to taste, then add the lemon juice to taste.
- Cool a little, then blend roughly.
- Reheat gently, then serve with a swirl of crème fraîche.

Beef & Green Split Pea

Fresh for...
January
13th

Ingredients

450g green split peas, soaked overnight and washed
450g shin of beef and soup bone (if available)
450g potatoes, peeled and roughly chopped
3 litres water
700g leeks, finely sliced
1 medium celeriac, peeled and cut into 4cm sticks

To garnish:
3 tablespoons celery leaves, chopped

Cooking time: 3:10 hours & minutes
Serves: 6

- Into a large saucepan add the pre-soaked split peas, beef and bone, potatoes and water.
- Cover, then bring to the boil and simmer for at least 2 hours, occasionally skimming off any scum.
- Remove the beef, then shred into small pieces.
- Squash the vegetables against the side of the pan with a wooden spoon.
- Return the meat to the pan along with the leeks and celeriac.
- Season to taste, then cover and simmer gently for 1 hour.
- Remove the soup bone, then serve hot, garnished with celery leaves.

Fresh for...
January
14th

Butternut Squash & Pancetta

Ingredients

100g pancetta, cubed
a handful fresh sage leaves
50g butter
2 medium onions, finely sliced
3 cloves garlic, sliced
1 large butternut squash, roughly chopped
1 litre water
125ml single cream

Cooking time	Serves
40 minutes	

- Fry the pancetta in a frying pan until crisp. Add the sage leaves, fry for a minute, then drain and set aside.
- Meanwhile, melt the butter in a saucepan, then add the onions, garlic and butternut squash.
- Sweat the vegetables for 10 minutes until softened, without browning.
- Add the water, then bring to the boil. Cover, then simmer for 15–20 minutes until soft.
- Blend until smooth, then add the set-aside pancetta and sage leaves.
- Reheat gently for 5 minutes, stir in the cream, then season to taste and serve.

Three Onion Soup

Fresh for...
January
15th

Ingredients

4 tablespoons extra virgin olive oil
750g red onions, finely sliced
340g shallots, finely sliced
3 teaspoons plain flour
2 teaspoons mustard
1.2 litres chicken stock
4 sprigs of fresh thyme
3 tablespoons Greek yoghurt

To garnish:
1 bunch spring onions, finely sliced

Cooking time	Serves
1:05 hour & minutes	4

- Heat the oil in a saucepan, then fry the red onions and shallots for 20–30 minutes, stirring frequently, until golden and caramelised.
- Stir in the flour and mustard, then cook gently for 2 minutes.
- Add the stock and thyme, then bring to the boil, stirring well.
- Cover and simmer for 30 minutes. Remove from the heat and remove the thyme sprigs.
- Stir in the yoghurt and season to taste.
- Scatter the soup with the spring onions, then serve.

Fresh for...
January
16th

Celeriac & Wild Mushroom

Ingredients

50g butter
1 medium onion, finely chopped
110g celeriac, peeled and roughly chopped
15g dried porcini or cep mushrooms, soaked for 20 minutes in 150ml boiling water
290ml water
200ml crème fraîche
1 tablespoon fresh dill, chopped

Cooking time	Serves
35 minutes	4

- Melt the butter in a saucepan, add the onion and celeriac, then cover and cook gently for 10 minutes, without browning.
- Strain the liquor from soaking the mushrooms into the pan. Chop the strained mushrooms, then add to the pan.
- Add the water, cover, then bring to the boil. Simmer gently for 15 minutes or until the vegetables are tender.
- Blend until smooth.
- Stir in the crème fraîche and dill, then season to taste.
- Reheat gently, and then serve.

Cream of Turnip with Smoked Ham

Fresh for...
January
17th

Ingredients

50g butter
1 medium onion, finely chopped
675g turnip, peeled and cut into 2.5cm dice
250g potatoes, peeled and cut into 2.5cm dice
1 thick lime slice, including skin
850ml vegetable stock
2 tablespoons crème fraîche
1 teaspoon chilli sauce (or to taste)
250g smoked ham, cut into 2.5cm slivers

To garnish:
slivers of smoked ham
1 lime, rind of

Cooking time	Serves
45 minutes	4

- Melt the butter in a saucepan, add the onion, turnip, potatoes and lime, then cover and cook for 5 minutes without browning.
- Add the stock, then cover and bring to the boil. Simmer gently for 30 minutes or until the vegetables are very tender.
- Blend until smooth, ensuring the lime is well puréed too.
- Return to a clean saucepan, then stir in the crème fraîche, chilli sauce and smoked ham. Season to taste.
- Reheat gently, then serve garnished with the smoked ham slivers and lime rind.

Fresh for...
January
18th

Carrot & Ginger

Ingredients

1 tablespoon olive oil
1 small onion, diced
8 medium carrots, diced
1 teaspoon ginger, puréed
500ml chicken stock

Cooking time	Serves
35 minutes	

- Heat the olive oil in a saucepan, add the onion, then cook gently for 5 minutes without browning.
- Add the carrots, ginger and stock, then bring to the boil. Cover and simmer for 20 minutes until the carrots are soft.
- Blend until smooth.
- Return to the pan, season to taste, then heat gently and serve.

Vietnamese Tofu & Noodles

Fresh for... January 19th

Ingredients

8 tablespoons groundnut oil
2 small onions, finely chopped
4 sticks lemongrass, outer leaves removed and finely chopped
5cm piece fresh ginger, peeled and finely chopped
4 cloves garlic, peeled and finely chopped
1.2 litres vegetable stock
8 fresh Kaffir lime leaves
225g tofu, cubed
1 packet (410g) fresh noodles

To garnish:
selection of leaves, torn (we use: baby spinach, coriander and mint)
bean sprouts
cucumber, cut into finely sliced strips
roasted raw peanuts

For the dressing:
2 tablespoons Thai fish sauce
4 tablespoons water
2 tablespoons sweet chilli sauce
1 lemon, juice of
2 garlic cloves, peeled and cut into slivers
sugar, to taste

Cooking time: 35 minutes

Serves: 4

- Put the oil into a saucepan, heat gently, then add the onion, lemongrass, ginger and garlic. Cook for 2 minutes, without browning.
- Add the vegetable stock and lime leaves, then simmer for 20 minutes.
- Add the tofu, then simmer for a further 5 minutes.
- Meanwhile, soak the noodles in boiling water for 5 minutes, then drain and divide into 4 soup bowls.
- Ladle the broth into the bowls, then top with the garnish ingredients.
- Place all the dressing ingredients in a bowl, then whisk well together. Serve as an accompaniment to the soup.

Fresh for...
January
20th

Russian Vegetable Soup*

Ingredients

50g butter
1 medium onion, finely chopped
225g potatoes, peeled and sliced
110g parsnips, sliced
110g carrots, sliced
50g cabbage, finely sliced
2 tablespoons freshly chopped flat-leaf parsley
half a teaspoon of dried mixed herbs
nutmeg, freshly grated, to taste
1.2 litres vegetable stock

To garnish:
1 small leek, cut into 5cm strips

Cooking time	Serves
50 minutes	4

- Melt half the butter in a saucepan, add the vegetables, then cover and cook gently for 10 minutes, without browning.
- Add the parsley, herbs, nutmeg and stock, then bring to the boil. Cover, then simmer gently for 30 minutes.
- Blend until smooth, then season to taste.
- Meanwhile, melt the remaining butter, then fry the leek strips until crisp. Drain on kitchen paper.
- Reheat the soup, then serve garnished with the crisp leek strips.

* Reproduced with the kind permission of Orion Books from the Cranks Recipe Book by Cranks Restaurants.

Jersusalem Artichoke & Carrot

Fresh for...
January
21st

Ingredients

25g butter
1 medium onion, finely chopped
400g Jerusalem artichokes, peeled and chopped
350g carrots, 240g roughly chopped, 110g grated
1 stick celery, roughly chopped
900ml vegetable stock
110ml milk

To garnish:
1 tablespoon sunflower oil
3 rashers unsmoked streaky bacon, chopped
150ml single cream

Cooking time: 35 minutes
Serves: 4

- Melt the butter in a saucepan, add the onion, then cover and cook gently until soft, without browning.
- Add the artichokes, roughly chopped carrots and celery, then cook gently for 2 minutes.
- Add the vegetable stock, then cover and bring to the boil. Simmer gently for 20 minutes until the vegetables are tender.
- Meanwhile, heat the oil for the garnish and sauté the chopped bacon over a moderate heat until crisp. Drain on kitchen paper.
- Blend the soup until smooth, then return to a clean saucepan.
- Stir in the grated carrot and milk, season to taste, then cover and simmer gently for a further 5 minutes.
- Serve garnished with a swirl of cream and sprinkled with crispy bacon.

Fresh for...
January
22nd

Roasted Butternut Squash

Ingredients

900g butternut squash, halved and seeds removed
40g butter
350g potatoes
1.2 litres vegetable stock
100ml single cream

To garnish:
3 tablespoons sunflower seeds, toasted

Cooking time	Serves
1:25 hour & minutes	6

- Preheat the oven to 160°C/325°F/Gas Mark 3.
- Place the butternut squash in a roasting tin with 25g of the butter dotted around it. Bake for 1 hour until softened and slightly caramelised.
- Melt the remaining butter in a saucepan, add the potatoes and stock, then simmer for 20 minutes until the potatoes are tender.
- Allow the butternut squash to cool a little, then scoop the flesh out of its skin into the saucepan with the potatoes.
- Blend until smooth, then pour into a clean saucepan, stir in the cream, then season to taste.
- Reheat gently, then serve garnished with the toasted sunflower seeds.

Thai Prawn & Noodle Broth

Fresh for...
January
23rd

Ingredients

18 tiger prawns, raw, with shells
1 litre fish stock
2 sticks lemongrass, finely sliced
10g (bunch) coriander, leaves and stalks separated
4 cloves garlic, peeled and finely sliced
2 tablespoons soy sauce
2cm piece fresh root ginger, peeled and finely sliced
1 large red chilli, deseeded and finely sliced
100g medium egg noodles
1 lime, juice of
3 spring onions, finely sliced diagonally
1 tablespoon mint leaves, shredded

Cooking time	Serves
30 minutes	

- Remove the heads and shells from the prawns, leaving the tails on, then remove the veins.
- Place all the shells in a large pan, then add the fish stock and 1 litre of water. Add the lemongrass, coriander stalks and half the garlic. Bring to the boil, skim, then simmer for 20 minutes.
- Strain the stock into a clean pan, then add the soy sauce, ginger, chilli and remaining garlic.
- Add the noodles and prawns, then simmer for 3–4 minutes until the noodles and prawns are cooked.
- Add the lime juice, then serve sprinkled with the spring onions, coriander and mint.

Fresh for...
January
24th

Beef Stroganoff

Ingredients

50g butter
4 tablespoons sunflower oil
2 medium onions, finely sliced
400g chestnut mushrooms, finely sliced
1 clove garlic, finely sliced
750g fillet steak, cut into thin slivers
3 tablespoons brandy
3 x 142ml tubs soured cream
3 tablespoons lemon juice
1–2 teaspoons paprika
Worcestershire sauce, to taste
1–2 tablespoons fresh parsley, chopped

Cooking time	Serves
25 minutes	6

- Heat a large, heavy-bottomed frying pan over a medium heat, add the butter and 2 tablespoons of oil, then add the onions and fry for 5–10 minutes until soft.
- Add the mushrooms and garlic, then fry quickly until tender. Pour into a dish and set aside.
- Heat the pan once again until hot, adding a little oil. Fry the steak in batches over a high heat until lightly browned.
- Return all the steak to the pan, add the brandy, then stir to soak in all the pan juices and cook off the alcohol.
- Return the mushrooms and onions to the pan, then add the soured cream, lemon juice and paprika. Add the Worcestershire sauce, then season to taste.
- Heat gently, then serve sprinkled with a little more paprika and parsley.

Fresh for...
January 25th

Haggis, Neeps & Tatties

Ingredients

half a small haggis, wrapped in foil
25g butter
3 small shallots, finely chopped
2 medium potatoes, diced
1 small swede, diced
425ml vegetable stock
1 tablespoon fresh parsley, chopped
3 tablespoons whisky

Cooking time	Serves
45 minutes	

- Add the haggis to a saucepan of water, then simmer for 40 minutes (or according to the instructions on the pack).
- Meanwhile, melt the butter in a saucepan, add the shallots, then cook until softened, without browning.
- Add the potatoes, swede and stock, then bring to the boil. Cover, then simmer gently for 30 minutes until the vegetables are tender. Season to taste.
- Remove the haggis from its pan and remove the foil. Divide across the serving bowls, creating small piles in the centres.
- Ladle the soup into the bowls, sprinkle with parsley and a splash of whisky, and then serve.

Fresh for...
January
26th

Sweet Potato, Cauliflower & Spinach Dhal

Ingredients

1 tablespoon olive oil
1 large onion, finely diced
2 cloves garlic, crushed
1 teaspoon ground cumin
1 teaspoon ground coriander
1 teaspoon turmeric
1 teaspoon hot chilli powder
2cm piece fresh root ginger, peeled and grated
250g red lentils
900ml hot vegetable stock
2 large sweet potatoes, peeled and diced into 2cm cubes
1 medium cauliflower, cut into small florets
1 bay leaf
235g spinach leaves, washed
200g low fat yoghurt
20g fresh coriander, chopped
1 lemon, cut into wedges

Cooking time	Serves
35 minutes	

- Heat the oil in a pan, then fry the onions over a medium heat for 5–10 minutes.
- Add the garlic, spices and ginger, then fry for a further 2–3 minutes to release the aromatic flavours.
- Add the lentils and hot stock, stir, then scrape the base of the pan to mix all the spices.
- Add the sweet potato, cauliflower and bay leaf and bring to the boil. Cover, then simmer gently for 15 minutes.
- Gently stir in the spinach to avoid breaking up the other vegetables, cover, then cook for a further 3–5 minutes to wilt the spinach.
- Stir through the yoghurt and fresh coriander, season to taste, then serve garnished with lemon wedges.

Leek & Potato

Fresh for...
January
27th

Ingredients

25g butter
half a small onion, diced
3 small leeks, finely diced
2 medium floury potatoes (such as Maris Piper), diced
600ml water
2 new waxy potatoes (such as Estima), diced into small cubes
50ml single cream
75ml milk

Cooking time: 50 minutes
Serves

- Melt the butter in a saucepan, add the onion and two-thirds of the leeks, then sweat for 10 minutes until the onion starts to soften.
- Stir in the floury potatoes, then cook for 5 minutes.
- Add the water and bring to the boil. Cover and simmer for 10 minutes until the potatoes and leeks are soft.
- Blend until smooth, then stir in the waxy potatoes and remaining leeks. Cook gently for a further 10 minutes until the potatoes and leeks are soft, stirring frequently.
- Stir in the cream and milk, then reheat gently.
- Season to taste using salt and ground white pepper, then serve.

Fresh for...
January
28th

Bacon, Jerusalem Artichoke & Porcini Mushroom

Ingredients

25g dried porcini mushrooms
25g unsalted butter
1 small onion, diced
1 clove garlic, chopped
100g bacon lardons
150g mushrooms, sliced
8 Jerusalem artichokes, peeled and diced
360ml vegetable stock
2 tablespoons double cream
1 teaspoon parsley, chopped

Cooking time: 45 minutes + overnight soaking

Serves

- Soak the dried porcini mushrooms in enough hot water to cover them and leave overnight.
- Melt the butter in a pan, then add the onion, garlic and bacon lardons. Cook for 5 minutes or until lightly browned.
- Add the sliced mushrooms to the pan, then cook for a further 5 minutes.
- Add the Jerusalem artichokes and cook for 3 minutes.
- Drain the porcini mushrooms and add to the pan along with the vegetable stock. Cover, then cook for 30 minutes.
- Blend until smooth.
- Return to the pan, add the cream and parsley, then season to taste. Reheat gently and serve.

Minestrone with Meatballs

Fresh for...
January 29th

Ingredients

2 tablespoons olive oil
1 medium onion, chopped
1 clove garlic, crushed
1 tablespoon tomato purée
1 red pepper, deseeded and diced
1 x 400g tin chopped tomatoes
300ml chicken stock
50g small pasta shapes
sugar, to taste
1 tablespoon fresh basil, chopped

For the meatballs:
250g minced beef, lean
1 handful white breadcrumbs, fresh
half an onion, grated
half an egg, beaten
1 teaspoon fresh oregano, chopped
1 tablespoon olive oil

Cooking time: 40 minutes
Serves: 4

- For the meatballs: combine all the meatball ingredients together in a bowl, then shape into small balls (about the size of a cherry). Fry in olive oil until cooked, then set aside.
- For the soup: heat the oil in a pan, then add the onion and cook gently for 5 minutes until soft, without browning.
- Add the garlic, tomato purée and red pepper, then cook for a further 5 minutes.
- Add the tomatoes, stock and pasta, then season to taste with salt, pepper and sugar. Cook for 15 minutes until pasta is soft.
- Add the meatballs and basil, reheat gently for 5 minutes, then serve.

Fresh for...
January
30th

Chicken & Lemon (Greek Avgolemone)

Ingredients

2 chicken breasts
2 litres chicken stock
125g long-grain rice
2-3 lemons, juice of, to taste
3 eggs

Cooking time	Serves
45 minutes	

- Place the chicken and stock in a saucepan, then cover and cook gently for 20 minutes to poach the chicken. Remove the chicken, shred using 2 forks, then set aside.
- Add the rice and lemon juice and season to taste, then cook for 15 minutes until the rice is cooked.
- Meanwhile, beat the eggs in a bowl, add 3 ladles of stock from the saucepan, gently, whisking at all times.
- Remove the saucepan from the heat, then add the beaten eggs, stirring continuously to thicken the soup.
- Add the poached chicken, season to taste, adding more lemon juice if required. Reheat gently, then serve.

Chestnut Mushroom & Parsley

Fresh for...
January
31st

Ingredients

25g butter
1 medium onion, finely chopped
1 garlic clove, finely chopped
40g plain flour
700ml vegetable stock
250g chestnut mushrooms, sliced
3 tablespoons fresh flat-leaf parsley, finely chopped
75ml single cream

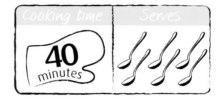

Cooking time: 40 minutes
Serves: 6

- Melt half the butter in a saucepan, then add the onion and garlic, cover, and cook gently for 5 minutes, without browning.
- Add the flour and cook gently for 1 minute, stirring continuously.
- Gradually add the stock, stirring all the time.
- Add half the mushrooms and the parsley. Cover, bring to the boil and simmer gently for 10–15 minutes until the vegetables are tender. Blend until smooth.
- In the remaining butter, fry the remaining mushrooms for 5 minutes until they begin to brown, then add to the blended soup. Simmer gently for a further 3 minutes.
- Stir in the cream, season to taste, then serve.

Fresh for...
February
1st

Tenderstem Broccoli & Dolcelatte*

Ingredients

2 tablespoons olive oil
1 small onion, finely chopped
2 cloves garlic, crushed
1 small potato, diced
500g tenderstem broccoli, cut into 5cm pieces
1 litre hot vegetable stock
130g Dolcelatte cheese, diced
1 tablespoon parsley, finely chopped
4 tablespoons double cream
30g shelled walnuts, finely chopped

Cooking time: 25 minutes
Serves: 6

- Heat the oil in a saucepan, add the onion, garlic and potato, then sweat for 10 minutes without browning.
- Add the broccoli and hot stock, then bring to a rapid boil. Cover and simmer for 6–8 minutes until the broccoli is just tender but has not lost its colour.
- Add the Dolcelatte and parsley, then stir until the cheese has melted.
- Blend before reheating, and season to taste.
- Serve with a drizzle of cream and a scattering of walnuts.

* Dolcelatte® is a registered trademark of Galbani.

Red Onion Soup
with Goat's Cheese Toasts

Fresh for...
February
2nd

Ingredients

4 tablespoons olive oil
25g butter
1.3kg red onions, finely sliced
3 cloves garlic, crushed
1 tablespoon thyme, finely chopped
100ml Marsala wine or port
1.2 litres hot beef stock

For the goat's cheese toasts:
300g goat's cheese log, cut into thin slices
half a pain parisien or French bread, cut diagonally into 1cm slices

- Heat the oil and butter in a wide, heavy-based saucepan, then fry the onions over a medium heat for 25–30 minutes, stirring frequently to avoid sticking.
- Add the garlic and thyme, then fry for 2–3 minutes. Add the Marsala wine or port, then continue to cook until the liquid has reduced by half.
- Add the hot stock, then cover and simmer for 20 minutes.
- Meanwhile, make the goat's cheese toasts. Ensure your bread slices fit into your soup bowls and that the goat's cheese log is the same width as the bread (if it's not, then crumble the goat's cheese rather than slicing it).
- Lightly toast the bread on both sides and place a slice of goat's cheese onto each toast.
- Continue to grill until the cheese has started to melt and take on some colour.
- Season the soup to taste, then serve with the goat's cheese toasts on top.

Fresh for...
February
3rd

Chilli Con Carne Soup

Ingredients

5 tablespoons olive oil
2 medium onions, finely diced
2 cloves garlic, crushed
3 green chillies, finely diced
1 teaspoon ground coriander
1 teaspoon ground cumin
1 teaspoon ground cinnamon
2 cardamom pods, bruised with a knife
1 red pepper, finely diced
800g braising steak, cut into 1–2cm chunks
1 x 400g tin chopped tomatoes
2 tablespoons tomato purée
1 x 410g tin red kidney beans, drained and rinsed
750ml beef stock
30g dark chocolate, broken into chunks

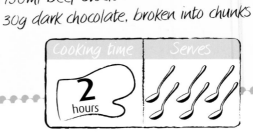

Cooking time: 2 hours

Serves

- Heat 3 tablespoons of oil in a large saucepan, add the onions and garlic, then cook gently for 10 minutes until softened.
- Add the chilli, coriander, cumin, cinnamon and cardamom pods, then stir gently.
- Add the red pepper before cooking for a further 5 minutes. Pour into a bowl and set aside.
- Return the pan to a high heat and, using the remaining oil, brown the steak in batches.
- Return all the steak to the pan, add the spicy onions, tomatoes, tomato purée, red kidney beans and stock, then partially cover and simmer over a low heat for 1½ hours until the meat is really tender.
- Add the chocolate and stir until melted, then season to taste and serve.

Fresh for...
February
4th

Yellow Split Pea & Bacon

Ingredients

170g yellow split peas
1 potato, diced
half an onion, diced
pinch of white pepper
375ml vegetable stock
40g celeriac, diced
1 carrot, diced
1 clove garlic, crushed
1 bay leaf
pinch turmeric
500g cooked smoked bacon, diced

Cooking time	Serves
45 minutes	

- In a large saucepan, place 100g of the yellow split peas, then add all the other ingredients, except the bacon.
- Bring to the boil and then simmer for 20 minutes.
- Remove the bay leaf, then blend until smooth.
- Add the remaining yellow split peas and the bacon, then cook gently for a further 20 minutes, or until the peas have softened.

Fresh for...
February
5th

Broccoli & Horseradish

Ingredients

Knob of butter
1 small onion, chopped
110g potato, peeled and cubed
850ml vegetable or chicken stock
1 lime, zest plus juice
270g broccoli, chopped
1 tablespoon fresh parsley, chopped
1 tablespoon fresh chives, chopped
2 tablespoons double cream
(1 tablespoon horseradish sauce or to taste)

Cooking time: 55 minutes
Serves

- Melt the butter in a saucepan, then cook the onion and potato gently for 5 minutes without browning.
- Add the stock and lime, then cover, bring to the boil and simmer gently for 30 minutes until the vegetables are tender.
- Meanwhile cook the broccoli in boiling water for 10 minutes, or until tender but still green.
- Cool the potato mixture a little, then blend until smooth.
- Pass through a sieve, then add the broccoli and blend briefly so you can still see bits of broccoli.
- Return to the pan, then add the herbs, cream and horseradish to taste. Season to taste and serve.

Red Lentil & Butternut with Marrow Chips

Fresh for...
February
6th

Ingredients

50g butter
1 medium onion, finely chopped
675g butternut squash, peeled and cut into 2.5cm pieces
1 bay leaf
1 litre fortified stock (see below)
225g red lentils, soaked for 30 minutes, then rinsed in plenty of cold water

For the fortified stock:
50g butter
1 small onion, roughly chopped
140g carrots, roughly chopped
140g celery, roughly chopped
425ml vegetable stock
570ml water

To garnish:
1 small marrow or courgette, deseeded and cut into 10cm long very fine chips
150ml crème fraîche
2 tablespoons fresh coriander leaves, chopped

Cooking time: 1:30 hour & minutes
Serves: 4

- To make the stock: melt the butter in a saucepan, add the onion, carrot and celery, then cover and cook gently for 5 minutes, without browning.
- Add the stock and water, then cover, bring to the boil, and simmer gently for 30 minutes.
- Strain into a bowl without pressing the vegetables too firmly.
- To make the soup: melt the butter in a saucepan, add the onion, butternut squash and bay leaf, then cover and cook for 15 minutes without browning.
- Add the stock and the pre-soaked and rinsed lentils, then season to taste.
- Cover, bring to the boil, then simmer for 30 minutes until the vegetables are tender.
- Blend until really smooth, then reheat gently.
- While reheating, deep fry the marrow chips until lightly brown and crisp. Remove from the pan to kitchen paper and sprinkle with a little salt.
- Serve the soup garnished with a swirl of crème fraîche, a generous pinch of the marrow chips and chopped fresh coriander leaves.

Fresh for...
February
7th

Chinese Leaves & Green Pepper

Ingredients

2 tablespoons extra virgin olive oil
50g butter
225g green peppers, deseeded and finely diced
2 medium onions, finely chopped
half a head of Chinese leaves, finely shredded
2 tablespoons plain flour
425ml chicken stock
425ml milk
3 tablespoons single cream

- Heat the oil and butter in a saucepan, add the green pepper, onion and Chinese leaves, then cook for 5 minutes.
- Stir in the flour, then cook for a further minute.
- Add the stock, bring to the boil, then simmer until the vegetables are cooked.
- Pour in the milk, then blend until smooth. Reheat gently.
- Add the cream, season to taste, then serve.

Pak Choi & Chilli

Fresh for...
February
8th

Ingredients

565ml water
200g pak choi, sliced
70g broccoli, small florets
half a fresh red chilli, chopped
1 teaspoon ginger purée
1 medium potato, diced
1 small onion, finely chopped
1 clove garlic, chopped
1 leek, finely sliced
50g spinach, chopped
2 teaspoons Demerara sugar
1 stick celery, chopped
half a red pepper, deseeded and sliced

Cooking time	Serves
40 minutes	

- Pour the water into a saucepan and add the pak choi (175g only at this stage), broccoli, chilli, ginger, potato, onion, garlic, leek, spinach, sugar and celery, then bring to the boil.
- Once boiling, cover, then simmer for 20 minutes or until all the vegetables are soft.
- Blend until smooth.
- Return to the pan, add the remaining pak choi and red pepper, then season to taste.
- Cook gently for a further 7 minutes, and then serve.

Fresh for...
February
9th

Smoked Chicken Chowder

Ingredients

100g smoked streaky bacon, diced
1 tablespoon olive oil
1 small onion, diced
1 stick celery, chopped
1 large potato, diced
800ml water
100g sweetcorn, fresh or frozen
100ml single cream
100g cooked smoked chicken, diced
1 tablespoon fresh parsley, chopped

Cooking time	Serves
40 minutes	4

- Fry the bacon until crisp and golden, drain on kitchen paper, then set aside.
- Heat the oil in a saucepan, add the onion and celery, then cook gently for 5–10 minutes until softened, without browning.
- Add the potato and water, bring to the boil, then cover and simmer for 10–15 minutes until the potato is almost tender.
- Add the sweetcorn, then cook for a further 5–7 minutes.
- Add the cream, smoked chicken and bacon, then heat and stir until thoroughly warmed through.
- Season to taste with pepper only (the chicken and bacon are already salty enough), then sprinkle with parsley and serve.
- For a smooth soup, simply add a little milk and blend.

Spiced Carrot & Lentil

Fresh for...
February
10th

Ingredients

1 tablespoon olive oil
1 small onion, diced
pinch of ground nutmeg
1 teaspoon mild curry powder
8 carrots (6 roughly chopped, 2 finely diced)
370ml vegetable stock
55g red lentils
3 tablespoons coconut milk
30ml single cream
1 tablespoon fresh coriander, chopped

Cooking time: 55 minutes
Serves: 4

- Heat the oil in a saucepan, then add the onion, nutmeg and curry powder. Fry gently for 5–10 minutes, or until the onion is softened.
- Add the roughly chopped carrots and stock, then bring to the boil and simmer gently for 20 minutes.
- Blend until smooth.
- Return to the heat, then add the red lentils and diced carrots. Bring back to the boil, then simmer gently for a further 20 minutes.
- Add the coconut milk, cream and coriander, then simmer for a further 5 minutes.
- Season to taste, then serve.

Fresh for...
February 11th

Lovers' Dish
Mussel, Tomato & Basil

Ingredients

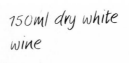

4 tablespoons olive oil
5 shallots, finely sliced
2 cloves garlic, finely sliced
500g plum tomatoes, peeled, deseeded and chopped
small bunch fresh basil
1kg uncooked mussels, cleaned and debearded*
150ml dry white wine

Cooking time	Serves
25 minutes	2

- Heat 2 tablespoons of olive oil in a saucepan, then fry the shallots and half of the garlic until lightly browned.
- Add the tomatoes and half the basil leaves, then cook over a medium to high heat until reduced to a thick sauce (around 15 minutes).
- Heat the remaining olive oil in a large saucepan, fry the rest of the garlic briefly, then toss the mussels into the oil.
- Pour in the white wine, then cover and cook until the mussels have opened.
- Tip the mussels into a colander with a bowl underneath to reserve the juices, then quickly remove at least half of the mussels from their shells.
- Add all the mussels to the sauce, along with the reserved cooking liquor, then reheat well.
- Add the remaining basil, season well and serve with a drizzle of extra virgin olive oil.

* Tap any open mussels sharply with a knife. If they do not begin to close, discard them, as they may not be fresh.

Spice Up Your Night
King Prawn, Chilli & Ginger

Fresh for...
February
12th

Ingredients

1 stick lemongrass
half a tablespoon of red Thai curry paste
250ml hot fish stock
1 red chilli, finely sliced
1cm piece fresh root ginger, grated
200ml coconut milk
14 raw king prawns
1 tablespoon fish sauce
1 tablespoon lime juice
1 teaspoon sugar
a few sprigs of fresh mint, shredded
5g fresh coriander leaves, shredded

Cooking time	Serves
10 minutes	2

- Remove the tough outer layer of the lemongrass, bash with a knife to bruise and release the flavour, then cut in half.
- Place the lemongrass, curry paste, hot stock, chilli, ginger and coconut milk in a saucepan, then simmer gently for 5 minutes.
- Add the king prawns, fish sauce, lime juice and sugar, then simmer for a further 3 minutes until the prawns are cooked.
- Remove the lemongrass pieces, then serve topped with the mint and coriander.

Fresh for...
February
13th

Cupid's Arrow
Asparagus Spears with Parma Ham

Ingredients

25g butter
1 leek, sliced
half a stick of celery, sliced
half a tablespoon of plain flour
250g asparagus, tips cut into 6cm lengths, stalks into 3cm lengths
350ml chicken stock
2 slices Parma ham
25ml double cream

Cooking time	Serves
25 minutes	2

- Melt the butter in a saucepan, then add the leek and celery. Cover and cook for 10–15 minutes until softened, without browning.
- Add the flour, stir, then cook for a further minute or so.
- Add the asparagus stalks and stock.
- Cover and simmer for 5–7 minutes until the asparagus is just tender but retains its colour and bite.
- Meanwhile, heat the grill, season the asparagus tips to taste, then drizzle over a little olive oil.
- Place the asparagus tips and Parma ham slices under the grill until the asparagus is slightly charred and the Parma ham is crispy.
- Blend the soup until completely smooth, then add the cream while gently reheating. Season to taste.
- Pour the soup into bowls and place the asparagus tips and Parma ham on top.

Love & Hearts

Artichoke Hearts with Parmesan Croutons

Fresh for...
February
14th

Ingredients

For the soup:
25g butter
1 small onion, chopped
240g tinned artichoke hearts, cut into chunks
2 teaspoons fresh thyme, chopped
1 bay leaf
350ml chicken stock
75ml single cream
2 teaspoons chives, snipped

For the croutons:
1 ciabatta, sliced at an angle
1 clove garlic
25g Parmesan, grated

Cooking time	Serves
30 minutes	

- Melt the butter in a saucepan, add the onion, then cook for 5 minutes.
- Add the artichokes, thyme and bay leaf, then sweat for a further 5 minutes until tender but without browning.
- Add the stock, then cover and simmer for 10–15 minutes until really tender.
- Remove the bay leaf, then blend until very smooth. Reheat gently, adding the cream, then season to taste.
- To make the croutons: toast each slice of ciabatta, then rub with the garlic clove.
- Serve the soup with a scattering of chives, a floating crouton with Parmesan sprinkled over the top and a drizzle of olive oil.

Fresh for...
February
15th

Salmon & Watercress

Ingredients

Knob of butter
1 leek, diced
300ml fish stock
2 medium potatoes, diced
pinch of white pepper
100g cooked salmon, flaked
35g watercress, finely chopped
150ml whole milk
35ml double cream

Cooking time	Serves
55 minutes	4

- Melt the butter in a saucepan, add the leeks, stock and half the potatoes, and season to taste with salt and white pepper.
- Bring to the boil, then simmer for 25 minutes.
- Blend until smooth.
- Add the remaining potato, then simmer gently for a further 20 minutes.
- Add the salmon and watercress, then cook gently for 5 minutes.
- Stir in the milk and cream, reheat gently, and then serve.

Crushed Velvet Wild Mushroom drizzled with Truffle Oil

Fresh for...
February
16th

Ingredients

15g dried porcini mushrooms
25g butter
1 tablespoon olive oil
3 shallots, thinly sliced
1 clove garlic, crushed
250g mixed mushrooms (chestnut, chanterelle, girolle), cleaned and sliced
2 teaspoons fresh thyme, finely chopped
250ml chicken stock
50ml double cream

To garnish:
1 tablespoon olive oil
100g mixed mushrooms
a squeeze of lemon juice
2 teaspoons fresh parsley, chopped
heart-shaped croutons
truffle oil, to taste

Cooking time: 40 minutes

Serves

- Soak the porcini mushrooms in 150ml of boiling water for 30 minutes, then strain to remove any grit and reserve the liquor.
- Roughly chop and set to one side.
- Meanwhile, heat the butter and oil in a frying pan, add the shallots and garlic, then sweat until softened.
- Add the 250g mixed mushrooms and thyme, then fry until browned.
- Transfer to a saucepan, then add the porcini mushrooms, reserved liquor and stock.
- Bring to the boil, then cover and simmer gently for 15–20 minutes.
- Meanwhile, reheat the frying pan to create the garnish. Add the olive oil and mixed mushrooms to the pan, then fry quickly until brown. Season to taste, then add the lemon juice and parsley.
- Blend the soup until completely smooth, then gently reheat while adding the cream.
- Divide the soup into bowls, garnish with the mushrooms, then serve with heart-shaped croutons and a good drizzle of truffle oil.

Fresh for...
February
17th

Oyster, Tomato & Saffron

Ingredients

3 tablespoons olive oil
3 cloves garlic, crushed
half a red onion, chopped
half a bulb of fennel, finely sliced
half a leek, chopped
725ml fish stock
200g chopped tomatoes
200g tomato passata
generous pinch of saffron, soaked in 2 tablespoons hot water
half a red chilli, finely diced
a few sprigs of thyme
1 bay leaf
half an orange, zest of
3 tablespoons fresh parsley, chopped
250g turbot or other white fish, filleted and cut into large chunks
12 oysters, shelled
12 large raw prawns, shelled

Cooking time	Serves
35 minutes	4

- Heat the oil in a saucepan, add the garlic, red onion, fennel and leek.
- Fry for 5–10 minutes, stirring frequently, until softened.
- Add the stock, chopped tomatoes, passata, soaked saffron, chilli, thyme, bay leaf, orange zest and 2 tablespoons of the parsley.
- Bring to the boil, then simmer uncovered for 15 minutes.
- Add the turbot and cook gently for 5 minutes.
- Add the oysters with their juices and prawns, then cook for a further 3–5 minutes until all the fish is cooked.
- Season to taste, sprinkle with the remaining parsley, then serve.

Smoked Mackerel & Horseradish

Fresh for...
February
18th

Ingredients

50g butter
1 medium onion, finely chopped
1 clove garlic, crushed
2 medium potatoes, diced
750ml water
280g smoked mackerel, skin removed and flaked
1 tomato, peeled, deseeded and chopped
1 teaspoon lemon juice
1 tablespoon fresh parsley, chopped
1 tablespoon fresh chives, chopped
3 tablespoons double cream
3 tablespoons horseradish sauce

Cooking time: 40 minutes
Serves: 4

- Melt the butter in a saucepan, add the onion, garlic and potatoes, then cook gently for 10 minutes until softened.
- Add the water, bring to the boil, then cover and simmer for 15 minutes until the potatoes are tender.
- Add two-thirds of the mackerel.
- Blend until smooth.
- Return to the pan, heat gently, then add the remaining mackerel, tomato, lemon juice and herbs, reserving a few for the garnish.
- Season to taste.
- Mix the cream, horseradish and remaining herbs together, ladle the soup into the serving bowls, then finish with a spoonful of the herby horseradish cream.

Fresh for...
February
19th

Creamy Chicken

Ingredients

25g butter
1 tablespoon olive oil
1 medium onion, diced
1 small clove garlic, crushed
2 medium potatoes, diced
750ml chicken stock
1 tablespoon white wine
140g cooked chicken breast, diced
2 tablespoons plain flour
2 tablespoons double cream
100ml milk

Cooking time	Serves
45 minutes	3

- Melt the butter in a saucepan, add the oil, onion and garlic, then cook for 5–10 minutes until the onion is soft.
- Add the potatoes and stock, bring to the boil, then cover and simmer for 25 minutes.
- Blend until smooth, then add the wine and cooked chicken.
- Mix the flour with a little water to form a paste and add to the pan. Whisk it in, then stir until simmering and thickened.
- Add the double cream and milk, season to taste, and then serve.

Italian Peasant Soup

Fresh for...
February
20th

Ingredients

4 tablespoons extra virgin olive oil
2 medium onions, finely chopped
400g potatoes, peeled and diced
1 bulb fennel, sliced
110g carrots, diced
3 large cloves garlic, crushed
1 tablespoon sun-dried tomato paste
half a medium red pepper, deseeded and finely diced
1.2 litres vegetable stock
450g ripe tomatoes, skinned and deseeded
4 tablespoons shredded fresh basil
25g butter
175g chestnut mushrooms, sliced
1 tablespoon sun-dried tomatoes, cut into thin strips

To garnish:
3 tablespoons freshly grated Parmesan
3 tablespoons fresh basil, shredded

Cooking time: 45 minutes
Serves: 6

- Heat the oil in a saucepan, add the onion, potatoes, fennel, carrots and garlic, then cook gently for 10 minutes, without browning.
- Add the sun-dried tomato paste, red pepper, stock and tomatoes.
- Cover, bring to the boil, then simmer gently for 20–30 minutes until the vegetables are tender.
- Blend briefly to a coarse purée, then add the shredded fresh basil.
- Separately, melt the butter in a frying pan and fry the mushrooms until crisp and brown.
- Add to the soup, together with the strips of sun-dried tomatoes.
- Season to taste, then serve with Parmesan and lots of fresh basil.

Fresh for...
February
21st

Broccoli, Cauliflower & English Mustard

Ingredients

1 tablespoon olive oil
1 large leek, diced
2 cloves garlic, crushed
5 broccoli florets (150g)
300ml vegetable stock
1 parsnip, diced
5 cauliflower florets (150g)
1 teaspoon English mustard
1 tablespoon fresh parsley, chopped
1 teaspoon fresh mint, chopped
60ml whole milk
2 tablespoons double cream

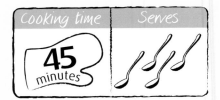

Cooking time	Serves
45 minutes	4

- Heat the olive oil in a saucepan, add the leeks and garlic, then cook gently for 5–10 minutes, until softened.
- Add the broccoli, stock, parsnip, cauliflower and English mustard, and season to taste.
- Bring to the boil, then simmer gently for 20–25 minutes, or until the vegetables have softened.
- Blend until smooth.
- Add the parsley and mint, stir in the milk and cream, then cook for a further 5 minutes before serving.

Sorrel & Oyster

Fresh for...
February
22nd

Ingredients

1.75 litres fish stock
12 fresh oysters, removed from their shells
225g fresh sorrel leaves, finely shredded

To garnish:
150ml single cream

- Pour the stock into a large saucepan, then cover and bring to the boil.
- Season to taste.
- Add the oysters, and cook for 1 minute.
- Distribute the sorrel between the serving bowls, then ladle over the broth and oysters.
- Serve immediately with a drizzle of cream.

Fresh for...
February
23rd

Split Pea & Leek

Ingredients

60g butter
1 medium onion, finely chopped
2 large leeks, finely sliced
2 medium potatoes, peeled and roughly chopped
110g green split peas, soaked overnight in plenty of water
1.2 litres chicken stock

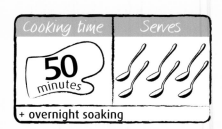

Cooking time: 50 minutes + overnight soaking
Serves: 6

- Melt the butter in a saucepan, then add the onion and leeks. Cover and cook gently until soft, without browning.
- Stir in the potatoes, green split peas and stock.
- Cover, bring to the boil, then simmer gently for 40 minutes until the split peas are tender.
- Blend until smooth.
- Season to taste, then reheat gently and serve.

Fresh for...
February
24th

Crispy Bacon & Mature Cheddar

Ingredients

15g butter
1 large onion, finely chopped
1 garlic clove, crushed
700g potatoes, peeled and roughly chopped
900ml vegetable stock
6 rashers bacon, diced
110g mature Cheddar cheese, grated
50ml single cream

Cooking time	Serves
40 minutes	

- Melt the butter in a saucepan, add the onion, then cook gently until soft, without browning.
- Add the garlic, potato and vegetable stock.
- Bring to the boil, then simmer for 20 minutes until the vegetables are tender.
- Meanwhile, fry the bacon until crispy.
- Blend the soup until smooth, then pour into a clean pan.
- Add the cheese and cream, then reheat gently.
- Stir in the crispy bacon, reserving a little for the garnish.
- Season to taste, then serve garnished with the reserved bacon.

Fresh for...
February
25th

Smoked Haddock Chowder

Ingredients

25g butter
1 small onion, finely chopped
400g potatoes, peeled and roughly chopped
725ml fish stock
200g natural uncooked smoked haddock, skinned and flaked
75ml single cream
salt
cayenne pepper

To garnish:
1 egg, hard-boiled and finely chopped
2 tablespoons finely chopped fresh flat-leaf parsley

Cooking time: 40 minutes
Serves

- Melt the butter in a saucepan, add three-quarters of the onion and 225g of the potatoes, then cook gently for 5 minutes, without browning.
- Add the stock, cover, then bring to the boil and simmer gently for 15 minutes until the vegetables are tender.
- Blend until smooth, then return to a clean pan. Add the remaining vegetables, cover, then simmer gently for 10 minutes until the vegetables are tender.
- Remove from the heat, add the fish, stir in the cream, then add salt and cayenne to taste. Take care as the smoked haddock is quite salty already.
- Reheat gently for 5 minutes, then serve garnished with the hard-boiled egg and parsley.

Sweet Potato & Orange

Fresh for...
February
26th

Ingredients

20g butter
1 large onion, finely chopped
500g sweet potatoes, peeled (of which 375g roughly chopped, 125g diced into 1cm cubes)
200g potatoes, peeled and roughly chopped
2 tablespoons freshly squeezed orange juice
700ml vegetable stock
half a teaspoon ground coriander
150ml milk

To garnish:
1 tablespoon sunflower oil
3 rashers bacon
150ml crème fraîche

Cooking time: 50 minutes
Serves

- Melt the butter in a saucepan, add the onion, cover, then cook gently until soft, without browning.
- Add the roughly chopped sweet potatoes, potatoes, orange juice, vegetable stock and ground coriander.
- Cover, bring to the boil, then simmer for 30 minutes until the vegetables are tender.
- Add the milk, then blend until smooth. Season to taste.
- Return to a clean pan, stir in the diced sweet potato, then cover and bring to the boil. Simmer for 15 minutes until the sweet potatoes are tender.
- Meanwhile, heat the oil in a frying pan, fry the bacon until crisp, then drain on kitchen paper.
- Serve the soup garnished with tablespoons of crème fraîche and topped with crispy bacon. This soup is also delicious chilled.

Fresh for...
February
27th

Red Kidney Bean & Tamarind

Ingredients

400g red kidney beans, washed
3 litres water
2 fresh bay leaves
half a stick of cassia (if unavailable use cinnamon stick)
2 tablespoons extra virgin olive oil
half a teaspoon black mustard seeds
4 garlic cloves, finely chopped
3 large onions, finely chopped
15 grinds of fresh black pepper
4 tablespoons tomato purée
3 teaspoons dried parsley
3 teaspoons fresh thyme, chopped
2 sprigs of fresh rosemary, chopped
half a lemon, juice of
4 tablespoons tamarind purée
salt

Cooking time	Serves
4 hours	6
+ overnight soaking	

- Soak the red kidney beans in plenty of water overnight.
- Drain the beans and put in a saucepan with the water at least 4 hours before the soup is to be eaten.
- Bring to the boil, then simmer gently, partially covered, for two hours, or until the skins come away from the beans, which will appear to split and become floury.
- Using a potato masher, mash one-quarter of the beans in the saucepan. (These will thicken the soup.)
- Add the bay leaves and cassia or cinnamon.
- Heat the oil in a separate pan and add the mustard seeds. When they begin to pop, briefly mash them with the back of a spoon, then add the garlic.
- Cook for 2 minutes, stirring and watching they do not brown.
- Add the onions, grind in the pepper, then fry until golden.
- Add to the kidney beans and stir well.
- Add the tomato purée, parsley, thyme and rosemary.
- Add the lemon juice and tamarind purée, then add the salt.
- Cover and simmer gently for 1 hour, adding more water if necessary.

Broccoli & Stilton

Fresh for...
February
28th

Ingredients

25g butter
1 tablespoon olive oil
1 small leek, diced
1 clove garlic, crushed
1 small potato, diced
450g broccoli florets
800ml vegetable stock
100g–150g Stilton cheese
100ml double cream

Cooking time	Serves
25 minutes	4

- Heat the butter and oil in a saucepan, add the leek, garlic and potato, then cover and cook gently for 10 minutes until soft.
- Add the broccoli florets and stock, then bring to the boil. Cover and cook for a further 6–8 minutes until the broccoli is just tender and has retained its colour.
- Stir in the Stilton until almost melted, then add the cream.
- Blend until smooth, season to taste and serve.
- If you're a Stilton fan, crumble extra over the top.

Fresh for...
March
1st

Roasted Garlic, Turnip & Chervil

Ingredients

50g butter
1 medium onion, finely chopped
4 large garlic cloves, unpeeled and roasted
1 stick celery, finely chopped
1 turnip, grated
225g potatoes, peeled and thinly sliced
900ml chicken stock
2 tablespoons double cream
2 tablespoons fresh chervil, finely chopped (or 1.5 tablespoons fresh parsley and half a tablespoon of tarragon)

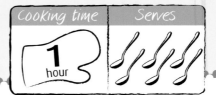

Cooking time	Serves
1 hour	6

- Melt the butter in a saucepan, add the onion, then cover and cook gently until soft, without browning.
- Peel the roasted garlic, then add to the pan with the celery, turnip and potatoes. Cook for 2 minutes, then add the stock.
- Cover, bring to the boil, then simmer gently until the vegetables are tender.
- Blend until smooth.
- Return to a clean saucepan, then reheat gently, adding the cream and chervil.
- Season to taste and serve.

Fresh for...
March
2nd

Aussie Roo Soup

Ingredients

75g butter
2 medium onions, finely chopped
275g kangaroo meat, finely chopped
3 garlic cloves, crushed
4 medium carrots, chopped
2 large potatoes, peeled and chopped
2 sticks celery, chopped
2 litres game or beef stock
3 tablespoons fresh flat-leaf parsley, finely chopped

To garnish:
1 tablespoon sunflower oil
3 rashers unsmoked streaky bacon, chopped

Cooking time: 1 hour

Serves

- Melt the butter in a saucepan, add the onion, then cover and cook gently for 5 minutes, without browning.
- Add the kangaroo meat, then brown gently.
- Add all the vegetables, cook for 2 minutes, then add the stock and parsley.
- Cover, bring to the boil, then simmer gently for 45 minutes until the meat is tender.
- For the garnish, heat the oil in a frying pan, then fry the bacon until crispy. Drain on kitchen paper.
- Serve the soup garnished with crumbled crispy bacon.

Fresh for...
March
3rd

Lettuce & Spring Onion

Ingredients

25g butter
175g spring onions, chopped
250g potatoes, peeled and chopped
1.5kg iceberg lettuce, chopped
570ml vegetable stock
3 teaspoons lemon juice (or to taste)
25g fresh parsley, chopped
450ml milk
275ml single cream

Cooking time: 40 minutes
Serves: 4

- Melt the butter in a saucepan, add the spring onions, then cover and cook gently for 5 minutes, without browning.
- Add the potatoes, lettuce, vegetable stock and lemon juice, to taste. Cover, bring to the boil, then simmer gently for 15 minutes until the vegetables are tender.
- Blend until smooth, then return to a clean pan.
- Stir in the parsley, then cover and simmer gently for a further 5 minutes.
- Stir in the milk and cream and season to taste. Reheat gently, then serve.

Fresh for...
March
4th

Borlotti Bean, Pancetta & Pasta

Ingredients

2 tablespoons olive oil
1 medium onion, finely diced
1 carrot, finely chopped
1 stick celery, finely chopped
2 cloves garlic, crushed
1 litre chicken stock
1 x 410g tin borlotti beans, rinsed and drained
1 bay leaf
100g pancetta, cubed
1 tablespoon fresh rosemary, finely chopped
1 tablespoon tomato purée
80g small pasta tubes or macaroni

Cooking time	Serves
25 minutes	4

- Heat the oil in a saucepan, add the onion, carrot, celery and garlic, then cook gently for 10 minutes until softened.
- Add the stock, borlotti beans and bay leaf, then bring to the boil, cover and simmer for a further 15 minutes.
- Meanwhile, fry the pancetta in a frying pan. Once the fat starts to run, add the rosemary. Continue to fry until the pancetta is dark and golden.
- Transfer a quarter of the soup (a couple of full ladles) to a bowl, then blend.
- Return the blended soup to the pan, along with the tomato purée, pasta, pancetta and rosemary.
- Cover and simmer for a further 10 minutes until the pasta is cooked.
- Season to taste and then serve.

Fresh for...
March
5th

Beef, Ale & Wild Mushroom

Ingredients

2 tablespoons olive oil
200g braising steak, cut into thin slivers
1 medium red onion, cut into small wedges
2 cloves garlic, crushed
1 tablespoon flour
284ml brown ale
2 sprigs of thyme
565ml beef stock
300g mushrooms (we used 100g of each shiitake, oyster and button)
1 tablespoon redcurrant jelly

Cooking time: 1:30 hour & minutes

Serves: 4

- Heat 1 tablespoon of the olive oil in a saucepan, then add the braising steak. Cook until sealed and lightly coloured, then remove and set aside.
- Add the remaining olive oil, red onion and garlic to the pan, then cook until lightly caramelised.
- Add the flour, then cook for 1 minute, stirring all the time.
- Add the ale, thyme and stock, then bring to the boil.
- Add the steak and mushrooms, then cover and simmer gently for 1 hour 15 minutes.
- Add the redcurrant jelly, then season to taste and serve.

Fresh for...
March
6th

Moroccan Lamb & Chickpea

Ingredients

2 tablespoons olive oil
1 x 350g lamb shank
1 medium onion, finely chopped
2 celery sticks, chopped
2 cloves garlic, crushed
half a teaspoon ground cinnamon
a good pinch of saffron
half a teaspoon ground ginger
half a teaspoon turmeric
a few grates of nutmeg (or a pinch of ground nutmeg)
3 plum tomatoes, chopped
60g green lentils, rinsed
1 tablespoon tomato purée
750ml chicken stock
80g tinned chickpeas
1 lemon, juice of
a small handful fresh coriander, chopped

Cooking time	Serves
2 hours	

- Preheat the oven to 180°C/350°F/gas mark 4.
- Heat the oil in a large casserole dish, add the lamb shank and fry until browned.
- Add the onion, celery and garlic, then fry for a further 10 minutes until softened and golden.
- Add the spices, stir for a few minutes, then add the tomatoes, lentils, tomato purée and stock.
- Cover and then cook in the preheated oven for 1 hour and 15 minutes.
- Add the chickpeas and return to the oven for a further 30 minutes until the pulses are tender.
- The lamb should now be tender enough to pull off the bone. Shred a little, then return to the casserole dish, adding the lemon juice and coriander.
- Season to taste, reheat gently on the hob, then serve.

Fresh for...
March
7th

Fish Stew

Ingredients

- 40g butter
- 2 medium onions, diced
- 1 tablespoon plain flour
- 300ml fish stock
- 120ml double cream
- 120ml white wine
- 40g Parmesan cheese, grated
- 200g salmon fillet, cut into 5cm cubes
- 200g skinned smoked haddock fillet, cut into 5cm cubes
- 100g scallops, cleaned and shelled (halved if large)
- 275g fresh tomatoes
- 125g cooked king prawns, peeled
- a small bunch fresh basil, roughly chopped
- a small bunch fresh parsley, roughly chopped

Cooking time: 50 minutes

Serves: 6

- Preheat your oven to 140°C/275°F/gas mark 1.
- Meanwhile, melt the butter in a casserole dish, stir in the onion, then cook for 10 minutes until soft and golden.
- Add the flour, mix for 1 minute, then stir in the fish stock, cream and wine.
- Whisk as it comes to the boil.
- Transfer to the oven for 10 minutes, then stir in the Parmesan and season to taste.
- Place the salmon and haddock chunks in a single layer in an ovenproof dish, then pour over the stock mix and cover with foil.
- Increase the oven to 180°C/350°F/gas mark 4, then cook for 15 minutes. Add the scallops and cook for a further 10–15 minutes.
- Meanwhile, blanch the tomatoes by dropping them into a bowl of boiling water for 30 seconds, drain, then peel away the skins. Remove the seeds and cut into chunky strips.
- Remove the dish from the oven, stir in the prawns, tomatoes and fresh herbs, then season to taste.
- Warm through for 2–3 minutes, then serve.

Fresh for...
March
8th

Minestrone

Ingredients

2 tablespoons olive oil
2 medium carrots, diced
2 red onions, diced
1 leek, diced
2 celery sticks, chopped
1 dessertspoon fresh thyme, chopped
1 dessertspoon fresh rosemary, chopped
1 clove garlic, finely sliced
1 x 400g tin chopped tomatoes
1–1.5 litres stock
1 x 410g tin cannellini beans
200g savoy cabbage, cored and shredded (ensure shreds are not too long for ease of eating)
75g small pasta shapes (we use macaroni)

Cooking time: 1 hour
Serves

- Heat the oil in a saucepan, then add the carrots, onions, leek, celery, thyme, rosemary and garlic.
- Cover, then cook, without browning, for 15 minutes until tender.
- Add the tomatoes, then cook for 5 minutes until the juice has reduced slightly.
- Add the stock and cannellini beans, bring to the boil, then simmer for a further 15 minutes. Skim off any red froth if necessary.
- Add the savoy cabbage and pasta, then simmer for a further 5–10 minutes (the cabbage should retain its dark green colour). Season to taste, then serve.

Fresh for...
March
9th

Tomato, Pepperoni & Parmesan

Ingredients

2 tablespoons olive oil
1 small onion, diced
1 carrot, diced
50g diced pepperoni
1 teaspoon smoked paprika
half a teaspoon sugar
270g tinned chopped tomatoes
1 teaspoon tomato purée
1 teaspoon fresh oregano, chopped (or pinch of dried oregano)
1 bay leaf
450ml chicken stock
grated Parmesan cheese

Cooking time	Serves
20 minutes	4

- Heat the olive oil in a saucepan, add the onion, then fry gently for 5–10 minutes.
- Add the carrot and pepperoni, then cook gently for a further 10 minutes.
- Add the paprika and sugar, season to taste, then cook for 5 minutes.
- Add the tomatoes, tomato purée, oregano, bay leaf and stock, then cook gently for 15–20 minutes.
- Season to taste, then serve garnished with the Parmesan.

Pear, Roquefort & Spinach

Fresh for...
March
10th

Ingredients

50g butter
1 large onion, finely chopped
1 large potato, finely chopped
2 cloves garlic, crushed
750ml water
250g spinach
2 pears, diced
50g Roquefort cheese, diced

Cooking time	Serves
30 minutes	4

- Melt the butter in a saucepan, then add the onion, potato and garlic.
- Cover and cook gently for 10 minutes, without browning.
- Add the water, then bring to the boil. Add the spinach, bring back to the boil, then cook for 5 minutes.
- Blend until smooth, then return to the pan.
- Blend the pears until smooth, then add to the soup and stir in well.
- Add the Roquefort, then season to taste. Heat gently for 3 minutes, then serve.

Fresh for...
March
11th

Cauliflower, Mustard & Gorgonzola

Ingredients

2 tablespoons vegetable oil
1 medium onion, finely chopped
1 tablespoon plain flour
284ml vegetable stock
284ml milk
1 medium cauliflower, cut into small florets
160g Gorgonzola cheese, cubed
1 teaspoon wholegrain mustard

Cooking time	Serves
40 minutes	4

- Heat the oil in a saucepan, add the onion, then cook until softened, without browning.
- Add the flour, then cook for 1 minute.
- Gradually add the stock and milk, stirring constantly.
- Add the cauliflower, bring to the boil, then cover and simmer for 20 minutes until the cauliflower is tender.
- Remove from the heat, add the Gorgonzola, then stir until melted.
- Blend until smooth, then return to the pan.
- Season to taste, then reheat gently for 3 minutes.
- Stir in the mustard and serve.

Fresh for...
March
12th

Roasted Parsnip, Lemon & Vanilla

Ingredients

6 parsnips, roughly diced
2 tablespoons olive oil
1 small onion, finely chopped
1 lemon, zest of
quarter of vanilla pod, seeds removed
625ml vegetable stock
185ml milk

Cooking time	Serves
45 minutes	

- Preheat your oven to 190°C/375°F/gas mark 5.
- Roast the parsnips in 1 tablespoon of olive oil for 20 minutes until softened and coloured.
- Meanwhile, heat the remaining olive oil in a saucepan, add the onion, then cook gently for 10 minutes until softened.
- Add the lemon zest, vanilla pod and stock, then bring to the boil.
- Add the roasted parsnips, cover, then simmer gently for a further 15 minutes.
- Blend until smooth, then return to the pan.
- Add the milk and season to taste. Reheat gently and serve.

Fresh for...

March

13th

Beetroot & Rhubarb

Ingredients

25g butter

300g rhubarb, chopped

300g cooked beetroot, diced

500ml vegetable stock

Cooking time	Serves
35 minutes	4

- Melt the butter in a saucepan, add the rhubarb, then cook gently until softened.
- Add the beetroot and stock, then bring to the boil.
- Cover and simmer for 10–15 minutes until the vegetables are tender.
- Blend until smooth.
- Return to the pan, season to taste, then serve.

Spring Greens

Fresh for...
March
14th

Ingredients

50g butter
2 medium potatoes, diced
half a leek, finely sliced
1 onion, finely chopped
500ml vegetable stock
200g spring greens, washed and shredded
250ml milk

Cooking time	Serves
40 minutes	

- Melt the butter in a saucepan, add the potatoes, leek and onion, then cover and cook for 10 minutes until softened, without colouring.
- Add the stock, bring to the boil, then cover and simmer for 15 minutes.
- Add the spring greens and cook for a further 35 minutes until the greens are tender.
- Blend until the soup has a coarse texture.
- Return to the pan, add the milk, then season to taste.
- Reheat gently, then serve.

Fresh for...
March
15th

Chocolate & Rhubarb Swirl

Ingredients

For the rhubarb soup:

300g rhubarb, chopped
100ml apple & blackberry juice
3 tablespoons clear honey
100ml white wine
half a teaspoon cornflour, mixed with a little cold water
1 or 2 drops rosewater (optional)

For the chocolate soup:

75g dark chocolate (good quality), broken into small chunks
150ml milk
150ml double cream
2 egg yolks
half a teaspoon cornflour, mixed with a little cold water
2 tablespoons golden caster sugar

Cooking time: 40 minutes

Serves

- To make the rhubarb soup: place the rhubarb, apple & blackberry juice, honey and white wine into a saucepan. Bring to the boil, then cover and simmer gently for 10 minutes until the fruit is softened.
- Blend until smooth, then return to the pan. Add the water and cornflour mix, then stir over a low heat until thickened. Add 1 or 2 drops of rosewater to taste, then set aside.
- To make the chocolate soup: place the chocolate, milk and cream in a bowl, then place over a pan of simmering water, stirring until the chocolate has melted.
- In a clean bowl, whisk together the egg yolks, cornflour mix and sugar.
- Pour the warmed chocolate milk onto the egg mixture, whisking as you pour. Once thoroughly mixed together, return the mixture to the pan.
- Stir continuously over a low heat until the mixture starts to thicken and bubble.
- If not to be served immediately, place some cling film over the chocolate soup to prevent a skin forming.
- Pour the chocolate soup into bowls, ripple with the rhubarb soup, then serve.

Red Lentil, Lemon & Thyme

Fresh for...
March
16th

Ingredients

2 tablespoons extra virgin olive oil
1 large onion, finely chopped
1 garlic clove, crushed
150g red lentils, washed
570ml vegetable stock
1 x 400g tin chopped tomatoes
2 teaspoons tomato purée
2 tablespoons fresh thyme, finely chopped
half a lemon, juice of (or to taste)

To garnish:
6 small sprigs of fresh thyme

Cooking time	Serves
40 minutes	6

- Heat the oil in a saucepan, add the onion and garlic, then cook gently for 1 minute without browning.
- Add the lentils, then stir to coat well in the oil.
- Add the stock, then bring to the boil. Skim off any scum.
- Add the tinned tomatoes, tomato purée and three-quarters of the thyme.
- Bring back to the boil, then cover and simmer for 15–20 minutes, stirring occasionally.
- Season to taste, then add the remaining freshly chopped thyme.
- Add the lemon juice little by little, to taste.
- Serve garnished with sprigs of thyme.

Fresh for...
March
17th

Lamb & Guinness

Ingredients

2 tablespoons extra virgin olive oil
2 medium onions, finely chopped
275g boned shoulder of lamb, finely diced
1.2 litres beef stock
275ml Guinness
3 sticks celery, diced
3 carrots, diced
50g pearl barley, washed
110g red lentils, washed
3 medium potatoes, about 450g, peeled and diced
pinch of dried mixed herbs

To garnish:
150ml natural yoghurt
6 fresh basil leaves

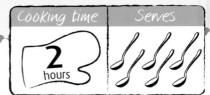

Cooking time: 2 hours
Serves: 6

- Heat the oil in a saucepan, add the onion, then cook gently until golden.
- Remove the onion from the pan and set aside. In the same pan, brown the lamb.
- Stir in the stock and the Guinness.
- Return the onion to the pan, then add the celery, carrots, barley and lentils.
- Partially cover, then simmer for 1 hour, stirring from time to time.
- Add the potatoes and herbs, season to taste, then simmer for a further 10–15 minutes until the potatoes are tender.
- Serve garnished with a dash of yoghurt and the basil leaves.

Fresh for...
March
18th

Celery & Cashew Nut

Ingredients

75g butter
2 heads of celery, roughly chopped (save the leaves for garnishing)
4 garlic cloves, finely chopped
150g unsalted cashew nuts
1.5 litres vegetable stock

To garnish:
50g unsalted cashew nuts, roughly chopped

Cooking time: 45 minutes
Serves

- Melt the butter in a saucepan, add the celery and garlic, then cover and cook gently for 10 minutes, without browning.
- Chop the nuts finely in a food processor, then add to the pan along with the stock.
- Cover, bring to the boil, then simmer for 30 minutes until the vegetables are tender.
- Blend until smooth, then pass the soup through a sieve into a clean saucepan.
- For the garnish: add the chopped cashew nuts to a frying pan over a high heat. Shake frequently until the nuts brown, then cool.
- Reheat the soup gently, then serve garnished with toasted cashew nuts and chopped celery leaves.

Fresh for...

March

19th

Mexican Style Black-eyed Beans*

Ingredients

350g black-eyed beans, washed and soaked in cold water overnight
1 medium onion, roughly chopped
1 medium carrot, roughly chopped
1 stick celery, roughly chopped
1.4 litres light chicken or vegetable stock
1–2 garlic cloves, chopped
3 tablespoons tomato purée
3 teaspoons Mexican chilli paste
2 teaspoons fresh oregano, chopped

To garnish:
1 tablespoon sunflower oil
2–3 rashers smoked streaky bacon, chopped
2 tablespoons fresh oregano, finely chopped

Cooking time	Serves
2:10 hours & minutes	4
+ overnight soaking	

- Place the drained beans, onion, carrot and celery in a large saucepan. Add the stock, garlic, tomato purée and chilli paste.
- Cover, then simmer gently for 2 hours or until the beans are tender, adding salt and the oregano 10–15 minutes before the end.
- Meanwhile, for the garnish: heat the oil in a saucepan, then fry the bacon until crispy. Drain on kitchen paper.
- Blend half the soup, then mix with the other half in the saucepan.
- Season to taste.
- Reheat, then serve sprinkled with the crispy bacon and fresh oregano.

* Reproduced by kind permission of Creative Food Processor Cookery, Nicola Cox, Ebury Press, 1986.

Chicken, Cumin & Corn-on-the-cob

Fresh for... March 20th

Ingredients

1.3–1.5kg chicken, cut into 6–8 serving pieces
1.7 litres chicken stock
1 large onion, peeled
1 small bay leaf
half a teaspoon ground cumin
half a teaspoon dried thyme
600g potatoes, peeled and finely sliced
3 large cobs of corn, cut into 5cm rounds
150ml double cream

To garnish:
1 avocado, peeled, stoned and thinly sliced
150ml soured cream
5 teaspoons capers, rinsed, drained and squeezed dry

Cooking time	Serves
1:30 hour & minutes	6

- Place the chicken pieces in a large saucepan, then add the stock.
- Slowly bring to a simmer, then skim off any impurities.
- Add the onion, bay leaf, cumin, thyme and salt, then simmer gently for 30 minutes until the chicken is cooked.
- Transfer the chicken to a warm serving dish.
- Remove the meat from the bones and cut into small pieces.
- Strain the cooking liquor and return it to a clean saucepan.
- Boil the stock over high heat until it is reduced by one-third.
- Add the potatoes, then cook for 15 minutes until the potatoes are tender.
- Mash half of the potatoes against the side of the saucepan to thicken the soup.
- Add the corn and chicken pieces, then simmer for 5–10 minutes.
- Stir in the cream and season to taste. Serve garnished with the avocado slices, soured cream and capers.

Fresh for...
March
21st

Salmon & Dill

Ingredients

- 250ml double cream
- 2 tablespoons olive oil
- 1 medium onion, finely diced
- 570ml fresh vegetable stock
- 200ml dry white wine
- 3 medium potatoes, peeled and diced into 1cm cubes
- 300g fresh salmon (tail fillet), skinned and cut into 3.5cm chunks
- 1–2 tablespoons dill, chopped

Cooking time	Serves
45 minutes	4

- Allow the cream to come to room temperature.
- Meanwhile, heat the oil in a saucepan, add the onion, then cover and cook gently for 5 minutes, without browning.
- Add the stock, wine and potatoes, then season to taste.
- Bring to the boil, then simmer for 15 minutes without covering, until the potatoes are tender but not too soft.
- Add the cubed salmon, then bring back to the boil.
- Add the dill, then remove from the heat and leave to stand for a couple of minutes. The hot stock will continue to cook the salmon.
- Add the cream, heat through gently, then serve.

Fresh for...
March
22nd

Carrot & Cardamom

Ingredients

30g butter
1 large onion, finely chopped
1 garlic clove, crushed
6 (450g) carrots, peeled and cut into equal size chunks
1 level tablespoon plain flour
850ml vegetable stock
15g creamed coconut
1 tablespoon lemon juice
seeds of 8 cardamom pods, crushed
1 teaspoon sugar

To garnish:
shredded coconut

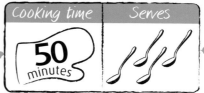

Cooking time	Serves
50 minutes	

- Melt the butter in a saucepan, then add the onion, garlic and carrots. Cover and cook gently for 5 minutes, without browning.
- Add the flour, then cook gently for 2 minutes.
- Stir in the stock, creamed coconut and lemon juice.
- Cover, bring to the boil, then simmer gently for 15 minutes until the carrots are tender.
- Blend until smooth. Add the cardamom and sugar, then season to taste.
- Toast the shredded coconut by heating it gently in a dry pan, until lightly browned, then set aside for the garnish.
- Reheat the soup gently, then serve garnished with the toasted coconut shavings. This soup tastes delicious chilled.

Fresh for...
March
23rd

Ceviche

Ingredients

900g firm white fish, e.g. seabass, red mullet, cod, haddock, skinned and cut into 1cm cubes
8 limes, juice of
2 garlic cloves, crushed
4 tablespoons red wine vinegar
4 tablespoons fruity extra virgin olive oil
290ml iced water
1 large red onion, finely sliced
1 bunch spring onions, white part only, finely sliced
4 large ripe tomatoes, peeled and chopped into small pieces
1 yellow pepper, deseeded and finely chopped
2–3 large red chillies, halved, deseeded and finely sliced
3 tablespoons fresh coriander leaves, chopped

Cooking time	Serves
20 minutes	4
+ marinating time	

This recipe is best made the day before as the longer the marinating time the better.

- Place the fish in a bowl, then cover with the lime juice.
- Stir gently, ensuring each fish cube is coated in the lime juice, then marinate for 4 hours or, if possible, overnight in the refrigerator.
- Blend the garlic, red wine vinegar and olive oil together, then pour into a bowl.
- Stir in the water, then toss with the red onion, spring onions, tomatoes, yellow pepper, chillies and a handful of chopped coriander leaves. Allow to infuse for 4 hours or overnight in the refrigerator.
- When ready to serve, toss all the ingredients together, including the remaining coriander leaves, then season to taste.

Spinach & Coconut

Fresh for...
March
24th

Ingredients

2 tablespoons olive oil
2 small onions, finely chopped
3 garlic cloves, crushed
2 sprigs of fresh thyme
2 teaspoons fresh chives, finely chopped
500g spinach leaves, washed
1.2 litres chicken or vegetable stock
275–450ml coconut milk, to taste
1 fresh green chilli, deseeded and finely sliced (or to taste)

Cooking time	Serves
25 minutes	

- Heat the oil in a saucepan, add the onion and garlic, then cover and cook gently for 5 minutes, without browning.
- Add the thyme, chives, spinach leaves, stock, coconut milk and chilli to taste.
- Cover, then simmer gently for 15 minutes.
- Blend until smooth.
- Season to taste, reheat gently, then serve.

Fresh for...
March
25th

Lamb Tagine

Ingredients

5 tablespoons olive oil
2 onions, finely sliced
3 cloves garlic, crushed
1 teaspoon ground cinnamon
1 teaspoon ground cumin
1 teaspoon ground ginger
1 teaspoon chilli powder
1 teaspoon ground coriander
1kg lamb leg steaks, cut into 3cm cubes
1 tablespoon flour
1 x 400g tin chopped tomatoes
2 bay leaves
1 x 410g tin chickpeas, drained and rinsed
250g prunes, quartered
500ml lamb stock
3 tablespoons fresh coriander, chopped

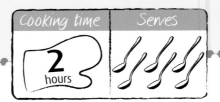

Cooking time: 2 hours
Serves

- Heat 3 tablespoons of oil in a large casserole dish, add the onions, then cook gently for 5–10 minutes until softened.
- Add the garlic, cinnamon, cumin, ginger, chilli and coriander, then stir for 1–2 minutes. Remove from the pan and set aside.
- In the remaining oil, brown the lamb in batches over a high heat.
- Return the meat and the spicy onions back to the pan, sprinkle with flour, stir, then cook for 1–2 minutes.
- Add the tomatoes, bay leaves, chickpeas, prunes and stock. Scrape the bottom of the pan to prevent sticking.
- Bring to a simmer, then cover and simmer gently for 1½ hours or until the lamb is very tender.
- Season to taste, then serve sprinkled with fresh coriander.

Chicory Soup

Fresh for...
March 26th

Ingredients

50g butter
2 heads of chicory, sliced
1 medium onion, finely sliced
110g parsnip, roughly chopped
400g potato, peeled and sliced
570ml vegetable stock
1 blade of mace
1 bay leaf
lemon juice, to taste
275ml milk
150ml double cream

To garnish:
chicory shreds
6 sprigs of fresh flat-leaf parsley

Cooking time	Serves
1 hour	6

- Melt the butter in a saucepan, then add the chicory (reserve a few shreds for garnishing), onion, parsnips and potatoes.
- Cover and cook gently for 10 minutes, without browning.
- Add the stock, mace blade and bay leaf, then bring to the boil.
- Simmer for 30 minutes.
- Remove the mace blade and bay leaf, then blend until smooth.
- Add the lemon juice, milk and cream, then season to taste.
- Reheat, then garnish with the reserved chicory shreds and parsley sprigs.

Fresh for...
March
27th

Cream of Chicken with Lemon & Tarragon

Ingredients

40g butter
1 medium onion, finely chopped
110g chicken breast meat, cut into small pieces
2 teaspoons dried tarragon
25g plain flour
570ml vegetable stock
1 lemon, grated zest and juice of
2 teaspoons soy sauce
150ml double cream

Cooking time	Serves
1 hour	6

- Melt the butter in a saucepan, add the onion, then cover and cook for 15–20 minutes.
- Add the chicken pieces and tarragon, then cook for 5 minutes.
- Stir in the flour, then cook for 1 minute.
- Gradually add the stock, lemon zest, lemon juice and soy sauce, then cover and cook until the chicken is tender.
- Remove from the heat, allow the soup to cool slightly, then gently stir in the cream (there's a chance the soup may curdle a little but don't be put off by this as it is still delicious).
- Reheat gently, then serve.

Fresh for...
March
28th

Lamb & Ale with dumplings

Ingredients

1 tablespoon extra virgin olive oil
1 large red onion, finely chopped
2 rashers smoked streaky bacon, finely diced
2 teaspoons brown sugar
225g boned leg of lamb, cut into 4cm slivers
20g rolled oats
570ml stock (see below)
2 dessertspoons seedless bramble conserve
2 large leeks, whites of, shredded

For the stock:
570ml chicken stock
1 small bottle strong Scottish ale
1 bay leaf
1 garlic clove
6–8 juniper berries
6 whole shallots

For the dumplings:
50g self raising flour
25g shredded suet
pinch of salt
water

Cooking time: 1:10 hour & minutes
Serves: 4

- For the stock: place all the stock ingredients in a saucepan, bring to the boil, then simmer until the liquid has reduced to 570ml. Strain and set aside.
- For the soup: heat the oil in a large saucepan, add the onion and bacon and a sprinkling of brown sugar, then heat gently until they begin to brown.
- Add the lamb and brown. Then add the oats, stock and conserve. Cover, bring to the boil, then simmer for 20–30 minutes until the lamb is tender.
- Meanwhile, for the dumplings: mix the dumpling ingredients with enough water to make a soft dough, divide into 12, then shape into balls.
- Add the leeks to the soup and rest the dumplings on the surface of the soup.
- Cover and simmer for 10 minutes until the leeks are just soft and the dumplings risen and cooked. Season to taste and serve.

Fresh for...

March

29th

Bacon, Broccoli & Celeriac

Ingredients

1 tablespoon olive oil
4 rashers smoked dry-cured bacon, diced
2 small onions, finely chopped
1 small celeriac, peeled and finely chopped
1 small broccoli, cut into small florets
700ml vegetable stock
1 bay leaf
1 teaspoon thyme, finely chopped
1 teaspoon rosemary, finely chopped
100g baby leaf spinach

Cooking time	Serves
45 minutes	4

- Heat the olive oil in a saucepan, then fry the bacon until crispy. Remove and set aside on kitchen paper.
- Add the onions to the saucepan, then cook gently until softened, without browning. Add the celeriac and broccoli, then cook for a further 5 minutes.
- Add the crispy bacon, vegetable stock and herbs, then bring back to the boil.
- Cover and simmer for 15–20 minutes until the vegetables are tender.
- Remove the soup from the heat, add the spinach leaves, stirring them in to wilt them.
- Blend until smooth, then return to the pan. Season to taste, reheat gently and serve.

Hungarian Lamb

Fresh for...
March
30th

Ingredients

1 tablespoon olive oil
175g lamb fillet, cut into cubes
1 medium onion, finely chopped
1 clove garlic, crushed
600ml lamb stock
200g tinned chopped tomatoes
half a teaspoon smoked paprika
1 bay leaf
half a teaspoon caraway seeds, lightly crushed
1 small stick celery, chopped
1 small carrot, diced
1 small potato, diced
75g swede, diced
half a red pepper, diced
1 heaped tablespoon mini pasta
1 tablespoon tomato purée
1 tablespoon fresh parsley, chopped

Cooking time	Serves
1:15 hour & minutes	4

- Heat the oil in a saucepan, add the lamb, onion and garlic, then fry until the meat is browned and the onions golden.
- Add the stock, tomatoes, paprika, bay leaf and caraway seeds, stir, then bring to the boil.
- Cover and simmer gently for 30 minutes.
- Add the vegetables and mini pasta, then cover and simmer for a further 20–30 minutes until the vegetables are tender.
- Stir in the tomato purée and parsley, then season to taste.
- Reheat gently, then serve.

Fresh for...
March
31st

White Onion

Ingredients

35g butter
1 tablespoon olive oil
3 medium white onions, finely sliced
1 large clove garlic, crushed
140ml white wine
500ml chicken stock
140ml single cream
1 teaspoon sugar
1 tablespoon fresh parsley, chopped

Cooking time	Serves
1:40 hour & minutes	

- Melt the butter and heat the olive oil in a pan, add the onions and garlic, then cover and cook over a low heat for 30 minutes without colouring. Stir occasionally.
- The onions should now be nice and soft, with some moisture in the pan from the steam.
- Uncover the pan and continue to cook gently for a further 30 minutes, by which time the onions should be greatly reduced, but still very pale.
- Add the white wine to the pan, then the stock. Cover and simmer for a further 30 minutes.
- Blend half the soup until smooth.
- Return the blended soup to the pan, add the cream, sugar and parsley and season to taste. Heat through for 5 minutes and serve.

Fresh for...
April
1st

Tomato, Chorizo & Chickpea

Ingredients

dash of olive oil
1 small onion, diced
1 clove garlic, crushed
half a green pepper, diced
60g chorizo, diced
250ml vegetable stock
200g tinned chopped tomatoes
200g passata
130g cooked chickpeas

Cooking time: 35 minutes

Serves

- Heat the olive oil in a saucepan, add the onion, then cook gently for 5–10 minutes.
- Add the garlic, green pepper and chorizo, then cook for a further 5 minutes.
- Add the stock, tomatoes, passata and chickpeas, then cover and simmer gently for 20 minutes.
- Season to taste, then serve.

Fresh for...
April
2nd

Serrano Ham & Broad Bean

Ingredients

500g broad beans, podded (half for the soup, half for garnishing)
3 tablespoons olive oil
1 medium onion, diced
2 cloves garlic, sliced
1 bay leaf
100g Serrano ham (or Parma ham), finely diced
200g peas, fresh or defrosted
1 litre chicken stock
1 tablespoon flat-leaf parsley, chopped

To garnish:
70g Serrano ham, cut into fine slivers
broad beans

Cooking time	Serves
25 minutes	4

- Blanch half the broad beans in boiling water for 3 minutes until tender, then plunge into cold water. Slip off and discard their outer skins, then put aside to use as garnish.
- Heat the olive oil in a saucepan, add the onion, then cook gently for 10 minutes until softened.
- Add the garlic, bay leaf and Serrano ham, then fry for 2–3 minutes. Add the peas and the remaining unblanched broad beans, then stir to heat through.
- Add the hot stock, quickly bring to the boil, then simmer for 3 minutes until the peas and broad beans are tender.
- Remove from the heat, add the parsley, then blend until smooth. Reheat and season to taste with pepper only. (The ham is already well salted.)
- To serve: place a small pile of the blanched broad beans set aside earlier in each bowl, then garnish with the slivers of Serrano ham and a drizzle of olive oil.

Ham & Pearl Barley

Fresh for...
April
3rd

Ingredients

2 tablespoons olive oil
1 medium onion, finely diced
30g green lentils
30g red split lentils
30g pearl barley
2 medium carrots, diced
800ml ham or chicken stock
250g cooked ham
200g tinned haricot beans, rinsed and drained
1 medium potato, peeled and diced
1 tablespoon fresh parsley, chopped

Cooking time	Serves
1:20 hour & minutes	4

- Heat the oil in a saucepan, then fry the onion for 10 minutes until transparent.
- Rinse the lentils and pearl barley, then add to the saucepan along with the carrots and stock.
- Bring to the boil, then cover and simmer for 30 minutes.
- Shred the ham into bite-sized pieces, then add the ham, haricot beans and potato to the saucepan. Simmer for a further 30 minutes.
- Check that all the pulses are thoroughly cooked, adding extra stock or water to adjust the consistency if required.
- Season to taste, stir in the parsley, then serve.

Fresh for...
April
4th

Chocolate Soup

Ingredients

725ml milk
250ml double cream
500g good quality dark chocolate, coarsely chopped
50g caster sugar
8 egg yolks
200ml whipping cream, whipped
6 tablespoons skinned hazelnuts, chopped
1 orange, finely grated rind of
6 teaspoons Grand Marnier

Cooking time: 30 minutes + chilling time
Serves: 6

- Bring the milk and cream to the boil, add the chocolate and stir until melted, then set aside.
- Heat the sugar with 1 tablespoon of water to make a syrup. When the sugar has melted, bring to the boil for 1 minute.
- Start to whisk the egg yolks, then gradually pour the syrup over the egg yolks while whisking continuously.
- Once the sugar has been incorporated, continue to whisk until the mixture is cold. The mixture will double in volume. Fold in the whipped cream.
- Toast the chopped hazelnuts by frying gently in a dry pan (i.e. non-oiled), until lightly browned all over.
- Mix the egg mixture with the chocolate sauce. Divide the mixture between the bowls, then sprinkle the toasted hazelnuts and grated orange zest over the top. Drizzle sparingly with Grand Marnier, then chill well. Delicious served with ice-cream.

Fresh for...
April
5th

Parsley Soup

Ingredients

300g fresh parsley
100g butter
4 large leeks, sliced
600g potatoes, peeled and diced
1.5 litres vegetable stock
150ml crème fraîche
nutmeg, few grates, or 1 teaspoon ground nutmeg

Cooking time	Serves
25 minutes	

- Wash the parsley well, then separate the stalks and leaves. Roughly chop all the stalks and half the leaves.
- Melt the butter in a saucepan, add the leeks, then cook gently for 5 minutes.
- Add the parsley stalks and chopped leaves, along with the potatoes and stock. Bring to the boil, then cover and simmer for 15–20 minutes.
- Add the remaining parsley leaves, then simmer for a further 2 minutes before removing from the heat.
- Blend the soup until smooth, then reheat gently while stirring in the crème fraîche. Add the nutmeg to taste, then season to taste with salt and pepper and serve.

Fresh for...
April
6th

Artichoke Hearts & Pancetta

Ingredients

1 small onion, diced
1 medium potato, diced
1 stick celery, diced
160g cooked cannellini beans
25g pancetta
550ml water
1 x 400g tin artichoke hearts, quartered
1 tablespoon white wine
small bunch parsley, chopped
pinch of ground turmeric
5 tablespoons double cream

Cooking time	Serves
40 minutes	4

- Place the onion, potato, celery, cannellini beans, pancetta and water into a saucepan, then bring to the boil.
- Cover and cook for 20 minutes until the vegetables are soft.
- Blend until smooth.
- Return to the pan, add the artichoke hearts, white wine and parsley, then cook gently for a further 10 minutes.
- Add the turmeric and cream, then season to taste. Reheat gently, then serve.

Spinach, Stilton & White Wine

Fresh for...
April
7th

Ingredients

50g butter
1 small onion, finely chopped
1 leek, finely chopped
2 sticks celery, finely chopped
2 tablespoons plain flour
5 tablespoons white wine
500ml vegetable stock
250g Stilton cheese, crumbled
50g spinach, washed and chopped
125ml milk
2 tablespoons single cream

Cooking time	Serves
40 minutes	4

- Melt the butter in a saucepan, add the onion, leek and celery, then cover and cook for 10 minutes, without browning.
- Add the flour, then cook for 1 minute. Stir in the white wine to make a sauce, then add the stock. Bring to the boil, then cover and simmer gently for 25 minutes.
- Remove the soup from the heat, then add two-thirds of the Stilton, stirring until melted.
- Blend until smooth.
- Place the spinach in a pan with 1cm of boiling water, cover and steam for 3 minutes until tender, then drain well.
- Return the blended soup to the pan, add the milk, then season to taste.
- Reheat gently, add the cooked spinach and cream, then serve.

Fresh for...
April
8th

Cauliflower & Almond

Ingredients

40g ground almonds
1 tablespoon olive oil
1 small onion, finely chopped
1 stick celery, finely chopped
500ml vegetable stock
1 medium cauliflower, cut into small florets (reserve some for garnish)
140ml milk
pinch of nutmeg, grated, to taste

Cooking time	Serves
30 minutes	

- In a non-stick frying pan, dry-fry the ground almonds over a low to medium heat, stirring constantly until they colour lightly (this helps to bring out their flavour), remove and set to one side.
- Heat the olive oil in a saucepan, add the onion and celery, then cook gently for 10 minutes until softened.
- Add the stock and ground almonds, then bring to the boil.
- Add the cauliflower florets (reserving 4 for later), then cook for a further 5 minutes until the cauliflower is just tender.
- Blend until smooth.
- Return to the pan, add the milk, season to taste, then add the remaining cauliflower florets. Reheat gently for 5 minutes until the florets are tender.
- Add the grated nutmeg to taste, and serve.

Savoy Cabbage & Bacon

Fresh for...
April
9th

Ingredients

300g savoy cabbage, shredded
25g butter
100g dry-cured bacon, roughly chopped
1 clove garlic, crushed
1 small onion, finely chopped
1 medium potato, diced
600ml vegetable stock
150ml single cream
100g bacon lardons

Cooking time: 40 minutes
Serves: 4

- Select 75g of the shredded cabbage which has a good colour, then cook in boiling salted water for 2–3 minutes until *al dente*. Refresh in cold water then set aside.
- Melt the butter in a saucepan, add the dry-cured bacon, followed by the garlic and onion.
- Cook for 5 minutes until softened, without browning.
- Add the potato and stock, bring to the boil, then cover and simmer for 10 minutes.
- Add the remaining uncooked cabbage, then cook for a further 3–5 minutes until tender but still retaining its colour.
- Blend until smooth.
- Return to the pan, add the cream, then season to taste. Reheat gently, then add the reserved cooked cabbage.
- Meanwhile, fry the lardons until browned and crispy.
- Place the crispy lardons in the serving bowls, ladle the soup over them and serve.

Fresh for...
April
10th

Lamb Kleftico

Ingredients

1 tablespoon olive oil
1 onion, diced
1 clove garlic, crushed
110g floury potatoes (e.g. Maris Piper), diced
500ml lamb stock (see below or use a cube)
150g tinned chopped tomatoes
1 teaspoon fresh oregano, or pinch of dried
half a teaspoon fresh rosemary, chopped, or small pinch of dried
1 bay leaf

For the fried vegetables:
2 tablespoons olive oil
50g onion, diced
50g potato, diced
50g aubergine, diced

For the stock:
leftover lamb joint (e.g. leg or shoulder)
1 bay leaf
1 carrot, chopped
1 onion, chopped
1 leek, chopped
a handful fresh parsley
10 peppercorns

Cooking time: 1:45 hour & minutes

Serves

- For the stock: place the leftover lamb into a saucepan, cover with water, and then add the remaining stock ingredients. Simmer gently for 1 hour, skimming off any scum occasionally. Allow to cool, remove the lamb and pull away any meat from the bone and shred. Strain, discarding the vegetables and herbs, then set aside both the lamb and the stock.
- Heat the olive oil in another saucepan, add the onion, then cook gently for 5 minutes, until softened, without browning. Add the garlic, fry for a few minutes, then add the potato and stock. Season to taste, then simmer gently for 15–20 minutes until the potato is soft.
- Meanwhile, for the fried vegetables: heat the oil in a frying pan, add the vegetables, then fry for 5–10 minutes until golden and cooked through, then set aside.
- Blend until smooth, then add the tomatoes, oregano, rosemary, cooked lamb, bay leaf and fried vegetables. Reheat gently, season to taste, then serve.

Fresh for...
April
11th

Hot & Sour Mushroom

Ingredients

850ml vegetable stock
1 stick lemongrass, bruised
5 kaffir lime leaves, roughly torn
2 tablespoons light soy sauce
1 teaspoon sugar
2 tablespoons lemon juice
250g oyster mushrooms, roughly separated
1 carrot, peeled and cut into fine matchsticks
1 or 2 red or green chillies, deseeded and roughly sliced

For the Nam Prik Pow paste:
4 tablespoons sunflower oil
3 garlic cloves, finely chopped
3 shallots, finely chopped
2 large red chillies, deseeded and roughly chopped
150ml water
2 tablespoons sugar
1 teaspoon salt

To garnish:
2 tablespoons fresh coriander leaves
110g bean sprouts

Cooking time: 35 minutes
Serves

- To make the Nam Prik Pow paste: heat the oil in a pan, then fry the garlic until golden brown. Remove and set aside.
- In the same pan, fry the shallots until crisp and golden. Remove and set aside.
- In the same pan, fry the chillies until darkened, then blend with the garlic, shallots and water until smooth.
- In the same pan, reheat the oil and add the paste, sugar and salt. Mix well, then cook until the paste becomes a dark, reddish brown.
- To make the soup: pour the vegetable stock into a large saucepan, then add the Nam Prik Pow paste and the rest of the ingredients. Cover, bring to the boil, then simmer gently for 10 minutes until the mushrooms are tender but firm.
- Serve garnished with the coriander leaves and bean sprouts.

Fresh for...
April
12th

Tortilla Soup

Ingredients

1 tablespoon groundnut oil
1 medium onion, finely chopped
2 cloves garlic, finely chopped
4 ripe tomatoes, roughly chopped
1 red chilli, deseeded and chopped
1.5 litres chicken stock
30 corn tortilla chips

To garnish:
2 avocados, peeled, stoned and sliced
110g feta cheese, cubed
110g crème fraîche
fresh coriander leaves, chopped
4 limes, halved

Cooking time: 35 minutes
Serves: 4

- Heat the oil in a saucepan, then add the onion, garlic, chopped tomatoes and chilli.
- Cook gently for 5 minutes. Add 2 tablespoons of stock, then blend until smooth
- Add the remaining stock, bring to the boil, then simmer for 20 minutes. Add the tortilla chips, then simmer until they become soft.
- Serve garnished with avocado, feta cheese, crème fraîche, coriander leaves and a squeeze of lime juice.
- Cut the remaining 3 limes in half, and then serve with each bowl.

Fresh for...
April
13th

Citrus Berry Soup

Ingredients

500g blueberries
425ml plain low fat yoghurt
290ml fresh orange juice
4 tablespoons light crème fraîche
2 tablespoons grated lemon zest
(approx. 4 lemons)
1 teaspoon ground cinnamon

To garnish:
4 dessertspoons Greek yoghurt
4 teaspoons runny honey
or
whole blueberries
icing sugar for sprinkling

Cooking time	Serves
15 minutes	4
+ chilling time	

- Blend all the ingredients until smooth, then pass through a fine sieve.
- Chill well.
- Serve with a spoonful of Greek yoghurt and drizzle with honey, or a few blueberries and a sprinkling of icing sugar.

Fresh for...
April
14th

Nettle Soup

Ingredients

25g butter
1 medium onion, finely chopped
2 garlic cloves, crushed
400g potatoes, peeled and finely chopped
450g freshly picked nettle tops*
1 litre vegetable stock
150ml double cream
freshly grated nutmeg

Cooking time: 35 minutes
Serves: 4

- Melt the butter in a saucepan, add the onion and garlic, then cover and cook gently for 10 minutes, without browning.
- Add the potatoes and nettles, then cook for 2 minutes.
- Add the stock, cover, then bring to the boil and simmer for 15 minutes.
- Blend until smooth.
- Return to a clean saucepan, stir in the cream, then season with freshly grated nutmeg, salt and pepper to taste. Reheat gently, then serve.

* When picking nettles, choose young leaves as the older ones can be very bitter. Grasp the nettle firmly by the stalk (it is the leaf which carries the sting). Once blanched the nettles will lose their sting – so you won't end up with a mouth full of blisters!

Fresh for...
April
15th

Arbroath Smokie & Scottish Cheddar

Ingredients

50g butter
2 medium onions, finely chopped
350g potatoes, peeled and chopped
1.2 litres water
1 pair Arbroath Smokies, skinned, boned and flaked
175g mature Scottish Cheddar cheese
125g carrots, coarsely grated
1 green pepper, coarsely grated
2 tablespoons double cream

To garnish:
fresh parsley, chopped

Cooking time	Serves
45 minutes	4

- Melt the butter in a saucepan, add the onion, then cover and cook gently until soft, without browning.
- Add the potatoes and water, then cover and simmer gently for 20 minutes until the vegetables are tender.
- Cool a little, add two-thirds of the flaked fish, then blend until smooth.
- Return to a clean saucepan, then reheat gently, stirring in the Cheddar cheese, carrots, green pepper, the remaining flaked fish and the double cream.
- Season to taste, then garnish with freshly chopped parsley.

Fresh for...
April
16th

Spring Vegetable & Pesto

Ingredients

25g butter
2 leeks, finely sliced
1 clove garlic, crushed
1 potato, diced
250g peas, fresh or frozen
400ml vegetable stock
50g broad beans, fresh or frozen
1 handful baby spinach leaves
1 tablespoon basil pesto

Cooking time	Serves
40 minutes	4

- Heat the butter in a saucepan, add the leeks, then cover and cook gently for 5–10 minutes, until softened, without browning.
- Add the garlic, fry for a few minutes more, then add the potato, 200g peas and vegetable stock. Cover and simmer gently for 15–20 minutes, until the potatoes are cooked.
- Blend until smooth.
- Add the remaining peas, broad beans, spinach leaves and pesto, then season to taste.
- Reheat gently for 5 minutes, then serve.

Fresh for... April 17th

Wood Pigeon & Morel Mushroom

Ingredients

1 tablespoon olive oil
2 medium shallots, finely sliced
4 pigeon breasts, sliced
90g morel mushrooms
1 tablespoon red wine vinegar
2 teaspoons redcurrant jelly
100ml red wine
2 tablespoons Madeira wine
550ml beef stock

Cooking time: 40 minutes

Serves:

- Heat the oil in a saucepan, add the shallots, then cook for 5 minutes or until a light golden brown.
- Add the pigeon breasts, cook for 1 minute, then add the morel mushrooms. Cook for a further 2 minutes on a gentle heat.
- Add the red wine vinegar, then reduce until it has nearly evaporated. Add the redcurrant jelly, red wine and Madeira, then simmer to reduce by half.
- Add the stock, bring to the boil, then cook for 10 minutes. Cover and simmer for a further 20 minutes.
- Season to taste, then serve.

Fresh for...
April
18th

Parsnip, Rhubarb & Ginger

Ingredients

50g butter
450g parsnips, peeled and roughly chopped
225g rhubarb, washed and roughly sliced
1 medium onion, finely sliced
2 teaspoons fresh root ginger, grated
1 tablespoon plain flour
850ml chicken stock
2 teaspoons light brown muscovado sugar

To garnish:
2 tablespoons fresh flat-leaf parsley, chopped

Cooking time: 35 minutes

Serves: 4

- Melt the butter in a saucepan, add the parsnips, rhubarb, onion and ginger, then cover and cook gently for 5 minutes, without browning.
- Add the flour, then stir well. Add the stock and sugar, then season to taste.
- Bring to the boil, stirring continuously. Lower the heat and simmer gently for 15 minutes until the vegetables are tender.
- Blend until very smooth. Adjust the seasoning to taste, then reheat gently and serve garnished with chopped fresh parsley.

Celery, Potato & Mature Cheddar Cheese

Fresh for...
April
19th

Ingredients

50g butter
1 medium onion, finely chopped
1 large head of celery, finely chopped
450g potatoes, peeled and sliced
725ml chicken stock
150ml double cream

To garnish:
50g mature Cheddar cheese, grated

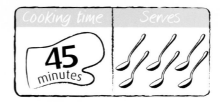

Cooking time: 45 minutes

Serves: 6

- Melt the butter in a saucepan, add the onion, celery and potatoes, then cover and cook gently for 10 minutes, without browning.
- Add the stock, then season well. Cover, bring to the boil and simmer gently for 30 minutes until the vegetables are tender.
- Blend half the soup finely and the other half of the soup coarsely.
- Return the soup to the pan, stir in the cream, then season to taste.
- Reheat gently and serve sprinkled with grated cheese.

Fresh for...
April
20th

Red Pepper & Goat's Cheese

Ingredients

2 medium onions, finely chopped
1.7 litres vegetable stock
75ml dry white wine
8 medium red peppers, deseeded and coarsely chopped
1 large cooking apple, peeled, cored and coarsely chopped
2 teaspoons dried basil
150g soft rindless goat's cheese

To garnish:
half a baguette, cut into 2cm slices
110g soft rindless goat's cheese

Cooking time	Serves
55 minutes	6

- Boil the onions in 5 tablespoons of stock for 10–15 minutes until the stock has evaporated and the onions have browned and are beginning to stick to the bottom of the pan, but do not burn them.
- Add the wine, scraping all the brown bits off the bottom of the pan, then simmer for 3 minutes.
- Add the red peppers, apple, basil, salt, pepper and the remaining stock, then simmer, partially covered, for 30 minutes until the vegetables are tender.
- Blend until smooth, then pass through a sieve. Return to a clean pan and reheat gently.
- Add the goat's cheese to the soup, then whisk until melted. Season to taste.
- For the garnish: toast the baguette slices, then spread each slice with the goat's cheese.
- Finally grill the slices until the goat's cheese is bubbling and browning. Rest the croutons on top of each bowl of soup and serve.

Persian Beef, Spinach & Spring Onion

Fresh for...
April
21st

Ingredients

1.2 litres water
225g minced beef
1 large onion, sliced
75g yellow split peas (soaked for 1 hour in plenty of water)
half a teaspoon ground turmeric
half a teaspoon freshly ground black pepper
1 teaspoon salt
225g long-grain rice
350g fresh spinach, chopped
25g chopped fresh dill
75g chopped green spring onion tops
150ml natural yoghurt

To garnish:
half a medium onion, finely sliced
2 tablespoons sunflower oil
1 tablespoon chopped fresh mint

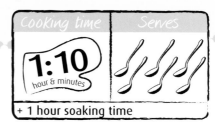

Cooking time	Serves
1:10 hour & minutes	4

+ 1 hour soaking time

- Pour the water into a saucepan and bring to the boil. Add the beef, onion, soaked yellow split peas, spices and salt. Cover, then simmer gently for 30 minutes.
- Add the rice and simmer for a further 20 minutes, stirring occasionally. Add the chopped spinach, dill and spring onion tops, then simmer for a further 10 minutes. Stir in the yoghurt, then season well.
- For the garnish (the garnish is essential with this soup): fry the onion in the oil over a moderate heat until golden brown, add the mint, then cook for a further 5 minutes until crisp. Drain on kitchen paper.
- Reheat the soup and serve with the crisp onion and mint sprinkled on top.

Fresh for... April 22nd

Spicy Lamb, Tomato & Chickpea

Ingredients

2 tablespoons extra virgin olive oil
1 large onion, finely chopped
275g boned shoulder of lamb, cut into small cubes
pinch of chilli powder
1 teaspoon ground turmeric
1 teaspoon ground cinnamon
150g tomato purée
1.5 litres water
1 teaspoon salt
1 x 410g tin chickpeas, rinsed
2–3 dessertspoons small pasta shapes
3 teaspoons dried mint
1 lemon, juice of

To garnish:
150ml natural yoghurt
2 tablespoons fresh flat-leaf parsley, finely chopped

Cooking time: 1:35 hours & minutes

Serves

- Heat the oil in a saucepan, add the onion, then cover and cook gently until soft, without browning.
- Add the meat and brown well. Add the spices and tomato purée. Cook for 2 minutes, stirring frequently.
- Gradually add the water over a period of 15 minutes in order to maintain a thick consistency. Then add the salt, cover and simmer for 30–40 minutes.
- Add the chickpeas, then simmer for a further 5 minutes. Stir in the pasta and simmer for 7 minutes. Add the mint and simmer for 1 minute.
- Stir in the lemon juice and serve garnished with a swirl of natural yoghurt and a sprinkling of fresh parsley.

Lentils, Spinach & Spring Herbs

Fresh for...
April
23rd

Ingredients

25g butter
1 large onion, finely chopped
1 garlic clove, crushed
1 stick celery, finely chopped
110g red or brown lentils, washed
1.2 litres vegetable stock
225g fresh spinach
6 tablespoons fresh herbs, chopped (any combination of herbs can be used but we use the following: flat-leaf parsley; chives; tarragon; thyme and marjoram)
1 teaspoon lemon juice
150ml Greek yoghurt

To garnish:
Greek yoghurt
reserved chopped fresh herbs

Cooking time: 45 minutes
Serves: 6

- Melt the butter in a saucepan, add the onion, garlic and celery, then cover and cook gently for a few minutes, without browning.
- Add the lentils and stir to coat well. Add the stock, cover, bring to the boil, then simmer for 20–30 minutes until the lentils are soft.
- Add the spinach and 5 tablespoons of your fresh herb combination to the soup (reserving 1 tablespoon for garnishing), then cook for 1 minute until the spinach has wilted.
- Add the lemon juice and most of the yoghurt, then blend until smooth.
- Return to the pan, reheat gently, then serve garnished with a dollop of yoghurt and the remaining herbs.

Fresh for...
April
24th

Butternut Squash, Orange & Ginger

Ingredients

4 tablespoons olive oil
1 large onion, finely sliced
1 clove garlic, crushed
1 medium butternut squash, peeled and roughly chopped
pinch of ground ginger
565ml vegetable stock
100ml orange juice
6 tablespoons single cream

Cooking time	Serves
45 minutes	4

- Heat the oil in a saucepan, add the onion and garlic, then cook until soft, without browning.
- Add the butternut squash and ginger, then cook gently for a further 5 minutes.
- Add the stock and orange juice, bring to the boil, then cover and simmer for 25–30 minutes until the butternut squash is tender.
- Blend until smooth, then return to the pan.
- Add the cream, season to taste, then reheat gently for 5 minutes and serve.

Fresh for...
April
25th

Plum Tomato & Basil

Ingredients

80g tomato purée
2 teaspoons caster sugar
2 tablespoons olive oil
1 teaspoon basil purée
500g passata with onion & garlic
400ml water
1 x 400g tin chopped tomatoes with garlic & herbs
1 tablespoon fresh basil, chopped

Cooking time	Serves
25 minutes	

- Place all the ingredients, except the fresh basil, in a saucepan. Stir well, then bring to the boil.
- Cover and simmer for 20 minutes.
- Season to taste, then stir through the fresh basil and serve.

Fresh for...

April

26th

Tuscan Bean

Ingredients

275g mixed dried beans, washed (including chickpeas, soya, black-eyed, pinto, haricot and kidney beans)
1 tablespoon extra virgin olive oil
1 large onion, chopped
1 small leek, sliced
4 garlic cloves, crushed
275ml vegetable stock
900ml water
1 x 400g tin chopped tomatoes
20g fresh flat-leaf parsley, finely chopped
75g shelled fresh green peas, or frozen peas
75g mushrooms, sliced
1 teaspoon chopped fresh oregano

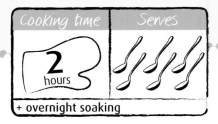

Cooking time	Serves
2 hours	6
+ overnight soaking	

- Soak the beans in plenty of cold water overnight. Drain, then place in a saucepan covered with water. Bring to the boil, then simmer gently for about 1 hour until the beans are tender. Drain.
- Heat the oil in a saucepan, add the onion, leek and garlic, then cover and cook gently until soft, without browning.
- Add the stock, water and cooked drained beans. Cover, then bring to the boil and simmer for 15 minutes.
- Add the tomatoes, parsley, peas, mushrooms and oregano, then cover and simmer for a further 15 minutes until the vegetables and beans are tender.
- Blend until smooth, then season to taste. Reheat gently for 10 minutes, then serve. This soup is even more delicious if eaten the day after cooking.

Cucumber, Pea & Mint

Fresh for... April 27th

Ingredients

2 tablespoons extra virgin olive oil
2 medium onions, finely chopped
1 garlic clove, crushed
175g potato, peeled and roughly chopped
400g frozen peas
450g cucumber, peeled and roughly chopped
425ml vegetable stock
1 tablespoon lemon juice
1 tablespoon fresh mint, chopped
50ml milk
200ml single cream

Cooking time: 45 minutes
Serves: 4

- Heat the oil in a saucepan, add the onions and garlic, then cover and cook gently for 10 minutes, without browning.
- Add the potato, peas and cucumber, then cover and cook gently for 2 minutes.
- Add the stock and lemon juice, then season to taste. Cover, bring to the boil, then simmer gently for 10 minutes until the vegetables are tender.
- Blend until smooth, then pass through a fine sieve for a silky consistency.
- Stir in the mint, milk and cream, then gently reheat.

Fresh for...
April
28th

Tomato, Spinach & Mascarpone

Ingredients

25g butter
1 medium onion, finely chopped
1 garlic clove, crushed
1 medium potato, roughly chopped
570ml vegetable stock
400g fresh tomatoes, roughly chopped
1 dessertspoon tomato purée
1 tablespoon Parmesan cheese, freshly grated
170g fresh spinach
3 tablespoons mascarpone cheese
150ml milk

To garnish:
2 tomatoes, diced
fresh basil leaves, torn

Cooking time	Serves
50 minutes	

- Melt the butter in a saucepan, add the onion and garlic, then cover and gently cook for 10 minutes, without browning.
- Add the potato and stock, then cover and simmer gently for 20 minutes until the vegetables are tender.
- Blend until smooth.
- Add the remaining ingredients, cover, bring to the boil and simmer gently for a further 15 minutes.
- Serve garnished with diced tomato and fresh basil.

Thai Spinach

Fresh for...
April
29th

Ingredients

25g butter
1 medium onion, finely chopped
1 medium potato, about 225g, roughly chopped
1 garlic clove, crushed
1 teaspoon ground cumin
1 litre vegetable stock
50g creamed coconut
250g fresh spinach
2 tablespoons fresh coriander, chopped
lemon or lime juice, to taste

Cooking time	Serves
45 minutes	4

- Melt the butter in a saucepan, then add the onion, potato and garlic. Cover and cook gently for 10 minutes, without browning.
- Stir in the cumin, then cook for 2 minutes. Add the vegetable stock, cover, then bring to the boil and simmer gently for 15 minutes.
- Stir in the creamed coconut and spinach, stand a little allowing the spinach to wilt, then blend until smooth. Season to taste.
- Reheat gently, stir in the coriander and lemon or lime juice, to taste, then serve.

Fresh for...
April
30th

Tomato & Tarragon

Ingredients

40g butter
1 tablespoon extra virgin olive oil
1 medium onion, finely chopped
1 stick celery, sliced
110g carrot, sliced
1 garlic clove, chopped
675g fresh ripe tomatoes, skinned and chopped OR 2 x 400g tins chopped tomatoes
2 tablespoons tomato purée
1 bay leaf
1–2 tablespoons fresh tarragon, chopped
1 litre chicken stock
1–2 teaspoons sugar, to taste
1 small strip lemon rind

Cooking time: 1 hour
Serves: 4

- Heat the butter and oil in a saucepan, add the vegetables and garlic, then cook gently for 2 minutes, without browning.
- Add the tomatoes, tomato purée, bay leaf, tarragon, chicken stock, sugar and lemon rind. Simmer gently, uncovered, for 20 minutes.
- Discard the strip of lemon rind and bay leaf, then blend until smooth.
- Pass through a fine sieve into a clean saucepan, then season to taste.
- Reheat gently, then serve.

Fresh for... May 1st

Crab Creole

Ingredients

2 tablespoons sunflower oil
1 medium onion, finely chopped
15g fresh root ginger, finely grated
225g very ripe tomatoes, peeled
pinch of saffron
1 sprig of fresh thyme
1 tablespoon tomato purée
500g fresh huss
500g whole uncooked prawns, peeled
200ml dry white wine
good pinch of sugar
1 whole cooked fresh crab
900ml fish stock
1 tablespoon fresh flat-leaf parsley, chopped
2 tablespoons fresh coriander, chopped

- Heat the oil in a saucepan, add the onion, then cover and cook gently until soft, without browning. Add the ginger, tomatoes, saffron, thyme and tomato purée.
- Add the huss and prawns, then add the wine and sugar. Cover, then simmer gently for 5 minutes.
- Add the crab meat, cover, then simmer for a further 5 minutes. Add the fish stock, cover, bring to the boil, then add the parsley and coriander and season to taste. Serve at once, very hot.

Fresh for...

May

2nd

Pea & Ham

Ingredients

25g butter
5 spring onions, sliced
500ml hot ham stock (from cube)
500g frozen peas
150g Wiltshire cured sliced ham, diced
100ml milk

Cooking time	Serves
20 minutes	4

- Melt the butter in a saucepan, add the spring onions, then fry for 2–3 minutes.
- Add the hot stock, bring to the boil, then add the peas.
- Keep on a high heat and quickly bring back to the boil. Once boiling, add the ham before reducing the heat and simmering for 5 minutes.
- Blend until smooth, add the milk, then reheat gently.
- Season to taste and serve.

Fresh for...

May

3rd

Cucumber, Yoghurt & Mint

Ingredients

3 large cucumbers
1 clove garlic, crushed
500ml Greek yoghurt
250ml single cream
1 lemon, juice of
600ml chicken stock
4 spring onions, chopped
Tabasco, to taste
2 tablespoons fresh mint, chopped
10g fresh dill, chopped

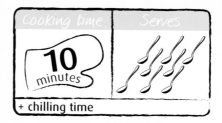

Cooking time: 10 minutes + chilling time

Serves

- Take half of one of the cucumbers, deseed and dice, then put aside for the garnish.
- Peel, deseed and roughly chop the remaining cucumbers, then place in a blender with all the other ingredients except the mint, dill and Tabasco.
- Blend until smooth, then chill for 3–4 hours.
- When you are ready to serve, check the seasoning, add the Tabasco as required, then serve garnished with the reserved cucumber, mint and dill.

Fresh for...
May
4th

Asparagus, Leek & New Potato Chowder

Ingredients

25g butter
1 leek, white part only, finely sliced
250g new potatoes, halved
500ml vegetable stock
500g asparagus, trimmed and cut into 2cm lengths
half a teaspoon of tarragon, finely chopped
150ml single cream
1 tablespoon parsley, finely chopped

Cooking time	Serves
35 minutes	4

- Melt the butter in a saucepan, add the leek, then cook for 5 minutes until soft.
- Add the potatoes and stock, then bring to the boil. Cover then simmer gently for 15 minutes until the potatoes are almost tender.
- Stir in the asparagus and tarragon, then cook for a further 3–5 minutes until asparagus is *al dente*.
- Remove one-third of the soup then blend until smooth.
- Return the blended soup to the pan, stir in the cream and parsley, then season to taste. Reheat gently for 3 minutes and serve.

Fresh for...
May
5th

Fish with Saffron & Cayenne

Ingredients

900g mixed fish and shellfish (e.g. whiting, mackerel, bass, crab, prawns, mussels, langoustine, eel etc.)
150ml extra virgin olive oil
2–3 medium onions, finely sliced
2 sticks celery, chopped
2 garlic cloves, crushed
1 bay leaf
1 sprig of fresh thyme
a few fresh sprigs of parsley
half an orange, rind of, cut into very fine strips
pinch of saffron threads dissolved in 1 tablespoon of water
pinch of cayenne pepper

Cooking time: 25 minutes
Serves

- Wash the fish then pat dry with kitchen paper. Fillet and skin the fish, if necessary, and cut into large, thick pieces. Remove any shellfish from their shells.
- Heat the oil in a saucepan, add the onion and celery, then cover and cook gently for 5 minutes, without browning.
- Add the remaining ingredients together with the fish in a layer, then add just enough water to cover.
- Cover, bring to the boil, then simmer very gently for 5 minutes.
- Add the shellfish and cook for a further 5 minutes. Season to taste, then serve.

Fresh for...

May

6th

Watercress, Pear & Brie

Ingredients

10g butter
1 small onion, diced
1 medium potato, diced
2 pears, cored and diced
490ml vegetable stock
120g watercress
65g Somerset brie, chopped into chunks
1 tablespoon double cream

Cooking time: 45 minutes

Serves: 4

- Melt the butter in a saucepan, add the onion and potato, then cook for 10 minutes, without browning.
- Add the pears and stock, then cook for 25 minutes until the onion and the potato are soft.
- Add the watercress, then cook for a further 3 minutes until it wilts. Add the brie, then cook for 1 minute.
- Blend until smooth, then season to taste.
- Add the double cream, then heat gently for 2 minutes and serve.

Sour Cherry Soup

Fresh for...
May
7th

Ingredients

550g fresh sour cherries, pitted (or 3 x 310g jars of preserved morello cherries, drained)
75g caster sugar (or to taste)
1 tablespoon lemon juice
450ml dry white wine
725ml water (include the juice from the jars of cherries, if used)
1 teaspoon ground cinnamon
150ml single cream

To garnish:
reserved cherry halves
150ml soured cream

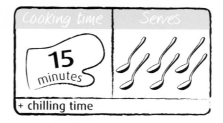

Cooking time	Serves
15 minutes	6

+ chilling time

- Cut 18 cherries in half, then set aside.
- Put the remaining cherries, sugar, lemon juice, white wine and water into a saucepan.
- Cover, bring to the boil, then simmer gently for 5–10 minutes.
- Add the cinnamon, cool a little, then blend until smooth. Stir in the cream, then chill well.
- Serve garnished with the cherry halves set aside earlier and a swirl of soured cream.

Fresh for...
May
8th

Simple Pea Soup

Ingredients

50g butter
1 small onion, finely diced
1 small leek, finely diced
1 stick celery, finely diced
750ml chicken stock
500g frozen peas

Cooking time	Serves
25 minutes	4

- Melt the butter in a saucepan, add the onion, leek and celery, and then cook gently for 10 minutes until soft and transparent.
- Add the stock, then simmer for 5 minutes.
- Add the peas, bring back to the boil, then simmer for a further 3–4 minutes until the peas are just tender.
- Blend until smooth, then season to taste and serve.

Courgette, Feta & Mint

Fresh for... May 9th

Ingredients

2 tablespoons olive oil
4–6 courgettes, cut into large chunks
1 clove garlic, crushed
600ml vegetable stock
75g feta cheese
1 tablespoon fresh mint, finely chopped
50ml double cream

- Heat the oil in a saucepan, add the courgettes and garlic, then cook over a medium heat for 20 minutes until soft and lightly browned.
- Add the stock, then simmer for 5 minutes.
- Add the feta cheese and mint, then stir over a low heat until the feta has almost melted.
- Blend until smooth.
- Reheat gently, adding the cream before serving. Garnish with extra feta and mint if desired.

Fresh for...
May
10th

King Prawn & Chorizo

Ingredients

1 tablespoon olive oil
1 medium onion, finely chopped
1 red pepper, deseeded and finely chopped
125g chorizo, diced
generous pinch of chilli flakes
1 tablespoon fresh thyme, chopped
2 cloves garlic, chopped
1 teaspoon smoked sweet paprika
800ml chicken stock
1 tablespoon tomato purée
200g tinned haricot beans, drained and rinsed
16 cooked king prawns
1 tablespoon flat-leaf parsley, chopped

Cooking time: 30 minutes
Serves

- Heat the oil in a saucepan, add the onion and red pepper, then cook for 5 minutes until they begin to soften.
- Add the chorizo, chilli flakes, thyme and garlic and stir frequently. Once the fat starts to run from the chorizo, add the paprika and keep stirring. The vegetables should have softened and the chorizo should be lightly browned.
- Add the stock, tomato purée and haricot beans, then simmer for a further 10 minutes.
- Add the king prawns, then cook for 3–5 minutes.
- Serve sprinkled with chopped parsley.

Asparagus, New Potato, Pea & Mint

Fresh for...
May
11th

Ingredients

2 bunches asparagus, reserve 12 tips for garnish, chop the remaining into 2cm pieces
50g butter
1 tablespoon oil
1 medium onion, diced
1 small leek, diced
200g new potatoes, peeled and diced
1 litre vegetable stock
1 tablespoon mint, chopped
250g peas, fresh or frozen
drizzle of lemon olive oil

Cooking time	Serves
35 minutes	6

- Steam the asparagus tips for 2–3 minutes until *al dente*, then refresh in cold water.
- Heat the butter and oil in a saucepan, add the onion and leek, then cook for 5 minutes. Then add the potato, cover and cook for a further 10 minutes, without browning, stirring occasionally to prevent sticking.
- Add the stock and chopped asparagus, bring to the boil, then cover and simmer for 3–5 minutes. Add the mint and peas then cook for a further 2 minutes.
- Blend until smooth. For a really silky finish, pass through a sieve.
- Reheat gently, season to taste, then serve with the asparagus tips on top and a drizzle of lemon olive oil.

Fresh for...
May
12th

Radish, Spring Onion & Lettuce

Ingredients

25g unsalted butter
1 medium potato, diced
1 small onion, diced
75g peas
520ml vegetable stock
100g lettuce, leaves removed and washed
3 spring onions, sliced
4 radishes, sliced
3 tablespoons double cream
1 teaspoon parsley, chopped

Cooking time	Serves
45 minutes	

- Melt the butter in a saucepan, add the potato and onion, then cook for 3 minutes until soft.
- Add the peas and stock, bring to the boil, then cover and simmer for 25 minutes.
- Add the lettuce, then cook, uncovered, for a further 5 minutes.
- Blend until smooth.
- Return to the pan, add the spring onion and radishes, then season to taste.
- Cook gently for 5 minutes, then add the cream and chopped parsley. Stir, and then serve.

Sweet Potato, Rhubarb & Apricot

Fresh for...
May
13th

Ingredients

25g unsalted butter
1 tablespoon olive oil
2 sweet potatoes, large cubes
2 spring onions, chopped
half a small green chilli, finely chopped
half a teaspoon ground coriander
half a lemon, zest of
half a lime, zest of
200g rhubarb, chopped
100g dried apricots, chopped
1 teaspoon brown sugar
100ml dry white wine
650ml vegetable stock
4 basil leaves, torn

Cooking time	Serves
40 minutes	4

- Heat the butter and oil in a saucepan, add the sweet potatoes, then cook gently until lightly coloured.
- Add the spring onions, chilli, coriander, lemon and lime zests, then cook for 3–4 minutes.
- Add the rhubarb, apricots, sugar, wine and stock. Bring to the boil, then cover and simmer for 15 minutes or until tender.
- Carefully remove 12 chunks of sweet potato from the soup and put to one side Blend the rest of the soup until smooth.
- Reheat gently, add the chunks of sweet potato and torn basil leaves, then season to taste and serve.

Fresh for…
May
14th

Wensleydale & Bacon

Ingredients

25g butter
110g smoked bacon, finely chopped
2 medium onions, finely chopped
2 large carrots, finely chopped
1 clove garlic, finely chopped
1.5 litres chicken stock
1 teaspoon paprika
250g Wensleydale cheese, grated

Cooking time	Serves
40 minutes	6

- Melt the butter in a saucepan, add the bacon, onion and carrot, then cook gently for 3–5 minutes.
- Add the garlic, then cook for a further 2–3 minutes. Add the chicken stock and paprika, cover, bring to the boil, then simmer for 20 minutes.
- Blend until smooth, then reheat slowly, adding the Wensleydale cheese, stirring well. Season with black pepper to taste. Don't add salt unless you are sure it needs it. Serve immediately.

Asparagus, Rosemary & Roasted Garlic

Fresh for...
May
15th

Ingredients

1 large glass jar
3 heads of garlic
570ml extra virgin olive oil
3 large sprigs of fresh rosemary
1 medium onion, finely sliced
450g fresh asparagus, cut into 5cm pieces
1 tablespoon plain flour
850ml vegetable stock
150ml single cream

To garnish:
2 tablespoons fresh flat-leaf parsley, chopped
1 lemon, zest of, grated

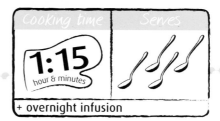

Cooking time	Serves
1:15 hour & minutes	

+ overnight infusion

- Preheat the oven to 180°C/350°F/gas mark 4.
- Sterilise a large glass jar by putting the clean jar in the oven for 10 minutes. Take out of the oven and allow to cool.
- To roast the garlic, remove any excess papery skin from the garlic heads, then place onto a small baking tin with 3 tablespoons of olive oil. Roast for 15–20 minutes until soft. Remove from the oven, then allow to cool. Trim off the top 1cm, then pack the garlic and sprigs of rosemary into the sterilised jar and completely cover the garlic with the remaining olive oil. Seal the jar and leave overnight.
- For the soup: heat 4 tablespoons of the infused garlic and rosemary oil from the jar in a saucepan, add the onion, then cover and cook gently for 5 minutes. Peel and finely chop 4 cloves of the infused garlic, add to the saucepan, and then cook gently for a further 5 minutes, without browning.
- Add the asparagus and cook gently for 2 minutes. Stir in the flour, then cook gently for a further 2 minutes. Gradually add the stock, stirring all the time. Cover, bring to the boil, then simmer gently for about 15–20 minutes until the asparagus is tender.
- Blend until very smooth, then pass through a fine sieve to remove any stringy fibres. Reheat gently, add the cream, then season to taste. Serve garnished with chopped parsley and lemon zest. This soup is also delicious served chilled.

Fresh for...
May
16th

Soupe au Pistou

Ingredients

1 small onion, peeled and studded with 2 whole cloves
4 litres water
1 small leek, finely sliced
175g carrots, cut into 2cm dice
110g pumpkin, cut into 2cm dice (optional)
275g ripe tomatoes, skinned, deseeded and roughly chopped (or 1 x 400g tin chopped tomatoes)
1 stick celery, cut into 2cm dice
sprig of thyme
1 bay leaf
225g potatoes, peeled and cut into 2cm dice
110g turnip, cut into 2cm dice
2 x 410g tins haricot beans, drained and rinsed
175g French beans, topped and tailed and cut into 5cm pieces
175g broad beans
275g courgettes, cut into 2cm dice
50g thick vermicelli or macaroni

For the pistou:
4 cloves garlic, peeled
pinch of salt
18 large basil leaves
150ml extra virgin olive oil
250g freshly grated Parmesan cheese

To garnish:
50g freshly grated Parmesan cheese
50g mature Dutch cheese, grated

Cooking time	Serves
40 minutes	4

- Put the onion into a saucepan, add the leek, carrots, pumpkin (if using), tomatoes, celery, thyme and bay leaf, then simmer gently for 15 minutes.
- Add the turnip, potatoes, haricot beans, French beans and broad beans, then bring to the boil. Once boiling add the courgettes and vermicelli or macaroni. Season to taste, then simmer for a further 15 minutes, or until the pasta is *al dente*. Discard the onion and bay leaf.
- For the pistou: put the peeled garlic cloves into a blender with a pinch of salt and the basil leaves. Bring to a purée, then slowly add the olive oil. Add the Parmesan and season to taste.
- To serve, put the pistou into a tureen and pour on the piping hot soup, stirring all the time. Ladle the soup into bowls and garnish with the mixed Parmesan and Dutch cheese.

Seafood Paella

Fresh for...
May
17th

Ingredients

5 tablespoons olive oil
1 large onion, finely chopped
2 cloves garlic, finely chopped
100g pimientos de piquillo (flame roasted peppers in a jar), cut into fine strips
400g Calasparra or paella rice, rinsed in cold water
200ml dry white wine
800ml fish stock
half a teaspoon sweet smoked paprika
large pinch of saffron, soaked in 150ml boiling water
4 vine tomatoes, skinned, deseeded and chopped
200g fresh mussels, cleaned and debearded
400g seafood selection (prawns, mussels, squid rings), fresh or frozen (defrosted if frozen)
100g peas, fresh or frozen
200g monkfish tail, cut into 3cm chunks
12 raw tiger prawns complete with tail section
3 tablespoons parsley, chopped
1 lemon, cut into wedges

Cooking time: 35 minutes
Serves: 6

- Heat 3 tablespoons of olive oil in a large saucepan, then add the onion, garlic and peppers. Cook gently for 15 minutes. Stir in the rice, then cook for 2–3 minutes, pour in the wine then stir until almost evaporated.
- Add most of the stock, the smoked paprika, saffron and tomatoes then cook for 10 minutes, stirring occasionally.
- Add the mussels in their shells, the seafood selection and peas, then stir, adding more stock if necessary.
- In a frying pan, heat the remaining oil and fry the monkfish for 2 minutes. Add the prawns and cook for a further 2 minutes until the prawns are pink.
- Transfer to the paella pan, season to taste and check that the rice is cooked; if not, add a little more boiling water and cook for a few minutes longer.
- Remove any unopened mussels, sprinkle with parsley and serve with lemon wedges.

Fresh for...

May

18th

Salmon, Tomato & Basil

Ingredients

25g butter
1 medium onion, finely chopped
3 garlic cloves, crushed
1 level teaspoon plain flour
900ml fish stock
300ml dry white wine
450ml milk
2 teaspoons tomato purée
pinch of cayenne pepper, or to taste
1 large bay leaf
200g fresh salmon, skinned, bones removed, diced into 2cm cubes
75g smoked salmon trimmings, cut into small pieces
700g ripe but firm tomatoes, skinned, deseeded and diced into 2cm cubes
1 tablespoon chopped fresh basil

To garnish:
150ml single cream
6 small sprigs of fresh basil
paprika

Cooking time: 30 minutes

Serves: 6

- Heat the butter in a saucepan, add the onion and garlic, then cover and cook gently for 5 minutes, without browning. Stir in the flour then cook for 2 minutes, stirring constantly.

- Gradually add the stock, white wine, milk, tomato purée, cayenne and bay leaf, then cover, bring to the boil and simmer gently for a further 10 minutes until the onions are soft. Remove the bay leaf then blend until smooth.

- Reheat gently, then when the soup is very hot, add the salmon, smoked salmon, tomatoes and basil. Simmer gently for 2 minutes until the salmon is just firm.

- Season to taste. (Take care as smoked salmon is already quite salty.)

- Serve garnished with a swirl of cream, the basil sprigs and a dusting of paprika.

Courgette & Brie

Fresh for...
May
19th

Ingredients

450g courgettes, sliced
2 medium potatoes, about 350g, peeled and chopped
1 onion, finely chopped
1.2 litres vegetable stock
225g Somerset brie, remove end rind and cut into pieces

Cooking time: 25 minutes

Serves

- Put all the ingredients except the brie into a large saucepan.
- Cover, bring to the boil, then simmer gently for 15 minutes until the vegetables are tender.
- Stir in the cheese until melted.
- Blend until smooth. Then season to taste and serve.

Fresh for...

May

20th

Petits Pois & Watercress

Ingredients

25g unsalted butter
1 medium onion, finely chopped
350g fresh petit pois (or frozen peas)
50g watercress
750ml vegetable stock
1–2 tablespoons fresh mint, chopped

Cooking time: 20 minutes

Serves

- Melt the butter in a saucepan, add the onion, then cook for 5 minutes until soft.
- Add the peas, watercress and stock and bring to the boil. Cover and simmer for 5 minutes until the peas are tender.
- Blend until smooth.
- Return to the pan, season to taste and reheat gently for 3 minutes.
- Add the mint, then serve.

Summer Vegetable & Pesto

Fresh for...
May
21st

Ingredients

2 tablespoons olive oil
2 cloves garlic, peeled and crushed
1 onion, finely chopped
2 sticks celery, finely diced
3 courgettes, diced
1.5 litres vegetable stock
120g peas, shelled
100g green beans, sliced into 2cm lengths
175g broad beans, shelled
1 tablespoon fresh basil, finely shredded
1 tablespoon fresh mint, finely shredded

To garnish:
50g Parmesan, finely grated
3 tablespoons fresh pesto

Cooking time: 25 minutes

Serves

- Heat the oil in a saucepan, add the garlic, onion and celery, then cook gently for 10 minutes, until soft.
- Add the courgettes and stock, bring to the boil, then cover and simmer for 5 minutes.
- Add the peas, green beans and broad beans, then simmer for a further 5 minutes.
- Remove from the heat, then stir in the basil and mint.
- Serve topped with Parmesan and drizzled with pesto.

Fresh for...

May

22nd

Gazpacho

Ingredients

4 cloves garlic
1.3kg sweet ripe tomatoes
1 red pepper, deseeded and finely chopped
1 yellow pepper, deseeded and finely chopped
1 small red onion, finely diced
75g ciabatta, crusts removed and cubed
4 tablespoons red wine vinegar
5 tablespoons olive oil
250ml tomato juice
Tabasco, to taste (optional)

To garnish:
crushed ice

Cooking time	Serves
10 minutes	6
+ chilling time	

- Crush the garlic to a smooth paste with a little salt, either using the back of a knife or a pestle and mortar.
- Blend all of the ingredients, except the tomato juice, until smooth.
- Sieve half the soup to give it a finer texture, then stir into the remaining half and add the tomato juice. Stir once again before chilling well.
- When chilled and you are ready to serve, season to taste, adding a little more olive oil and red wine vinegar to taste. Add a splash of Tabasco, to taste, if required.
- Serve chilled with a little crushed ice piled in the middle of the soup.

Fresh for...
May
23rd

Kitchen Herb Garden

Ingredients

50g butter
8 spring onions, sliced
2 cloves garlic, crushed
500g potatoes, peeled and diced
1.5 litres vegetable stock
200g fresh peas
3 baby gem lettuces, finely sliced
2 tablespoons fresh parsley, chopped
2 tablespoons fresh thyme, chopped
2 tablespoons fresh chives, chopped
2 tablespoons fresh mint, chopped
2 tablespoons fresh tarragon, chopped
200ml single cream
half a lemon, juice of

Cooking time	Serves
40 minutes	8

- Melt the butter in a saucepan, add the spring onion, garlic and potato, then cover and cook for 10 minutes, without browning.
- Add the stock and bring to the boil, then cover and cook for 15 minutes.
- Add the peas, half the lettuce and herbs, then cook for a further 3–5 minutes.
- Blend until smooth, then add the remaining lettuce, cream and lemon juice. Reserve a few herbs for garnishing, then add the rest to the pan.
- Reheat gently and then serve.

Fresh for...

May

24th

Watercress & New Potato

Ingredients

25g butter
1 medium onion, finely sliced
1 clove garlic, crushed
250g new salad potatoes, halved
800ml vegetable stock
400g watercress, hard stalks removed
3 tablespoons double cream
half a lemon, juice of
pinch of nutmeg, grated or ground to taste

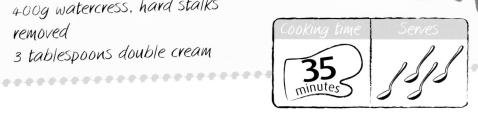

Cooking time: 35 minutes

Serves: 4

- Melt the butter in a saucepan, add the onion, garlic and new potatoes, then cover and cook gently for 10 minutes, without browning.
- Add the stock, bring to the boil, then simmer for 5 minutes.
- Add the watercress, return to the boil, then cook for 4 minutes, retaining the colour in the watercress.
- Remove from the heat, set aside some chunks of potato, then blend the rest of the soup until smooth.
- Return to the pan, add the reserved potato chunks and cream, then reheat gently for 3 minutes.
- Season to taste. Add the lemon juice, then add the grated nutmeg to taste and serve.

Fresh for...
May
25th

Spinach, Honey & Herbs

Ingredients

465ml vegetable stock
1 large carrot, finely chopped or grated
2 sticks celery, chopped
1 small onion, finely diced
285g baby spinach
1 tablespoon parsley, chopped
1 tablespoon chives, chopped
4 basil leaves
1 tablespoon honey
180ml tomato passata
Worcestershire sauce, to taste

Cooking time	Serves
30 minutes	4

- Place the stock in a saucepan, bring to the boil, then add the carrot, celery and onion. Cover and simmer for 15 minutes.
- Add the spinach, herbs, honey and passata, stir, then simmer rapidly for 5 minutes.
- Blend, but not too smoothly.
- Return to the pan, add the Worcestershire sauce, then season to taste.
- Reheat gently for 2–3 minutes and serve.

Fresh for...
May
26th

Lobster Bisque

Ingredients

1 small lobster, fresh & whole
40g unsalted butter
1 medium onion, sliced
30g plain flour
1 tablespoon tomato purée
2 tablespoons brandy or calvados
600ml fish stock
75ml double cream
1 teaspoon fresh parsley, chopped

Cooking time	Serves
1 hour	4

- Place the lobster in a saucepan of cold water then heat gently for 30 minutes, until the lobster is light pink in colour; do not allow to boil. Remove from the heat and allow to cool in the water.
- Once cool, remove the lobster from the water and place on a chopping board. Remove the claws, cut the lobster in half lengthways and remove the meat, taking care to avoid any discoloured meat (green, brown or black).
- Whilst the lobster is cooking, melt the butter in a saucepan, add the onion, then cook until soft without browning.
- Add the flour and tomato purée, stir in well, then cook for 30 seconds.
- Add the brandy or calvados, then reduce the volume by half. Add the stock and keep stirring until the soup comes to the boil and starts to thicken. Cover, then simmer gently for 25 minutes.
- Blend until smooth.
- Add the lobster meat and double cream, then season to taste. Reheat at a simmer for 3 minutes, sprinkle over the parsley and serve.

Fresh for...
May
27th

Broad Bean & Bacon

Ingredients

1 tablespoon olive oil
12 rashers smoked, streaky bacon, cut into strips
12 spring onions, roughly chopped
750ml vegetable stock
500g broad beans

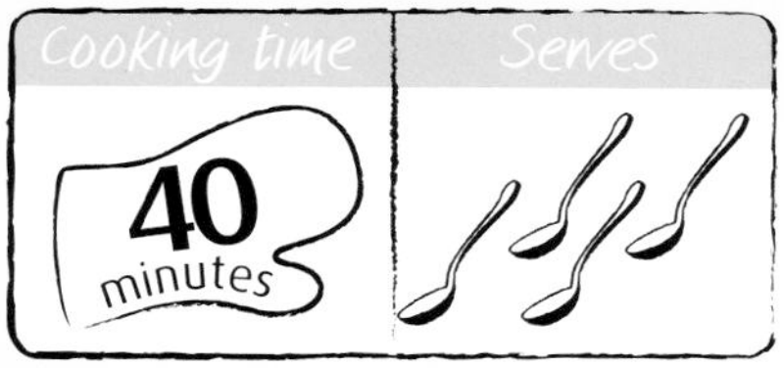

- Heat the oil in a pan, add the bacon and spring onions, then cook for 8–10 minutes until the bacon starts to crisp.
- Add some of the stock to the pan, then cook gently for a further 3 minutes.
- Add the broad beans and the remaining stock, then cook for 20 minutes.
- Blend until smooth.
- Reheat gently, season to taste and serve.

Fresh for...
May
28th

Pea, Herb & Lettuce

Ingredients

25g butter
300g fresh peas
1 small head of soft lettuce, torn into pieces
3 small spring onions, finely sliced
2 tablespoons parsley, roughly chopped
2 tablespoons coriander, roughly chopped
650ml vegetable stock
100ml single cream

Cooking time	Serves
20 minutes	4

- Melt the butter in a saucepan, add the peas, lettuce and spring onions, then cook gently until the lettuce has wilted.
- Add the herbs, cook for a further minute, then add the stock. Simmer gently for 3 minutes.
- Remove from the heat, set aside 2 ladles of soup, then blend the remaining soup until smooth.
- Return the blended and set-aside soup to the pan, then reheat gently for 3 minutes.
- Add the cream, season to taste, then reheat gently for 2 minutes and serve.

Fresh for...
May
29th

Orange & Saffron Vichyssoise

Ingredients

25g butter
3 young leeks (250g), finely chopped
1 clove garlic, sliced
250g Jersey Royal new potatoes, peeled and diced
750ml vegetable stock
5–6 strands of saffron, infused in 50ml boiling water
4 oranges, juice of, plus zest of 1 orange
caster sugar, to taste

To garnish:
Coriander, finely chopped

Cooking time	Serves
35 minutes	

- Melt the butter in a saucepan, add the leeks and garlic, then cook gently for 5 minutes, without browning.
- Add the potato, then cook for a further 2–3 minutes.
- Add the stock and infused saffron, bring to the boil, then cover and simmer for 15 minutes.
- Blend until smooth, then add the orange juice and pass through a sieve. Season to taste with salt, pepper and caster sugar (this will vary depending on the sweetness of your oranges). Then reheat gently and serve garnished with chopped coriander.
- To serve chilled: refrigerate for several hours, then serve in iced shot glasses, topped with chopped coriander and a few shreds of orange zest.

Fresh for...
May
30th

Watercress & Apple

Ingredients

25g butter
2 spanish onions, finely chopped
1 tablespoon medium curry powder
2 bunches watercress
1 tablespoon cornflour
570ml chicken stock
2 egg yolks
150ml hot double cream
290ml milk
1 eating apple, peeled, cored and sliced

To garnish:
2 eating apples, peeled, cored and finely diced
juice of 1 lemon
4 sprigs of watercress

Cooking time	Serves
25 minutes	4

- Melt the butter in a saucepan, add the onion, then cover and cook gently, without browning.
- Stir in the curry powder, then cook for 2 minutes, stirring. Add the watercress, reserving 1 large handful.
- Mix the cornflour with a little stock, until smooth, then add to the soup with the remaining stock.
- Bring to the boil, then simmer gently for 10 minutes. Add the reserved watercress leaves, then cook for a further 2 minutes.
- Whisk the egg yolks into the hot cream, then stir into the soup.
- Remove immediately from the heat, then blend with the milk and apple until completely smooth and mousse-like. Season to taste and chill well.
- Mix the diced apple with the lemon juice to retain its colour. Serve the soup garnished with the diced apple and sprigs of watercress. This soup is also delicious hot.

Gooseberry Soup

Fresh for...
May
31st

Ingredients

900g under-ripe gooseberries (if unavailable use gooseberries preserved in syrup, or frozen)
pinch of salt
4 level dessertspoons sugar (or to taste)
1 lemon, rind of, finely grated
2 teaspoons plain flour
275ml milk
150ml soured cream

Cooking time	Serves
20 minutes	4
+ chilling time	

- Put the gooseberries into a saucepan, add a dash of water, salt, sugar and lemon rind, then cover and simmer gently until the gooseberries are tender.
- Add the flour, then blend until smooth, passing through a sieve for extra silkiness.
- Stir in the milk and soured cream, adding a little more milk if necessary to achieve the right consistency.
- Cover, then simmer very gently for 5 minutes. Remove from the heat, allow to cool, and then refrigerate.
- Serve well chilled.

Fresh for...
June
1st

Roasted Red Pepper, Goat's Cheese & Rocket

Ingredients

8 large red peppers
1 head garlic
3 tablespoons olive oil
2 medium onions, finely chopped
2 carrots, peeled and diced
2 sticks celery, diced
1 teaspoon sweet smoked paprika
1.5 litres vegetable stock
50g rocket leaves
150g goat's cheese

Cooking time	Serves
1 hour	

- Preheat your oven to 230°C/450°F/gas mark 8.
- Cut the peppers in half, removing the seeds but leaving the stalks intact, then place in a roasting tin as a single layer with the skins facing upwards. Wrap the garlic head in foil and add to the tin, then roast for 30 minutes until the pepper skins are lightly charred.
- Place the peppers in a bowl, cover with cling film, then allow to cool. Once cooled, the skins should be easy to remove.
- Meanwhile, heat the oil in a saucepan, add the onions, carrots and celery, then cover and cook for 15–20 minutes until softened. Add the smoked paprika and stir.
- Add the stock and skinless peppers (as well as their juices) to the pan. Squeeze half the roasted garlic cloves from their skins and add to the pan (you can use the other half in a bruschetta or pasta dish later), bring to the boil then remove from the heat.
- Blend until smooth, season to taste, then serve with a small handful of rocket leaves and crumbled goat's cheese.

Fresh for...
June
2nd

Courgette & Tarragon

Ingredients

25g butter
4 medium courgettes, chunked
1-2 tablespoons tarragon, chopped
300ml vegetable stock
300ml milk

Cooking time	Serves
35 minutes	4

- Melt the butter in a saucepan, add the courgettes, then cook gently for 5 minutes.
- Add the tarragon, then cook gently for a further 5 minutes.
- Add the stock, which should almost cover the courgettes, bring to the boil, then cover and simmer for 15 minutes until the courgettes are tender.
- Add the milk, then blend until smooth.
- Season to taste, then reheat gently for 3 minutes and serve.

Fresh for...
June
3rd

Plum Soup

Ingredients

675g red plums
290ml good red wine
2 tablespoons lemon juice
pinch of ground cloves
half a teaspoon mixed spice
4 tablespoons sugar (or to taste)
1 level tablespoon cornflour
290ml buttermilk

To garnish:
75g plain chocolate
100ml double cream

Cooking time	Serves
25 minutes	4
+ chilling time	

- Place the plums in a saucepan with a little water, then cover and simmer for about 10–15 minutes or until tender.
- Pass the plums and juices through a sieve into a clean saucepan, then add the red wine, lemon juice, ground cloves, mixed spice and sugar to taste.
- Mix the cornfour with a little water until smooth, then stir well into the soup. Bring to the boil, stirring until the mixture thickens, and simmer gently for 2 minutes.
- Allow the soup to cool, stir in the buttermilk, then chill well.
- Melt the chocolate in a bain-marie or in a bowl placed over a pan of simmering water. Serve the soup garnished with swirls of the melted chocolate and cream.

Fresh for...
June
4th

Chicken & Asparagus

Ingredients

1 tablespoon olive oil
1 chicken breast
a knob of butter
1 small onion, diced
400ml chicken stock
2 small potatoes, diced
250g asparagus (reserve a few tips, cut the rest into 3cm pieces)
30ml single cream
1 tablespoon fresh parsley, chopped

Cooking time	Serves
55 minutes	4

- Heat the olive oil in a frying pan, add the chicken breast, and then fry gently, turning occasionally, for 15–20 minutes, until fully cooked through. Cool slightly, shred (using 2 forks), then set aside.
- Meanwhile, melt the butter in a saucepan, add the onion, then cook gently for 5–10 minutes.
- Add the stock and potato, bring to the boil, and simmer gently for 15 minutes, stirring occasionally.
- Add the asparagus pieces (excluding the tips) and cook gently for a further 5 minutes.
- Blend until smooth.
- Add the cream, asparagus tips, shredded chicken and fresh parsley. Reheat gently, season to taste and then serve.

Fresh for...
June
5th

Thai Green Curry Soup

Ingredients

For the paste:

1 stick lemongrass, chopped
2 green birds eye chillies, deseeded and chopped
2 shallots, peeled and chopped
2 cloves garlic, peeled and chopped
1 teaspoon ground cumin
1 teaspoon ground coriander
1 tablespoon Thai fish sauce
1 lime, zest and juice of

For the curry:

2 tablespoons olive oil
2 small chicken breasts, cut into strips
1 x 400ml tin coconut milk
500ml chicken stock
100g Basmati rice (washed before cooking to remove the starch)
large handful fresh basil, shredded
large handful fresh coriander leaves, shredded

Cooking time	Serves
20 minutes	4

- Place all the paste ingredients in a blender and blend to a fine paste.
- For the curry: heat the oil in a saucepan, add the chicken and paste, then cook gently for 3–4 minutes, taking care as it will spit.
- Add the coconut milk and stock. Bring to a simmer, then add the rice.
- Cover and simmer for 7–9 minutes until the rice is just cooked.
- Sprinkle with the shredded basil and coriander leaves, then serve and enjoy.

Fresh for...
June
6th

Fennel Soup with Lobster

Ingredients

2 tablespoons olive oil
1 stick celery, chopped
2 shallots, sliced
3 fennel bulbs, sliced
100ml dry white wine
700ml fish stock
1 bay leaf
100ml double cream
1 tablespoon fresh parsley, chopped
150g lobster flesh

Cooking time: 1 hour

Serves

- Heat the oil in a saucepan, add the celery, shallots and fennel, then cook for 10 minutes until softened.
- Add the wine, then simmer to reduce the liquid by half.
- Add the stock and bay leaf, and bring to the boil. Cover and simmer for 30–40 minutes until the fennel is tender.
- Remove the bay leaf, then blend until smooth. Pass through a sieve, using the back of a ladle to push it through.
- Reheat gently, add the cream, then season to taste.
- Serve the soup topped with a sprinkle of parsley and the lobster flesh.

Fresh for...

June

7th

Cullen Skink

Ingredients

100ml whole milk
426ml.vegetable stock
2 fillets smoked haddock
25g butter
1 small onion
1 medium potato, diced
1 teaspoon parsley, chopped
2 tablespoons double cream

- Heat the milk and half of the stock in a saucepan. Add the smoked haddock, then poach for 10 minutes until lightly cooked.
- Remove from the heat, then cool the fish in the liquid.
- In another saucepan, melt the butter, then add the onion and cook gently for 5 minutes, without browning.
- Add the potato and the remaining stock, then bring to the boil. Cover and simmer for 15 minutes until the potato is soft.
- Add the liquid from the poached haddock to the pan (but don't add the fish).
- Blend until smooth, then return to the pan. Now add the smoked haddock and parsley, then heat for 2 minutes. Add the double cream, season to taste, and then serve.

Fresh for...
June
8th

Wild Salmon Chowder

Ingredients

25g butter
1 small onion, finely chopped
500g new potatoes, halved
600ml fish stock
150g fresh peas
550g wild salmon, cooked and flaked
2 tablespoons chopped herbs (we use parsley, mint and chives)
4 tablespoons double cream
100g smoked salmon, thin strips

Cooking time	Serves
40 minutes	4

- Melt the butter in a saucepan, add the onion, then cook gently until softened.
- Add the new potatoes and stock, bring to the boil, then cover and simmer gently for 20 minutes until the potatoes are tender but intact.
- Remove from the heat, blend half the soup until smooth, and return to the pan. Add the peas, then cook for 2–3 minutes.
- Add the wild salmon, herbs and cream. Season to taste, then reheat gently.
- Place the smoked salmon strips in the serving bowls, then ladle the soup over the top and serve.

Fresh for...
June
9th

Butternut Squash, Cromer Crab & Chilli

Ingredients

2 tablespoons olive oil
1 medium onion, finely chopped
1 clove garlic, crushed
1 medium butternut squash, roughly chopped
1 stick lemongrass
pinch of chilli flakes
500ml vegetable stock
140ml coconut milk
120g white crab meat
1 tablespoon fresh coriander, chopped
squeeze of lime

Cooking time: 45 minutes

Serves

- Heat the oil in a saucepan, add the onion, garlic and butternut squash, then cook gently for 10 minutes.
- Take the stick of lemongrass, remove the tough outer layer, then bash with the back of a knife to release the flavours.
- Add the chilli flakes and lemongrass to the pan, then fry for 2–3 minutes.
- Add the stock, bring to the boil, then cover and simmer gently for 20 minutes until the squash is tender.
- Remove the lemongrass, then blend until smooth.
- Add the coconut milk, crab meat and most of the coriander.
- Season to taste, then reheat gently for 5 minutes.
- Add a squeeze of lime, to taste, sprinkle with the remaining coriander, and then serve.

Fresh for...
June
10th

Asparagus, Cucumber & Pea

Ingredients

250g asparagus, chopped (but reserve tips)
50g butter
1 medium onion, finely chopped
250g leeks, finely sliced
1 clove garlic, finely chopped
quarter of a cucumber, diced
125g fresh peas, shelled
750ml vegetable stock
3 tablespons chives, snipped
1 tablespoon of each, chopped: parsley, thyme, rosemary, coriander
1 dessertspoon sage leaves, chopped
1 dessertspoon mint leaves, chopped

Cooking time	Serves
25 minutes	4

- Place the asparagus tips in a little water, then steam for 3 minutes until *al dente.* Refresh in cold water and then leave to one side.
- Melt the butter in a saucepan, add the onion, leeks and garlic, then cook gently for 5 minutes, without browning.
- Add the chopped asparagus, cucumber and peas, stir, then cook for 2 minutes.
- Add the stock, rapidly bring to the boil, then cover and simmer for 5–7 minutes until the vegetables are just tender but retain their colour.
- Blend until smooth.
- Add the chopped herbs and asparagus tips, then season to taste. Reheat gently, then serve.

Fresh for...
June
11th

Baby Vegetable & Minted Lamb Broth

Ingredients

1 tablespoon fresh parsley, chopped
1 tablespoon olive oil
1 clove garlic, crushed
200g lamb fillet
1 litre vegetable stock
100g baby carrots, cut into batons
100g broad beans, shelled (weight is pre-shelled)
100g fresh peas
pinch of sugar
2 tablespoons fresh mint, chopped
1 tablespoon chives, chopped
5–6 radishes, cut into small wedges
4 spring onions, finely sliced

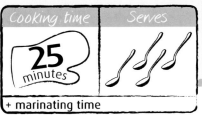

Cooking time	Serves
25 minutes	4
+ marinating time	

- Mix the parsley, olive oil and garlic together, then spoon over the lamb fillet. Leave to marinate for at least 30 minutes, preferably 2 hours, in the fridge. Remove the marinated lamb from the fridge and bring to room temperature 30 minutes before cooking.
- Season the lamb, then place in a preheated saucepan. Cook for 3–4 minutes on each side. This will leave it pink in the middle; cook for longer if required. Remove the lamb from the pan, cover with foil and set aside.
- Place the stock in the pan, bring to the boil, then add the carrots. Cover and boil for 2 minutes.
- Add the broad beans and peas, then cook for a further 3–5 minutes. At this stage the vegetables should be *al dente*.
- Add the sugar, most of the herbs, the radishes and spring onions, then season to taste. Cook for a further 3 minutes on a gentle heat.
- Finely slice the lamb across the fillet (aim for 5–7 slices per portion), then place in the serving bowls. Ladle the soup over the top, sprinkle with the remaining herbs, then serve.

Strawberry, Cream & Champagne

Fresh for...
June
12th

Ingredients

1kg ripe strawberries, washed, hulled and quartered (reserving 200g for garnish)
430ml champagne or sparkling wine
caster sugar or honey (if required)
1–2 teaspoons cornflour, mixed with a little water
285ml extra-thick single cream

Cooking time	Serves
30 minutes	
+ marinating time	

- Soak the strawberries set aside for garnishing in one-third of the champagne for at least 1 hour, at room temperature.
- Blend the remaining strawberries until smooth, then sieve into a saucepan to remove the seeds.
- Ripe strawberries should be sweet enough but if they need to be sweeter, add honey or sugar to taste.
- Add the remaining champagne to the pan, then gently bring to a simmer.
- Add the cornflour, stirring continuously until thickened, then stir in the cream.
- Serve warm or chilled, garnished with the champagne-soaked strawberries.

Fresh for...
June
13th

Tomato & Basil Vichyssoise

Ingredients

25g butter
1 small onion, finely chopped
1 large leek, washed and finely sliced
225g potato, peeled and roughly chopped
850ml vegetable stock
75g tinned chopped plum tomatoes
50g tomato purée
275ml milk
2 tablespoons fresh basil, chopped

Cooking time	Serves
25 minutes	

- Melt the butter in a saucepan, add the onion and leek, then cover and cook gently for 5 minutes, without browning.
- Add the potato and stock, then season to taste. Cover, bring to the boil, then simmer gently for 10 minutes until the potato is tender.
- Add the tomatoes and tomato purée, then cook gently for a further 3 minutes.
- Blend until very smooth, then stir in the milk and fresh basil.
- Adjust the seasoning to taste, then serve, or chill to serve cold later.

Fresh for...
June
14th

Fish Bouillabaisse

Ingredients

1 tablespoon sunflower oil
1 red onion, finely sliced
1 leek, white only, finely sliced
2 carrots, cut into fine strips
pinch of saffron
1 litre fish stock
2 tablespoons fresh flat-leaf parsley, chopped
2 tablespoons fresh dill, chopped
Pernod, to taste (approx a capful)
110g fresh skinned salmon fillet, cut into 1cm strips
110g fresh skinned lemon sole fillet, cut into 1cm strips
110g fresh skinned turbot fillet, cut into 1cm strips
60g cooked shelled prawns
60g cooked shelled mussels
60g scallops, trimmed of the white muscle

Cooking time	Serves
30 minutes	

- Heat the oil in a saucepan, add the vegetables, then fry for 10 minutes, until golden. Stir in the saffron and stock, then cover and simmer gently for 10 minutes.
- Add the parsley, dill and a dash of Pernod, then stir. Add the fish and shellfish, stir gently, then season to taste.
- Bring almost to the boil carefully, without stirring, as this may break up the fish, then serve.

Fresh for...
June
15th

Roasted Garlic Vichyssoise

Ingredients

100ml extra vigin olive oil
1 head of garlic, separated into unpeeled cloves
150g butter
4 leeks, washed and roughly chopped
900g Maris Piper, or similar, potatoes, peeled and roughly chopped
1.2 litres chicken stock
150ml double cream

To garnish:
2 tablespoons fresh chives, snipped

Cooking time	Serves
50 minutes	6

- Preheat your oven to 170°C/325°F/gas mark 3.
- Pour the oil into a small ovenproof dish, add the garlic, toss to coat it thoroughly in the oil, then cover and roast for 15–20 minutes until soft. Remove from the oven and leave to cool.
- Meanwhile, melt the butter in a saucepan, add the leeks, then cover and cook gently for 10 minutes until beginning to wilt but without browning, stirring frequently.
- Add the potatoes and stock. Cover, bring to the boil, then simmer gently for 15 minutes until the vegetables are tender. Peel the roasted garlic and add it to the pan.
- Blend until very smooth, then add the cream. If necessary, add a little water to thin to the required consistency.
- Season to taste, then reheat gently and serve garnished with the freshly snipped chives.

Prawns & Citrus Vegetable Julienne

Fresh for... June 16th

Ingredients

For the stock:

225g chicken livers, washed and drained well
2 chicken thighs, skinned
570ml water
1 small onion, roughly chopped
1 small carrot, peeled
1 small parsnip, peeled
1 small potato, peeled

For the soup:

6 tomatoes, skinned and roughly chopped
1 teaspoon Worcestershire sauce
1 teaspoon Dijon mustard
570ml chicken stock (see above)
25g medium oatmeal
half an orange, juice of
half a lemon, juice of
15g freshly grated root ginger
275ml water
half a grapefruit, flesh of, all pith and skin removed, cut into small pieces.
225g prawns, peeled and cooked
1 egg yolk, beaten

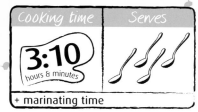

Cooking time: 3:10 hours & minutes + marinating time

Serves: 3

- Preheat the oven to 200°C/400°F/Gas Mark 6.
- To make the stock: put all the stock ingredients into a saucepan, then cover, bring to the boil and simmer gently for 1 hour. Gently remove the carrot, parsnip and potato, keeping them whole and set aside. Pass the liquid through a fine sieve into a clean bowl and reserve.
- To make the soup: put the tomatoes in a saucepan, then add the Worcestershire sauce and mustard. Cook gently for 10 minutes to break up the tomatoes.
- Bring the stock to the boil, then stir in the oatmeal. Add to the tomato mixture, then simmer gently for 30 minutes until the mixture is fairly thick but not gloopy.
- Meanwhile, prepare the vegetables reserved from the stock. Cut them into matchsticks. Put the carrots and potatoes into a small ovenproof dish, then pour over the orange juice. Put the parsnips in another small ovenproof dish, then pour over the lemon juice. Bake both dishes in the oven for 30 minutes.
- Put the ginger in a small saucepan with the water. Bring to the boil, then simmer gently for 10 minutes. Cool, then add the grapefruit pieces and prawns and leave to marinate for 30 minutes.
- When the tomato mixture is ready, remove from the heat and stir in the well-beaten yolk. Pass through a fine sieve, then add the baked vegetables and gingered grapefruit and prawns. Season to taste, then reheat and serve.

Fresh for...
June
17th

Carrot & Coriander

Ingredients

25g butter
1 medium onion, finely chopped
1 garlic clove, crushed
550g carrots (of which
  450g roughly chopped
  100g coarsely grated)
1 litre vegetable stock
pinch of freshly grated nutmeg
1 tablespoon chopped fresh coriander
150ml single cream

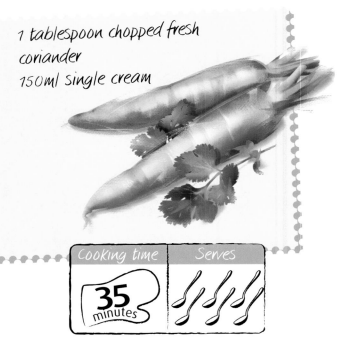

Cooking time	Serves
35 minutes	6

- Melt the butter in a saucepan, add the onion and garlic, then cover and cook gently for 10 minutes, without browning.
- Add the roughly chopped carrots, stock and nutmeg, then cover and bring to the boil. Simmer gently for 10–15 minutes until the vegetables are tender.
- Blend until smooth. Then add the grated carrots, coriander and cream. Season to taste, then serve.

Florentine Bean Soup

Fresh for...
June
18th

Ingredients

1kg fresh or 450g dried cannellini or borlotti beans, washed
8 tablespoons extra virgin olive oil
5 large garlic cloves (of which
 2 to be peeled and chopped
 2 to be crushed without peeling
 1 to be peeled only)
2 large onions, finely chopped
1 carrot, chopped
1 leek, chopped
1 stick celery, chopped
1 large ripe tomato, peeled, deseeded and chopped
1 ham bone
1.5 litres water
salt
half a teaspoon of beef extract
275g dark green cabbage leaves (ideally the black Tuscan cabbage cavolo nero), cut into large pieces
1 sprig of fresh rosemary
pinch of dried thyme

To garnish:
6 slices coarse white bread
5 tablespoons Parmesan cheese, freshly grated

Cooking time	Serves
1:55 hours & minutes	3

+ overnight soaking

- If using dried beans, soak them overnight. Once soaked, boil for 5–10 minutes, wash, then boil again for a further 5–10 minutes. Drain.
- Heat 3 tablespoons of oil in a saucepan, add the 2 chopped garlic cloves and the onions, then cover and cook gently for 5 minutes, without browning. Add the remaining vegetables, the ham bone, beans and water. Add a pinch or two of salt and the beef extract. Cover, bring to the boil, then simmer gently for 1 hour until the beans are tender.
- Remove the ham bone and 1 large ladleful of whole, cooked beans and set aside. Blend the rest until smooth. Add the reserved beans and stir in the cabbage. Cover, then simmer gently for 10 minutes, or until the cabbage is tender.
- Meanwhile, pour the remaining olive oil into a small saucepan, add the rosemary, thyme and the 2 unpeeled but crushed garlic cloves. Cook gently for 10 minutes. Strain the oil into the soup, then heat through for 3 minutes, stirring constantly.
- Toast the bread in the oven. Rub each side of the toast with the remaining peeled garlic clove. Place the toast in the base of each bowl, then ladle over the soup. Sprinkle with the Parmesan and serve.

Fresh for...
June
19th

Papaya & Ginger Gazpacho with Shiitake Mushrooms

Ingredients

2 tablespoons sunflower oil
2 large onions, finely sliced
4 garlic cloves, crushed
110g (approx 10–15cm) fresh root ginger, peeled and finely sliced
2 large papayas
500ml mango and orange juice
juice of 2 large limes

To garnish:
2 tablespoons sunflower oil
2 garlic cloves, crushed
225g shiitake mushrooms
2 tablespoons single cream
4 spring onions, finely sliced diagonally

Cooking time	Serves
30 minutes + chilling time	4

- Heat the oil in a saucepan, add the onion, garlic and ginger, then cover and cook gently for 10 minutes, without browning. Leave to cool.
- Meanwhile, cut the papaya in half lengthways. Discard the seeds and scoop out the flesh. Place the papaya, onion mixture, mango and orange juice and lime juice in a liquidiser and blend until very smooth. Season to taste, then chill well.
- When ready to serve, prepare the garnish. Heat the oil in a saucepan, add the garlic and cook gently for 2 minutes, without browning. Add the mushrooms, then fry over a moderate heat for 5 minutes, stirring frequently. Season to taste, then, while piping hot, spoon into the centre of each bowl of chilled soup.
- Drizzle cream over the mushrooms, sprinkle with spring onions and serve.

Black Bean, Carrot & Jalapeño

Fresh for...
June
20th

Ingredients

110g butter
2 onions, coarsely chopped
5 cloves garlic, coarsely chopped
6 bay leaves
500g carrots, coarsely chopped
25ml Jalapeño Tabasco sauce (or 1 tablespoon chopped Jalapeño chillies)
150ml sherry, or fortified wine
625g tinned black beans, drained and rinsed
3 tablespoons tomato purée
1 litre water

To garnish:
Cheddar cheese, grated

Cooking time: 55 minutes
Serves

- Melt the butter in a saucepan, add the onions, garlic and bay leaves then cook gently for 10 minutes, until the onions are soft. Add the carrots and Jalapeño sauce or chillies, then cover and cook for 5 minutes.
- Add the sherry, simmer for a further 15 minutes, then add the drained black beans and tomato purée. Season to taste, then cover with the water. Bring to the boil, then simmer for 20 minutes.
- Remove from the heat, then discard the bay leaves. Blend until smooth, then reheat gently.
- Season to taste, then serve garnished with grated Cheddar cheese.

Fresh for...
June
21st

Broad Bean & Prosciutto Ham

Ingredients

2 tablespoons olive oil
40g Prosciutto ham, diced
2 leeks
150g peas (fresh or frozen)
200g broad beans, shelled (fresh or frozen)
350ml ham stock
85ml double cream
a sprig of fresh mint, chopped

Cooking time	Serves
35 minutes	

- Heat 1 tablespoon of olive oil in a frying pan, add the Prosciutto, and then fry until crispy. Set aside on kitchen paper.
- Meanwhile, heat 1 tablespoon of olive oil in a saucepan, add the leeks and fry until soft. Then add the peas, 150g broad beans and stock, bring to the boil and simmer gently for 20 minutes.
- Blend until smooth.
- Add the remaining broad beans, crispy Prosciutto and cream, then cook for 10 minutes, or until the beans are soft.
- Add the mint, season to taste, then serve.

Sweet Potato Chowder

Fresh for...
June
22nd

Ingredients

25g butter
3 medium onions, sliced
2 cobs of corn, kernels removed
570ml milk
675g sweet potatoes, peeled and diced into 2.5cm cubes
150ml double cream

Cooking time	Serves
50 minutes	

- Melt the butter in a saucepan, add the onions, then cook gently for 5–10 minutes until soft, without browning.
- Meanwhile, place the corn kernels and the milk into a saucepan and simmer gently for 20 minutes, until tender.
- In a separate pan, simmer the sweet potatoes in plenty of salted water for 20 minutes, until tender.
- Add the cream to the corn and milk pan, then blend coarsely.
- Combine the onions, corn mixture and sweet potatoes in a clean saucepan.
- Reheat gently and then serve.

Fresh for...

June

23rd

Crab Bisque

Ingredients

2 large cooked crabs
110g butter
1 medium onion, finely chopped
1 medium carrot, finely chopped
2 medium sticks celery, finely chopped
4 garlic cloves, crushed
1 small bunch fresh tarragon or parsley, chopped
1 bay leaf
3 sprigs of fresh thyme
a few fresh parsley stalks
110g tomato purée
pinch of chilli powder to taste
150ml dry white wine
150ml brandy
1.5 litres water
75g plain flour
275ml double cream

Cooking time	Serves
1:05 hour & minutes	6

- Remove the meat from the crab, roughly chop, then set aside. Crush the shell and claws into small pieces using a rolling pin.
- Heat 25g butter in a saucepan, add the onion, carrot, celery, garlic, tarragon, bay leaf, thyme sprigs and parsley stalks, cover, then cook gently for 10 minutes until soft, but without browning.
- Stir in the tomato purée, chilli powder, crushed crab shell, wine and brandy. Pour in the water, then cover and bring to the boil. Simmer gently for 40 minutes with the lid ajar, then strain well.
- Melt the remaining butter in a clean saucepan, then stir in the flour. Gradually stir in the strained liquor. Add the reserved meat, then, stirring continuously, bring to the boil and simmer for 2 minutes.
- Stir in the cream, season to taste, then reheat gently and serve.

Spinach & Nutmeg

Fresh for... June 24th

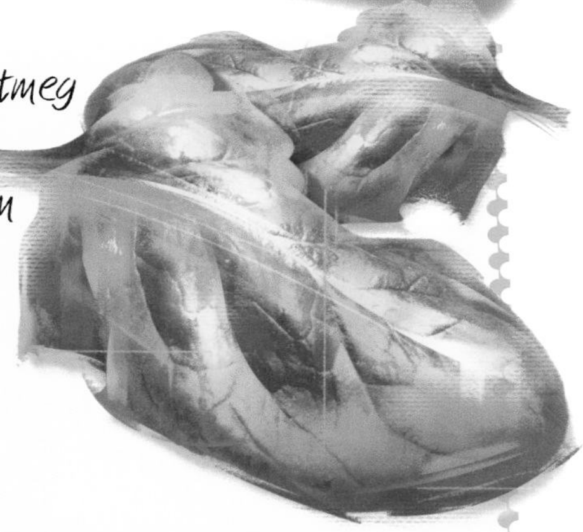

Ingredients

25g butter
1 large onion, finely chopped
25g plain flour
900ml vegetable stock
half a lemon, juice of (or to taste)
700g fresh spinach
freshly grated nutmeg
150ml milk
50ml single cream

Cooking time: 30 minutes

Serves: 6

- Melt the butter in a saucepan, add the onion, then cover and cook gently for 10 minutes, without browning.
- Stir in the flour, then cook gently for 2 minutes.
- Gradually add the stock, lemon juice, spinach and nutmeg.
- Cover, bring to the boil, then simmer for 5 minutes, until the spinach has wilted.
- Blend until smooth, then stir in the milk and cream.
- Season to taste, then reheat gently and serve.

Fresh for...
June
25th

Roasted Red Pepper, Sweetcorn & Chilli

Ingredients

3 medium fresh red chillies
2 medium red peppers
3 fresh cobs of corn
1.2 litres chicken stock
50g butter
1 large onion, finely chopped
1 medium leek, white part only, sliced
1 garlic clove, crushed
2 medium potatoes, about 350g, peeled and roughly chopped
150ml single cream

Cooking time: 2:10 hours & minutes
Serves: 6

- Preheat the oven to 200°C/400°F/ gas Mark 6.
- Place the chillies and red peppers in a roasting tin, then bake in the oven for 30 minutes.
- Place the corn in a saucepan, add the stock, then cover, bring to the boil and simmer for 30 minutes.
- Meanwhile, melt the butter in a saucepan, add the onion, leek and garlic, then cover and cook gently for 10 minutes, without browning.
- After 30 minutes, remove the chillies and red peppers from the oven. When cool enough to handle, skin and deseed them, dicing the chillies into small cubes and the red peppers into small even pieces, keeping them separate.
- Remove the corn cobs from the stock, then remove the corn from each cob, setting aside the stock and the corn kernels.
- Add the chillies, potatoes and stock to the onion, leek and garlic mixture, cover, bring to the boil, then simmer gently for 15–20 minutes until the vegetables are tender.
- Add the cream, corn and red pepper pieces, and then blend until smooth. Season to taste, then reheat gently and serve.

Kohlrabi with Caraway

Fresh for...
June
26th

Ingredients

25g butter
450g kohlrabi, peeled and chopped
40g plain flour
570ml vegetable stock
half a medium onion, finely chopped
15g fresh flat-leaf parsley, finely chopped
2 level teaspoons caraway seeds
50ml single cream

To garnish:
1 tablespoon sunflower oil
3 rashers smoked streaky bacon, finely sliced

Cooking time	Serves
40 minutes	6

- Melt the butter in a saucepan, add the kohlrabi, then cover and cook gently for 5 minutes, without browning.
- Add the flour, stir for 1 minute, then, still stirring, gradually add the stock. Cover, bring to the boil, then simmer gently for 20 minutes until the kohlrabi is tender. Blend until smooth.
- Boil the onion in plenty of water for 5 minutes, drain, then add to the soup with the parsley and caraway seeds. Cool slightly, stir in the cream, and then season to taste.
- For the garnish: heat the oil in a frying pan, then fry the bacon until crispy. Drain on kitchen paper.
- Gently reheat the soup and serve garnished with the crispy bacon.

Fresh for...
June
27th

Raspberry & Cranberry Soup

Ingredients

450g fresh or frozen raspberries
725ml cranberry juice
3 teaspoons arrowroot
1 teaspoon lemon juice
25–50g sugar

To garnish:
150ml soured cream

Cooking time	Serves
15 minutes	6
+ chilling time	

- Blend two-thirds of the raspberries with the cranberry juice, reserving one tablespoon of cranberry juice. Pass through a sieve into a saucepan to remove the pips and then bring to the boil.

- In a separate bowl, mix the arrowroot and the reserved tablespoon of cranberry juice until smooth.

- Pour the hot raspberry mixture over the arrowroot cream, stirring constantly. Then return the mixture to the pan. Stir over a gentle heat until the soup has thickened. Remove from the heat, then add the remaining raspberries, a little lemon juice and sugar to taste, then chill.

- Stir the soured cream to make it smooth, then add a swirl onto each bowl of chilled soup to serve.

Fresh for...
June
28th

Soup de Poissons

Ingredients

900g fish and shellfish, e.g. bass, bream, sole carcasses, crab, etc.
3 tablespoons extra virgin olive oil
1 large leek, finely sliced
1 medium onion, finely sliced
half a medium head of fennel, finely sliced
8 large garlic cloves, chopped
225g tomatoes, chopped
1 bay leaf
1 orange, rind of, cut into very fine strips
a pinch of saffron combined with 1 tablespoon warm water

For the Rouille:
110g red pepper
half a fresh red chilli, or to taste
8 garlic cloves, peeled
2 teaspoons chopped fresh thyme or basil
salt

For the Aioli:
8-10 garlic cloves, peeled
2 egg yolks, beaten well
1 lemon, juice of
1 teaspoon Dijon mustard
275ml oil (half groundnut and half olive oil)

To garnish:
Gruyère cheese, grated
croutons

Cooking time	Serves
1:10 hour & minutes	

- Wash the fish, then pat dry with kitchen paper. Fillet and skin the fish if necessary, then cut into large pieces. Remove any shellfish from their shells.
- Heat the oil in a saucepan, add the leek, onion, fennel and garlic, then cover and cook gently for 10 minutes, without browning.
- Add the tomatoes, bay leaf and orange strips, then season to taste. Cook for a further 5 minutes, then add the fish, cover with boiling water, and simmer vigorously for 5 minutes. Break up the fish with a wooden spoon to extract all the flavours.
- Simmer the broth for 30 minutes, stirring occasionally. Pass the soup through a fine sieve, pressing hard with a wooden spoon to squeeze out all the fish juices, but do not grind the solids through the sieve. Return the broth to a clean saucepan, and bring to the boil. Then stir in the saffron.
- For the rouille: blend all the rouille ingredients. For the aioli: blend the garlic, yolks, lemon juice and mustard in a liquidiser, then season to taste. With the machine still running, gradually add the oil until a thick, shiny, firm sauce is obtained.
- Reheat the soup gently, floating croutons coated with rouille or aioli on the top. Sprinkle with grated Gruyère cheese.

Fresh for...
June
29th

New Potato Salad Soup

Ingredients

25g butter
1 onion, diced
1 floury potato (e.g. Maris Piper), diced
400ml vegetable stock
1 teaspoon lemon juice
1 tablespoon white wine vinegar
150g new potatoes, diced into chunky cubes
75ml crème fraîche
half bunch of spring onions, sliced

Cooking time	Serves
40 minutes	

- Melt the butter in a saucepan, add the diced onion, then cook gently for 5 minutes, or until starting to soften.
- Add the diced floury potato, stock, lemon juice and white wine vinegar, and then season to taste. Simmer for 10–15 minutes, or until the potatoes are soft.
- Blend until smooth, and then add the chunky new potato cubes. Simmer for a further 15 minutes, or until the new potatoes are cooked through.
- Stir in the crème fraîche and spring onions, and then season to taste. Reheat gently, then serve.

Courgette, Pea & Spinach

Fresh for...
June
30th

Ingredients

- 25g butter
- 1 small onion, diced
- half a clove of garlic, crushed
- 2 medium floury potatoes (e.g. Maris Piper), diced
- 330ml vegetable stock
- 2 courgettes, diced
- 40g peas (fresh or frozen)
- fresh lemon juice, squeeze of
- half a teaspoon wild garlic (or chives), chopped
- 2 handfuls baby spinach leaves
- 1 teaspoon fresh tarragon, chopped
- 1–2 tablespoons crème fraîche

Cooking time	Serves
35 minutes	3

- Melt the butter in a saucepan, add the onion, then cook gently for 5–10 minutes, until softened.
- Add the garlic, then cook for a few minutes. Add the potato and stock and simmer for 15 minutes.
- Add the courgette, peas and lemon juice. Season to taste, then simmer for a further 5 minutes. Blend the soup until smooth.
- Add the wild garlic, spinach and tarragon, then stir in the crème fraîche. Reheat gently, and then serve.

Fresh for...
July
1st

Red Onion & Roasted Cherry Tomato

Ingredients

1.35kg cherry tomatoes
3 large garlic cloves, quartered
3 red onions, 1 chopped, 2 finely sliced
1 large handful fresh basil leaves
3 tablespoons olive oil
25g butter
2 teaspoons balsamic vinegar
2 heaped teaspoons dark brown sugar
300ml boiling water
1 tablespoon tomato purée

Cooking time	Serves
1:20 hour & minutes	

- Preheat the oven to 190°C/375°F/gas mark 5.
- Place the cherry tomatoes into a shallow roasting tin, add the garlic and chopped onion. Add 6 basil leaves to the tin, season, then add the olive oil, stir to coat, then roast for 50–60 minutes, until the tomatoes are soft and beginning to brown.
- Melt the butter in a saucepan, add the sliced onions, then fry gently until tender and caramelised. After 10 minutes, add the balsamic vinegar and sugar then cook for a further 2 minutes.
- Blend the roasted cherry tomatoes and onions with a little boiling water, then pass through a fine sieve. Add the tomato purée and any remaining water to the onions then season to taste.
- Tear the remaining basil leaves, stir into the soup, then reheat gently and serve.

Cream of Carrot & Kiwi with Orange Peppers

Fresh for...
July
2nd

Ingredients

50g butter
1 medium onion, roughly chopped
1 large garlic clove, crushed
1 large orange pepper, deseeded and finely chopped
450g carrots, roughly chopped
725ml chicken stock
290ml milk
half a teaspoon sugar
2 sprigs of fresh rosemary, finely chopped
4 kiwi fruits, peeled, quartered, then very thinly sliced

Cooking time	Serves
40 minutes	

- Melt the butter in a saucepan, add the onion and garlic, then cover and cook gently for 5 minutes, without browning. Add three-quarters of the orange pepper, then cook for 1 minute.
- Stir in the carrots and stock, then cover, bring to the boil and simmer gently for 15 minutes or until the vegetables are tender.
- Add the milk, then blend until smooth.
- Add the remaining orange pepper, sugar and rosemary, then season to taste.
- Cook gently for 10 minutes, stirring occasionally.
- Add the kiwi fruit, then warm through. Serve piping hot or chilled.

Fresh for...
July
3rd

Curried Banana Soup

Ingredients

50g butter
1 clove garlic, finely chopped
1 medium onion, finely chopped
1 tablespoon mild Madras curry powder
110g Basmati rice
1.25 litres chicken stock
250ml single cream
2 ripe bananas, peeled and cut into chunks
half a lime, juice of

To garnish:
sweet potato crisps (optional)

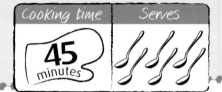

Cooking time: 45 minutes

Serves: 4

- Melt the butter in a saucepan, add the garlic and onion, then cook gently for 10 minutes until soft, without browning.
- Add the curry powder, then cook for a further 3 minutes.
- Add the rice and chicken stock, bring to the boil, then simmer for 25 minutes, until the rice is soft.
- Blend, then add the cream and bananas, then blend again until smooth.
- Add the lime juice, season to taste, then reheat gently and serve. Try garnishing with sweet potato crisps.

Fresh for...
July
4th

Pappa al Pomodoro

Ingredients

175ml extra virgin olive oil
4 cloves garlic, cut into fine slivers
4kg ripe tomatoes, skinned, quartered and deseeded or 2kg tinned plum tomatoes (drained off)
sugar to taste
570ml water
2 loaves stale Pugliese bread or ciabatta
1 large bunch fresh basil, torn

To garnish:
6 small sprigs of fresh basil

Cooking time	Serves
50 minutes	6

- Heat 2 tablespoons of the oil in a saucepan, add the garlic, then cook gently for a few minutes. Just as the garlic begins to brown, add the tomatoes, then simmer uncovered for 20–30 minutes, stirring occasionally, until the tomatoes become concentrated. Season to taste, adding sugar if necessary, then add the water and bring to the boil.
- Meanwhile, cut off most of the crust then break the remaining bread into large chunks. Add the bread to the tomato mixture and stir until the bread absorbs the liquid, adding more boiling water if it is too thick. Remove from the heat and allow to cool a little.
- Add the torn basil leaves and remaining extra virgin olive oil and stir. Allow to sit for 10 minutes before serving to allow the bread to absorb the flavour of the basil and oil. To serve, garnish with a few sprigs of fresh basil.

Fresh for...

July

5th

Watercress, Soya Bean & Pesto

Ingredients

1 tablespoon olive oil
8 spring onions, sliced
1 teaspoon garlic purée
800ml chicken stock
300g frozen soya beans
200g watercress
2 teaspoons lemon juice
3 tablespoons fresh pesto

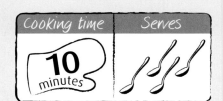

Cooking time	Serves
10 minutes	

- Heat the oil in a saucepan, add the spring onions and garlic purée, then fry for 3 minutes.
- Add the stock and soya beans, bring back to the boil, then cook for 2 minutes.
- Add the watercress, then cook for a further 3 minutes.
- Blend until smooth.
- Add the lemon juice and pesto, then stir through.
- Season to taste and serve.

Prawn, Celery & Lemon Vichyssoise

Fresh for...
July
6th

Ingredients

10g butter
1 small onion, finely sliced
350g celery, cut into 1cm slices
225g white of leek, sliced
450g potatoes, peeled and sliced
2 strips of lemon rind
seeds from 5 cardamom pods, crushed
pinch of celery salt
pinch of sugar
900ml chicken stock
150ml single cream
lemon juice, to taste
110g cooked peeled prawns, roughly chopped

To garnish:
slivers of lemon
sprigs of dill or fennel or 2 teaspoons finely chopped fresh flat-leaf parsley

Cooking time	Serves
40 minutes	4

- Melt the butter in a saucepan, add the onion, celery, leek and potatoes, then cover and simmer gently for 5 minutes, without browning.
- Stir in the lemon rind, cardamon seeds, celery salt, sugar and stock. Cover, bring to the boil, then simmer gently for 30 minutes until the vegetables are tender.
- Remove the lemon rind, blend until smooth, then pass through a sieve.
- Stir in the cream, then season to taste with salt, pepper and lemon juice. Add the prawns, then reheat gently, without boiling.
- Delicious served hot or chilled, garnished with slivers of lemon and sprigs of dill or fennel, or with pinches of chopped fresh parsley.

Fresh for...
July
7th

Slow Roasted Tomato & Basil

Ingredients

1kg ripe tomatoes, halved
1 red pepper, deseeded then cut into large strips
1 red onion, cut into 6 wedges
2 cloves garlic, unpeeled
2 tablespoons olive oil
2 tablespoons balsamic vinegar
1 teaspoon caster sugar
400ml vegetable stock
10g fresh basil leaves, chopped

Cooking time	Serves
1:05 hour & minutes	4

- Preheat your oven to 170°C/325°F/gas mark 3.
- Arrange the tomatoes, cut side up, in a roasting tin, then place the red pepper, onion and garlic cloves around the tomatoes. Drizzle with olive oil and balsamic vinegar, then season well.
- Sprinkle the sugar over the top, then roast for 1 hour. The tomatoes should have dried out a little and the pepper and onion should be soft.
- Peel the roasted garlic, then blend the roasted tomatoes, roasted vegetables, stock and basil until fairly smooth.
- Pour into a saucepan, reheat, season to taste and serve.

Cock-a-Leekie

Fresh for...
July
8th

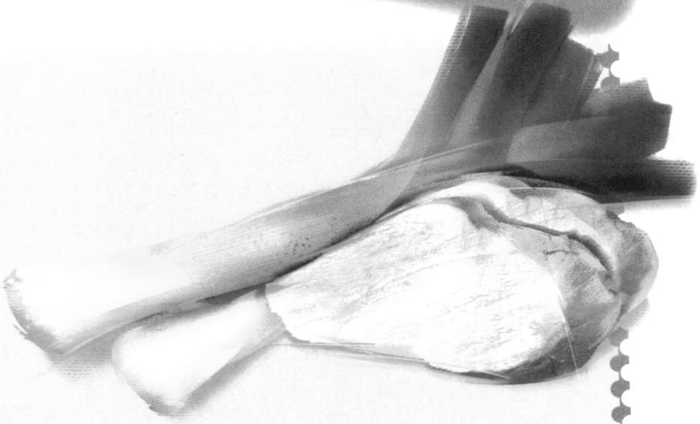

Ingredients

1 leek, sliced
1 medium potato, diced
1 small onion, chopped
565ml chicken stock
130g chicken, cooked and diced
1 teaspoon parsley, chopped
2 tablespoons double cream

Cooking time	Serves
45 minutes	4

- Place half of the leek and half of the potato in a saucepan, add all of the onion and stock, bring to the boil, then cover and simmer for 25 minutes.
- Blend until smooth.
- Add the remaining leek and potato, then cook for 15 minutes until soft.
- Add the cooked chicken and fresh parsley.
- Add the cream, season to taste, then stir. Cook for a further 5 minutes, then serve.

Fresh for...
July
9th

Summer Sorrel, Swiss Chard & Lemon Thyme

Ingredients

50g butter
3 shallots, finely chopped
150g sorrel leaves
250g Swiss chard, stalks removed, chopped
1 tablespoon lemon thyme
1 lemon, zest and juice of
1 dessertspoon dry sherry
250ml milk
half a teaspoon brown sugar
500ml chicken stock
1 level dessertspoon cornflour, mixed with a little cold water
4 tablespoons double cream

Cooking time	Serves
20 minutes	4

- Melt the butter in a saucepan, add the shallots, then cook gently for 5–10 minutes until softened, without browning.
- Add the sorrel, Swiss chard, lemon thyme and lemon zest, then stir to wilt the leaves.
- Add the sherry, milk, lemon juice, sugar and stock, bring to the boil quickly, then simmer for 2–3 minutes.
- Blend until smooth.
- Reheat gently for 2 minutes, then add the cornflour. Cook until thickened slightly, then season to taste. Finish with the cream and serve.

Summer Berry, Apple & Rhubarb

Fresh for... July 10th

Ingredients

300g rhubarb, cut into lengths
2 apples, peeled and chopped
450g mixed berries (we use a mix of: raspberries, blueberries, cherries, blackcurrants, blackberries)
75g caster sugar
300ml white wine
1 orange, zest of
2 tablespoons crème de cassis
lemon juice or honey
300g berries to finish (we use 100g each: raspberries, blueberries, cherries)

Cooking time: 40 minutes

Serves: 4

- Preheat your oven to 180°C/350°F/gas mark 4.
- In an ovenproof dish, place the rhubarb, apples and 450g mixed berries (reserve the additional 300g berries to use later). Sprinkle with sugar, then bake for 30–40 minutes until the rhubarb is tender. The fruits should be glossy and sitting in their own juices. Remove from the oven and allow to cool.
- Blend until smooth, then push through a sieve to remove pips from the fruit. Leave to one side.
- Meanwhile heat the wine and orange zest in a saucepan, then slowly bring to the boil to infuse the orange.
- Remove from the heat, discard the orange zest, then add the *crème de cassis*. Mix with the puréed fruits. Adjust the sweetness by adding lemon juice or honey, to taste.
- Add the reserved berries, stir, then serve warm. Tastes great chilled, too.

Fresh for...
July
11th

Broccoli & Crème Fraîche

Ingredients

25g butter
1 small onion, finely chopped
1 medium potato, diced
170g broccoli, cut into florets
1 courgette, large chunks
1 celery stick, sliced
540ml vegetable stock
2 tablespoons crème fraîche

Cooking time	Serves
30 minutes	4

- Melt the butter in a saucepan, add the onion and potato, then cook gently for 5–10 minutes, without browning.
- Add the rest of the vegetables, then cook gently for a further 2 minutes, again without browning.
- Add the stock, bring to the boil, then cover and simmer for 15–20 minutes until the vegetables are tender.
- Blend until smooth.
- Return to the pan, season to taste, then reheat gently for 3 minutes, stir in the crème fraîche and serve.

Broad Bean, Garlic & Herb

Fresh for...
July
12th

Ingredients

600g broad beans, removed from their pods
1 tablespoon olive oil
1 medium onion, finely chopped
2 cloves garlic, crushed
1 tablespoon basil, chopped
1 tablespoon parsley, chopped
1 tablespoon chives, chopped
750ml chicken stock

Cooking time	Serves
35 minutes	4

- Skin the broad beans by blanching them in boiling water for 2–3 minutes, refresh in cold water, then slip the skins off by squeezing each bean gently. This is time-consuming but essential for this soup!
- Heat the olive oil in a saucepan, add the onion and garlic, then cover and cook gently for 10–15 minutes until softened, without browning.
- Add the skinned broad beans, herbs and stock, bring to the boil, then simmer for 5 minutes.
- Blend half of the soup until smooth.
- Return to the pan, season to taste, then reheat for 3 minutes and serve.

Fresh for...

July

13th

Crab & Artichoke Hearts

Ingredients

25g butter
half a small leek, finely sliced
1 celery stick, diced
2 shallots, finely chopped
2 x 400g tins artichoke hearts
(2 x 240g drained weight)
500ml vegetable stock
1 tablespoon thyme, chopped
150ml single cream
170g white crab meat
1 tablespoon fresh parsley, chopped
1 tablespoon lemon juice

Cooking time	Serves
30 minutes	4

- Melt the butter in a saucepan, add the leek, celery and shallots, then cook gently for 10 minutes, without browning.
- Add the artichokes, stock and thyme, bring to the boil, then cover and simmer for 15 minutes.
- Blend two-thirds of the soup until smooth, and set aside.
- Blend the remaining third until it has a coarse and pulpy texture.
- Combine the blended soups in a pan, add the cream, crab meat, parsley and lemon juice.
- Season to taste, then reheat gently for 5 minutes and serve.

Fresh for...
July
14th

Spicy Sweet Potato

Ingredients

1 tablespoon olive oil
1 small onion, diced
2 teaspoons ground ginger
1 teaspoon ground coriander
pinch of cayenne pepper
pinch of cumin
pinch of cinnamon
pinch of mild curry powder
500ml vegetable stock
1 medium potato, diced
1 sweet potato, diced
2 teaspoons sugar
3 tablespoons plain yoghurt
lime juice, to taste

Cooking time	Serves
30 minutes	4

- Heat the olive oil in a saucepan, add the onion, then cook gently for 5–10 minutes.
- Add the spices, then fry for a few minutes.
- Add the stock, potato and sweet potato, then bring to the boil and simmer gently for 20 minutes.
- Blend until smooth.
- Season to taste, stir in the sugar and yoghurt, add the lime juice to taste, then serve.

Fresh for...
July
15th

Potato, Sorrel & Goat's Cheese

Ingredients

150g soft mild goat's cheese
25g butter
1 medium onion, finely chopped
1 clove garlic, crushed
2 medium potatoes, diced
750ml chicken stock
225g sorrel leaves
100ml single cream
1 tablespoon chives, snipped

- Remove the goat's cheese from the fridge and bring to room temperature.
- Heat the butter in a saucepan, then add the onion, garlic and potatoes. Cook gently for 10 minutes, without browning.
- Add the stock, bring to the boil, then cover and simmer for 10 minutes until the potatoes are tender.
- Add the sorrel leaves, then cook for a further 5 minutes.
- Blend until smooth.
- Add the cream, season to taste, then heat thoroughly, but don't let it boil.
- Divide the goat's cheese among the serving bowls, sprinkle with the chives, then ladle the soup over and serve.

Fresh for...
July
16th

Broad Bean & Smoked Chicken

Ingredients

200g cooked, smoked chicken breast (or roasted chicken breast)
25g butter
1 medium onion, finely chopped
2 small celery sticks, sliced
1 clove garlic, crushed
400g broad beans, removed from their pods
1 tablespoon fresh thyme, chopped
750ml chicken stock

To garnish:
100g broad beans (removed from their pods but in their skins)

Cooking time	Serves
30 minutes	

- For the garnish: take 100g of the broad beans, blanch in boiling water for 3 minutes, refresh in cold water, then remove the skins. Set aside to decorate the soup later.
- Finely slice one-quarter of the smoked chicken, then set aside for later; roughly chop the remaining chicken.
- For the soup: melt the butter in a saucepan, add the onion, celery and garlic, then cook gently for 5 minutes, without browning.
- Add the broad beans in their skins, the roughly chopped chicken, thyme and stock, then bring to the boil. Cover and simmer for 15 minutes.
- Blend until smooth. Return to the pan, then season to taste.
- Add the reserved skinned broad beans and sliced chicken, then heat for 5 minutes and serve.

Fresh for...
July
17th

Carrot, Sweetcorn & Elderflower

Ingredients

2 tablespoons olive oil
1 medium onion, finely diced
2 medium carrots, diced
2 celery sticks, finely sliced
700ml vegetable stock
1 tablespoon elderflower cordial
400g sweetcorn

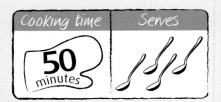

Cooking time	Serves
50 minutes	4

- Heat the olive oil in a saucepan, add the onion, carrots and celery, then cook for 10 minutes.
- Add the stock, bring to the boil, then add the elderflower cordial. Cover, then cook gently for 15 minutes or until the vegetables are tender.
- Blend until smooth.
- Add the sweetcorn, season to taste, then cook for a further 10 minutes and serve.

Bouillabaisse

Fresh for...
July
18th

Ingredients

3 tablespoons olive oil
3 cloves garlic, crushed
half a red onion, chopped
half a fennel bulb, finely sliced
half a leek, chopped
800ml fish stock
1 x 400g tin chopped tomatoes
400ml tomato passata
half a red chilli, finely diced
pinch of saffron, soaked in 2 tablespoons hot water
3 sprigs of thyme
1 bay leaf
half an orange, zest of
3 tablespoons fresh parsley, chopped
400g turbot, filleted, large chunks
350g large raw prawns, tail on
2 cooked crabs, meat only

Cooking time	Serves
35 minutes	4

- Heat the oil in a saucepan, add the garlic, red onion, fennel and leek, then cook gently, stirring frequently for 5–10 minutes until softened.
- Add the stock, chopped tomatoes, passata, chilli, saffron, thyme, bay leaf, orange zest and 2 tablespoons of the chopped parsley.
- Bring to the boil, then simmer for 15 minutes.
- Add the turbot, then cook for 5 minutes.
- Add the prawns and crab meat, then cook for a further 3–5 minutes until all the fish is cooked.
- Season to taste, sprinkle with the remaining chopped parsley and serve.

Fresh for…
July
19th

Beef Consommé with Avocado

Ingredients

340g shin of beef, diced into 2cm cubes
half a small chicken carcass, roughly chopped
1.5 litres beef stock
1 medium onion, peeled and roughly chopped
2 carrots, peeled and roughly chopped
large sprig of parsley
2 sprigs of fresh thyme
1 bay leaf
6 peppercorns
1 white of an egg, and the eggshell
1 tablespoon dry sherry
2 avocados
2 tablespoons extra virgin olive oil

Cooking time	Serves
2 hours	2
+ 1 hour chilling time	

- Put the beef, chicken, stock, vegetables, herbs and peppercorns into a saucepan, bring to the boil, then simmer gently, uncovered, for 1½–1¾ hours until reduced by half. Strain, then return to the heat.
- Beat the egg white until frothy, then whisk into the stock and add the eggshell. Reduce the heat to low, then simmer for 15 minutes.
- This begins the clarification of the consommé. Add the sherry, then heat for 5 minutes. Remove from the heat and leave to cool a little.
- Pour through a sieve double-lined with muslin; the consommé will now be clear.
- Halve the avocados, remove the stones and scoop the flesh into a bowl. Add the olive oil and mash to a smooth paste. Season to taste, then spoon into ramekins.
- Carefully pour the consommé into the ramekins, covering the avocado. Place the ramekins in the refrigerator for approximately 1 hour until set. Serve chilled.

Fresh for...
July
20th

Citrus Chicken & Sage

Ingredients

2 tablespoons olive oil
1 stick celery, diced
2 small leeks, diced
360ml chicken stock
1 small potato, diced
1 cooked chicken breast, shredded
1 orange, juice of and zest, grated
half a lemon, juice of, to taste
135ml milk
3 tablespoons double cream
1 teaspoon fresh sage, chopped (or a pinch of dried)

Cooking time	Serves
40 minutes	

- Heat the olive oil in a saucepan, add the celery and leeks, then cook gently for 10–15 minutes, until soft.
- Add the stock and potato, season to taste, then bring to the boil and simmer gently for 20 minutes.
- Blend until smooth.
- On a low heat, add the chicken, orange juice and zest and lemon juice, to taste. Simmer for 5 minutes.
- Add the milk, cream and sage, simmer gently for a further 5 minutes, and then serve.

Fresh for...
July
21st

Melon & Mint

Ingredients

3 Charentais melons
2 Galia melons
150ml dry white wine
150ml grape juice
2 lemons, juice of
2–3 sprigs of fresh mint, leaves shredded
crushed ice

Cooking time	Serves
20 minutes + chilling time	8

- Cut the melons in half, and scoop out the seeds over a bowl to catch any juices.
- Using a melon baller, scoop out 48 melon balls and set them aside.
- Remove the rest of the flesh from the melons and blend together with the wine, grape juice and lemon juice (you may need to do this in batches).
- Blend until smooth, then chill well.
- To serve, garnish each bowl with 6 melon balls, a few shredded mint leaves and some crushed ice.

Fresh for...
July
22nd

Salsa Soup

Ingredients

For the soup:
2 x 400g tins chopped tomatoes
2 cloves garlic, crushed
2 tablespoons olive oil
1 tablespoon fresh basil, chopped
half a red pepper, deseeded and finely diced

For the salsa:
450g plum tomatoes
140g cherry vine tomatoes, halved
1 small red onion, finely diced
2 red chillies, deseeded and finely diced
1 lime, juice of
2 tablespoons olive oil
20g fresh coriander, chopped
half a red pepper, deseeded and diced
2 corn cobs

Cooking time	Serves
45 minutes	

- Place all the soup ingredients in a saucepan, then bring to the boil and simmer for 20 minutes.
- Meanwhile, to prepare the salsa: plunge the plum tomatoes into boiling water for 30 seconds, then peel, deseed and dice. Place in a large bowl.
- Add all the other salsa ingredients to the bowl except for the corn, then set aside to marinate for at least 30 minutes.
- Heat your grill to a high setting, brush the corn cobs lightly with oil, then grill, turning frequently, until a dark golden colour and slightly charred. Allow the cobs to cool slightly, then cut off all the kernels.
- Serve the soup warm or chilled topped with a good spoonful of the salsa and some of the corn. Place bowls of tortilla chips, shredded cooked chicken, grated cheese and soured cream on the table for guests to help themselves.

Fresh for...
July
23rd

Chickpea, Chilli & Lime

Ingredients

2 tablespoons olive oil
1 medium onion, finely diced
10g fresh coriander, stalks and leaves separated and finely chopped
2 teaspoons ground cumin
2 red chillies, deseeded and finely chopped
2 cloves garlic, crushed
1 x 400g tin chopped tomatoes
1 x 410g tin chickpeas, drained
800ml vegetable stock
half a lime, zest and juice of

Cooking time	Serves
55 minutes	4

- Heat the oil in a saucepan, add the onion, then cook gently for 5–10 minutes until softened, without browning.
- Add the coriander stalks, cumin, chilli and garlic, then stir for a couple of minutes until aromatic.
- Add the tomatoes, cover, then cook gently for 15 minutes until the tomatoes have thickened.
- Add the chickpeas and stock, then bring to the boil, cover and simmer for a further 20 minutes.
- Blend two-thirds of the soup (if you prefer a completely smooth soup, then blend all of it).
- Return the blended soup to the pan, add the lime zest, lime juice and coriander leaves. Season to taste, reheat gently and serve.

Fresh for...
July
24th

Cress & Potato

Ingredients

15g butter
1 small onion, finely chopped
40g leek, thinly sliced
125g potato, peeled and chopped
700ml vegetable stock
200g cress
half a teaspoon grated nutmeg
100ml milk
75ml single cream

To garnish:
150ml natural yoghurt
cress

Cooking time: 30 minutes
Serves: 4

- Melt the butter in a saucepan, add the onion, then cover and cook gently for 10 minutes, until soft, without browning.
- Add the leek and potato, then cook for a further 5 minutes. Add the stock, bring to the boil, then simmer for 20 minutes until the vegetables are tender.
- Stir in the cress and nutmeg, then season to taste.
- Add the milk and cream, then blend until smooth.
- Reheat gently then serve garnished with natural yoghurt and cress.

Fresh for...

July

25th

Pea, Lettuce & Mint

Ingredients

50g butter
2 small onions, finely chopped
1 garlic clove, crushed
350g potatoes, peeled and roughly chopped
900ml chicken stock
125g shelled fresh green peas (if unavailable use frozen peas)
2 handfuls lettuce leaves (200g), shredded
1 small bunch mint, leaves shredded
150ml single cream

Cooking time: 30 minutes

Serves: 4

- Melt the butter in a saucepan, add the onions and garlic, then cover and cook gently until soft, without browning.
- Add the potatoes and stock, then cover and simmer gently for 20 minutes until the vegetables are tender.
- Add the peas, lettuce and mint leaves, then cover and simmer for a further 5 minutes.
- Blend until smooth, then stir in the cream.
- Season to taste, then serve warm or chilled.

Roasted Tomato & Red Pepper

Fresh for...
July
26th

Ingredients

6 medium red peppers, halved and deseeded
8 ripe tomatoes, skinned and halved
2 tablespoons extra virgin olive oil
1 teaspoon sugar
1 tablespoon fresh basil, chopped
1 medium onion, finely chopped
1 garlic clove, crushed
900ml vegetable stock

To garnish:
fresh basil, chopped

Cooking time	Serves
1:25 hour & minutes	6

- Preheat the oven to 190°C/375°F/gas mark 5.
- Place the red peppers skin side up in a roasting tin, add the tomatoes cut side up, then drizzle with 1 tablespoon of the olive oil.
- Sprinkle with sugar, then chopped fresh basil, then season. Bake in the oven for 1 hour.
- Heat the remaining olive oil in a saucepan, add the onion and garlic, then cover and cook gently for 15 minutes, without browning.
- Add the peppers, tomatoes and stock, then cover and bring to the boil.
- Blend until smooth, season to taste, then serve warm or chilled, garnished with lots of chopped fresh basil.

Fresh for…
July
27th

Cantaloupe Melon & Bitter Chocolate

Ingredients

1 large cantaloupe melon, flesh of, (about 1.5kg)
50g butter
1 tablespoon sugar
1 lemon, rind of, finely grated
good pinch of salt
900ml milk

To garnish:
3 tablespoons cantaloupe melon, diced
shavings of bitter chocolate

Cooking time	Serves
25 minutes	4

- Take enough of the melon flesh to cut 3 tablespoons of diced melon, and then coarsely chop the remaining melon.
- Melt the butter in a saucepan, add the coarsely chopped melon, sugar, lemon rind and salt, then cook gently for a few minutes.
- Add the milk, then cover, bring to the boil and simmer gently for 15 minutes.
- Blend until smooth, then chill well.
- Garnish each serving with diced melon and shavings of bitter chocolate.

Peach Soup Flambé

Fresh for... July 28th

Ingredients

275ml water
1.35kg ripe peaches or nectarines
110g sugar, plus 3 teaspoons
4 tablespoons lemon juice
1 teaspoon honey
1 teaspoon fresh rosemary, finely chopped
2 tablespoons soured cream

To garnish:
2 tablespoons soured cream
1 teaspoon sugar
3 tablespoons Cognac or Armagnac

Cooking time	Serves
50 minutes	4

- Fill a large saucepan with water, bring to the boil, then add the peaches. Simmer for 5–15 minutes, as necessary, to loosen their skins. Remove, then set aside to cool. Reserve 150ml of the cooking water. Peel the peaches, then cut them in half and remove the stones.
- Place 110g sugar and 275ml of water into a saucepan, then simmer gently to dissolve the sugar before the liquid comes to the boil. Once dissolved, bring the liquid to the boil and boil for 1 minute. Add 6 peach halves and poach very gently for 15 minutes. Allow to cool in the liquid.
- Place the remaining peaches in a separate saucepan with the reserved 150ml cooking water, add the lemon juice, honey, rosemary and 3 teaspoons sugar. Simmer gently, stirring frequently, for 10 minutes. Blend until smooth, then reheat gently and stir in 2 tablespoons of soured cream.
- Ladle the purée into soup bowls. Drain the peach halves and float cut side up in the centre of each bowl. Mix the soured cream and 1 teaspoon sugar together for the garnish, then spoon the mixture over the peach halves. Warm the Cognac or Armagnac and spoon over the peaches. Dim the lights, ignite the brandy and serve the soup with the flames dancing.

Fresh for...
July
29th

Scallop & Smoked Bacon Chowder

Ingredients

50g butter, preferably unsalted
2 small young leeks, very finely sliced
1 large potato, peeled and diced
2 rashers smoked streaky bacon, finely sliced
570ml fish or vegetable stock
340g frozen sweetcorn
1 heaped dessertspoon plain flour
200g crème fraîche
275ml single cream
14 medium scallops, chopped into quarters, or 500g small queen scallops (adding corals if preferred)
1 teaspoon honey
fresh parsley, chopped

Cooking time: 45 minutes
Serves

- Melt the butter in a saucepan, add the leeks, potato and bacon, then cook gently for 20 minutes. Add three-quarters of the stock, then cook for a further 10 minutes before adding the sweetcorn.
- Mix the flour with the remaining stock, then add to the saucepan. Heat gently until warmed through.
- Add the crème fraîche, cream and chopped scallops, then heat gently until the scallops are firm. Be careful not to cook them too quickly, or for too long, as they will become tough.
- Add the honey just before serving, season to taste, then sprinkle with fresh parsley and serve.

Mangetout & Yellow Split Pea

Fresh for... July 30th

Ingredients

25g butter
1 large onion, finely chopped
110g yellow split peas, soaked for 1 hour in plenty of water
900ml vegetable stock
250g mangetout

Cooking time	Serves
50 minutes	6
+ 1 hour soaking time	

- Melt the butter in a saucepan, add the onion, then cover and cook gently for 5 minutes, without browning.
- Add the soaked split peas, then stir to coat in the butter. Add the stock, cover, bring to the boil, then simmer for 30 minutes until tender. The time will vary according to the age and hardness of the split peas.
- Add the mangetout, then simmer for a further 5 minutes.
- Blend until smooth, then season to taste. Reheat gently, then serve.

Fresh for...
July
31st

Chinese Chicken & Sweetcorn

Ingredients

2 teaspoons white sugar
150g sweetcorn kernels, tinned or frozen
700ml chicken stock
2 tablespoons soy sauce
2 tablespoons cornflour
80g cooked chicken, shredded

Cooking time	Serves
20 minutes	4

- Place the sugar, two-thirds of the sweetcorn, stock and soy sauce into a saucepan. Then cook gently for 10 minutes.
- Blend the soup until smooth.
- Mix the cornflour with a little water, to form a paste, and then add to the soup, stirring frequently.
- Add the chicken and remaining sweetcorn, then reheat gently for 10 minutes and serve.

Fresh for...
August
1st

Summer Pistou

Ingredients

1 tablespoon olive oil
1 small onion, chopped
1 clove garlic, finely chopped
300ml vegetable stock
150g new potatoes
200g baby carrots
100g baby courgettes, cut into batons
2 tomatoes, skinned and chopped
100g fresh peas, shelled (or frozen)
1 tablespoon green pesto

Cooking time	Serves
30 minutes	4

- Heat the olive oil in a saucepan, add the onion and garlic, then cook gently for 5 minutes until soft, without browning.
- Add the stock, bring to the boil, then add the new potatoes. Cover, then simmer for 10 minutes.
- Add the carrots, courgettes and tomatoes, then cook for a further 8 minutes. Add a little water if required.
- Add the peas, then simmer for 5 minutes.
- Season to taste, add the green pesto and serve.

Fresh for...
August
2nd

Smoky Fish & Fennel Chowder

Ingredients

25g butter
1 medium onion, finely sliced
1 head of fennel (225g), finely sliced, reserving the fennel fronds for decoration
1 teaspoon fennel seeds
half a teaspoon turmeric
1 bay leaf
225g potato, peeled and diced small
half a lemon, juice and grated rind of
1 rounded tablespoon Dijon mustard
225g smoked cod or haddock
425ml milk
150ml water or dry white wine
1 dessertspoon plain flour
2 tablespoons Greek yoghurt

To garnish:
3 or 4 fennel fronds per person

Cooking time	Serves
30 minutes	4

- Melt the butter in a saucepan, add the onion, fennel, fennel seeds, turmeric and bay leaf, then cover and cook gently for 10 minutes, without browning.
- Add the potato, lemon rind and mustard, then cook for 2 minutes.
- Lay the fish on top of the vegetables, pour over the milk and water or wine, then bring to the boil. Cover and simmer gently for a further 10 minutes, then remove the pan from the heat.
- Remove the fish from the pan and flake it into a separate bowl. Mix the flour and yoghurt to a paste, then stir into the soup. Add the lemon juice, and season to taste.
- Bring back to the boil, stirring continuously. Serve garnished with the reserved fennel fronds.

Aubergine & Butter Beans with Mint & Pine Nuts

Fresh for...
August
3rd

Ingredients

2 large aubergines
3 tablespoons extra virgin olive oil
1 shallot, chopped
1 garlic clove, crushed
half a level teaspoon ground cumin
half a level teaspoon ground cinnamon
150g cooked butter beans
3 large plum tomatoes, skinned and chopped
500ml vegetable stock

To garnish:
2 tablespoons mint, chopped
2 tablespoons pine nuts, toasted

Cooking time	Serves
1 hour	4

- Preheat your oven to 200°C/400°F/ gas mark 6. Meanwhile, place the aubergines in a saucepan, cover with boiling water, then simmer for 10 minutes. Drain, then cut in half lengthways.
- Slash the cut sides in 3 places, then brush with 2 tablespoons of olive oil. Arrange on a baking tray, then bake in the oven for 10 minutes. Remove from the oven and cool. Remove the skins and dice the flesh into 2.5cm cubes.
- Meanwhile, heat the remaining olive oil in a saucepan, add the shallot and garlic, then cover and cook gently for 5 minutes, without browning.
- Stir in the cumin and cinnamon, then cook for a further 2 minutes. Add the butter beans, diced aubergine and chopped tomatoes.
- Season to taste, then cook for 2 minutes. Add the stock, cover, then simmer for a further 20 minutes until tender.
- Blend coarsely, then heat through.
- Serve liberally sprinkled with the mint and toasted pine nuts. (Toast by frying gently in a dry pan until lightly browned.)

Fresh for...
August
4th

Tomato Borscht

Ingredients

25g butter
1 small onion, finely chopped
1 garlic clove, crushed
225g raw beetroot, grated
1 teaspoon ground cumin
half a teaspoon ground cinnamon
225g fresh ripe tomatoes, skinned and roughly chopped
275ml tomato juice
1 tablespoon tomato purée
570ml vegetable stock
1 tablespoon soy sauce

Cooking time	Serves
30 minutes	4

- Melt the butter in a saucepan, add the onion, garlic and beetroot, then cover and cook gently for 10 minutes, without browning.
- Add the cumin, cinnamon, tomatoes, tomato juice, tomato purée and stock, then cover and simmer gently for 15 minutes until the vegetables are tender.
- Add the soy sauce and season to taste.
- Blend until really smooth, then reheat gently. Serve either hot or chilled.

Fresh for...
August
5th

Champagne & Camembert

Ingredients

120g ripe Camembert, diced
1 small knob of butter
1 tablespoon olive oil
1 clove garlic, crushed
100g shallots, finely chopped
1 small potato, finely diced
225ml champagne
565ml chicken stock
6 tablespoons single cream

Cooking time	Serves
40 minutes	

- Make sure the Camembert is at room temperature. If it is not ripe, simply remove the skin because this will not melt in your soup.
- Heat the butter and olive oil in a saucepan, add the garlic, shallots and potato, then cook for 10 minutes until softened, without browning.
- Pour in the champagne, then after a minute add the stock. Bring to the boil, then cover and simmer for 20 minutes, stirring occasionally, until the potato has broken down.
- Add the Camembert and allow it to melt over a low heat, stirring gently.
- Add the cream, season to taste, then heat gently for 2–3 minutes and serve.

Fresh for...
August
6th

Apple, Vine Tomato & Smoked Bacon

Ingredients

25g butter
1 tablespoon olive oil
1 small onion, finely diced
1 clove garlic, crushed
6 rashers smoked bacon, chopped
600g ripe vine tomatoes, skinned and chopped
2 small Cox's apples, peeled and diced
1 teaspoon brown sugar
500ml vegetable stock
4–6 fresh sage leaves, very finely sliced

Cooking time	Serves
1:20 hour & minutes	4

- Heat the butter and oil in a saucepan, add the onion and garlic, then cover and cook gently for 10 minutes, without browning.
- Add half the bacon, stirring to prevent it sticking, and cook for 2 minutes.
- Add the tomatoes, apples, sugar and stock, then bring to the boil. Cover and simmer gently for 1 hour, stirring occasionally.
- Blend until nearly smooth.
- Add the sage leaves, season to taste, then reheat gently for 2–3 minutes.
- Meanwhile, fry the remaining bacon until crispy. Place the bacon in the serving bowls, then ladle the soup over and serve.

Roasted Fennel & Somerset Cider

Fresh for...
August
7th

Ingredients

700g fennel bulbs
2 medium red onions
2 tablespoons olive oil
1 tablespoon coriander seeds
2–3 tablespoons lemon thyme, chopped
300ml dry Somerset cider
750ml chicken stock
150ml double cream

Cooking time	Serves
55 minutes	3

- Preheat the oven to 200°C/400°F/gas mark 6.
- Cut the fennel bulbs and red onions into 6 wedges, so that they are of similar sizes.
- Place in an ovenproof dish, drizzle with olive oil, sprinkle the coriander seeds and lemon thyme over, then toss to ensure all vegetables are covered. Roast for 30 minutes, stirring occasionally, until the vegetables are softened with some caramelised edges.
- Pour the cider over the vegetables and roast for a further 15 minutes. The cider should have reduced to a syrupy layer in the dish (don't allow it to dry out).
- Remove from the oven, then blend until smooth, adding the chicken stock as you blend (you may need to do this in batches).
- Sieve the soup, pushing it through with the back of a ladle. This takes a little time but is well worth it.
- Return the sieved soup to the pan, then add the cream. Season to taste, reheat for 3 minutes and serve.

Fresh for...
August
8th

Summer Salad

Ingredients

2 avocados, skin and stone removed
270g roundhead lettuce, roughly chopped
1 teaspoon coriander, chopped
2 tablespoons lime juice
410ml fresh apple juice
1 teaspoon parsley, chopped
100g cherry tomatoes (two-thirds cut in half)
2 spring onions, finely sliced

Time	Serves
15 minutes	4

- Place the avocado, lettuce, coriander, lime juice, apple juice, half the parsley and a third of the cherry tomatoes in a blender.
- Blend until smooth.
- Place the blended soup in a bowl, then add the remaining chopped parsley, spring onions and cherry tomatoes.
- Season to taste, then stir well and serve.

Sweet Potato & Red Pepper Chowder

Fresh for...
August
9th

Ingredients

1 tablespoon olive oil
1 small onion, finely diced
1 large sweet potato, diced
1 tablespoon plain flour
670ml vegetable stock
125g sweetcorn kernels
half a red pepper, deseeded and finely sliced
half a red chilli, deseeded and finely diced
2 spring onions, finely sliced
4 tablespoons double cream
1 teaspoon parsley, finely chopped

Cooking time	Serves
30 minutes	

- Heat the olive oil in a saucepan, add the onion and sweet potato, then cook gently for 5 minutes, without browning.
- Add the flour, then cook for 1 minute. Add the stock, bring to the boil, then cover and simmer for 15 minutes until the sweet potato is tender.
- Blend until smooth.
- Add the sweetcorn, red pepper, chilli and spring onions, then cover and simmer gently for 5 minutes.
- Add the cream and parsley, season to taste and serve.

Fresh for...
August
10th

Tomato & Mascarpone

Ingredients

2 tablespoons olive oil
1 medium onion, diced
half a clove of garlic, finely chopped
pinch of dried oregano
pinch of fresh rosemary, finely chopped
5 tablespoons tomato purée
320g passata
1 x 400g tin chopped tomatoes
1 tablespoon caster sugar
400ml water
3 tablespoons fresh basil leaves, chopped
1 heaped tablespoon mascarpone cheese

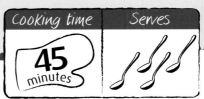

Cooking time	Serves
45 minutes	4

- Heat the oil in a saucepan, add the onion and garlic, then cover and cook for 10 minutes until soft, without browning.
- Stir in the oregano, rosemary and tomato purée, then cook for a further 5 minutes.
- Stir in the passata, chopped tomatoes, sugar and water and bring to the boil. Cover and simmer for 20 minutes.
- Stir in the basil, then blend until smooth.
- Reheat gently, season to taste, then stir in the mascarpone cheese. Continue to heat through gently, then serve.

Greek Salad Soup

Fresh for... August 11th

Ingredients

600g very ripe plum tomatoes
350g cherry tomatoes (of which 150g cut in half)
200ml passata
2 teaspoons balsamic vinegar
1 clove garlic, chopped
1 medium red onion, finely sliced
half a lemon, juice of
500g vine tomatoes
half a large cucumber, peeled, deseeded and diced into large cubes
2 tablespoons fresh oregano, chopped
1 tablespoon flat-leaf parsley, roughly chopped
240g marinated Kalamata olives
320g feta cheese, cubed

Time: 30 minutes + chilling time
Serves: 8

- Blend the plum tomatoes, whole cherry tomatoes, passata, balsamic vinegar and garlic, then sieve and chill.
- Half an hour before serving, make a Greek salad: put the red onion in a large bowl, then sprinkle over the lemon juice and allow to steep for 5 minutes.
- Cut the vine tomatoes through the middle and cut each half into quarters, before adding to the bowl.
- Add the cucumber, halved cherry tomatoes and herbs, then stir.
- Pour the chilled tomato soup into bowls, top with the Greek salad, then scatter over the olives and feta cheese and serve.

Fresh for...
August
12th

Grouse, Shallot & Thyme

Ingredients

1 x 400g grouse
6 rashers streaky bacon
2 tablespoons olive oil
200g carrots, diced
2 sticks celery, diced
200g swede, diced
150g shallots
250ml full-bodied red wine
600ml chicken stock
a few sprigs of thyme
1 tablespoon fresh rosemary, chopped
1 bay leaf
1 tablespoon fresh parsley, chopped

Cooking time	Serves
1:45 hour & minutes	4

- Preheat your oven to 150°C/300°F/gas mark 2.
- Remove any giblets or down feathers from the grouse. Season, then lay the streaky bacon across the breast, securing with string.
- Heat the oil in an ovenproof pan with a tight-fitting lid, add the grouse, then brown the skin on all sides. Remove from the pan and set aside.
- Add the vegetables to the pan, cook for 5 minutes, then add the wine and cook for a further 2 minutes.
- Return the grouse to the pan, add the stock and herbs (except the parsley), season to taste, then slowly bring to the boil.
- Cover the pan, then place it in the oven for 1½ hours, stirring occasionally.
- Remove the pan from the oven, take the grouse out and set aside to cool slightly.
- Once cooled, skin and then strip the meat from the bones. Return the shredded meat to the pan, season to taste, then reheat gently for 5 minutes. Stir in the parsley and serve.

Mango, Orange & Ginger

Fresh for... August 13th

Ingredients

3 large ripe mangoes, peeled and flesh placed in a bowl
1–2 oranges (freshly grated zest of half and juice of 1)
1 teaspoon fresh root ginger, grated
250ml natural yoghurt
500ml milk
1 dessertspoon balsamic vinegar

To garnish:
4 dessertspoons yoghurt
2 tablespoons fresh coriander leaves, chopped

Time	Serves
20 minutes + chilling time	4

- Put the mango pulp, orange zest and juice, and ginger into a blender, then blend until very smooth.
- Pass through a fine sieve into a clean bowl, then stir in the yoghurt, milk and balsamic vinegar. Season with salt to taste.
- Cover and chill well. Serve with a dollop of yoghurt and a sprinkle of chopped coriander leaves.

Fresh for...
August
14th

Spicy Corn Chowder

Ingredients

2 tablespoons extra virgin olive oil
1 medium onion, finely chopped
1 garlic clove, crushed
2 sticks celery, finely chopped
1 large carrot, very finely chopped
225g potato, peeled (half roughly, half finely chopped)
340g tinned sweetcorn, drained
half a teaspoon powdered ancho or red chilli
725ml water
1 small red pepper, deseeded and finely chopped
half a medium green pepper, deseeded and finely chopped
1 level teaspoon bottled jalapeño peppers
75ml double cream

Cooking time: 55 minutes
Serves: 4

- Heat the oil in a saucepan, add the onion and cook gently for 15 minutes until golden.
- Add the garlic, then cook for 1 minute. Next, add the celery, half of the carrot, the roughly chopped potato, half of the sweetcorn and the ancho chilli. Cook gently for 2 minutes.
- Add the water, cover, bring to the boil, then simmer gently for 15 minutes until the vegetables are tender.
- Blend until smooth, then stir in the red, green and jalapeño peppers and the remaining carrot. Add the finely chopped potato and remaining sweetcorn. Cover, bring to the boil, then simmer gently for 10 minutes.
- Stir in the double cream, season to taste, then reheat gently and serve.

Aubergine Soup with a Red Pepper Cream

Fresh for...
August
15th

Ingredients

For the soup:
2 tablespoons extra virgin olive oil
450g aubergine, coarsely chopped
1 small onion, finely chopped
1 large garlic clove, chopped
1 litre chicken stock

For the red pepper cream:
1 red pepper, quartered and deseeded
2 tablespoons single cream
chilli oil, to taste (optional)

Cooking time: 40 minutes

Serves

- Heat the oil in a saucepan, add the aubergine, onion and garlic, then cook gently for 20 minutes, without browning.
- Meanwhile, grill the red pepper until the skin has charred. Cool in a plastic bag, then skin the pepper. Blend with the cream, season to taste and add chilli oil, if required.
- Blend the aubergine and onion mixture a little, then add the stock and season to taste. Reheat. Then just before you are ready to serve, spoon the red pepper cream onto the soup.

Fresh for...
August
16th

Ratatouille Soup

Ingredients

1 tablespoon extra virgin olive oil
1 large onion, finely chopped
1 garlic clove, crushed
100g aubergine, diced into 2.5cm cubes
125g courgette, diced into 2.5cm cubes
60g green pepper, diced into 2.5cm cubes
60g red pepper, diced into 2.5cm cubes
110g fresh plum tomatoes, roughly chopped
3 tablespoons tomato purée
1 teaspoon brown sugar
pinch of cayenne pepper
900ml vegetable stock
20g sun-dried tomatoes, diced

Cooking time: 30 minutes
Serves: 4

- Heat the oil in a saucepan, add the onion, then cover and cook gently for 10 minutes, without browning.
- Add the garlic, half the aubergine, half the courgettes, then half each of the green and red pepper. Add all of the tomatoes, tomato purée, brown sugar, cayenne and stock. Cover and simmer for 10 minutes.
- Blend until smooth.
- Fill a saucepan with salted water and bring to the boil. Add the remaining vegetables and simmer for 1 minute. Drain, then add to the soup along with the sun-dried tomatoes. Reheat gently, then serve.
- This soup is delicious hot or chilled.

Summer Tomato

Fresh for...
August
17th

Ingredients

25g butter
1 medium onion, finely chopped
1 garlic clove, finely chopped
a pinch of paprika
900g ripe tomatoes, coarsely chopped
1 teaspoon lemon juice
350ml water
1 dessertspoon brown sugar (or to taste)
25ml milk
1 tablespoon single cream

To garnish:
150ml natural yoghurt
3 tablespoons fresh basil, chopped

Cooking time: 30 minutes + chilling time

Serves: 4

- Melt the butter in a saucepan, add the onion and garlic, then cover and cook gently for 10 minutes until soft, without browning.
- Add the paprika and tomatoes and cook for 10 minutes. Add the lemon juice, water and brown sugar to taste, then simmer for 5 minutes.
- Blend until smooth, then stir in the milk and cream.
- Season to taste, then chill well. Serve garnished with a dollop of yoghurt and sprinkled with fresh, chopped basil leaves.

Fresh for...
August
18th

Sorrel Soup

Ingredients

40g butter
1 large onion, finely chopped
900ml vegetable stock
225g fresh sorrel leaves
225ml single cream

Cooking time	Serves
15 minutes	6

- Melt the butter in a saucepan, add the onion, then cover and cook gently for 5 minutes, until soft, without browning. Add the stock and bring to the boil.
- Stir in the sorrel, cover, then cook for 1 minute until the leaves wilt a little.
- Blend until smooth, add the cream, then season to taste.
- This soup is delicious hot or chilled, garnished with a swirl of cream and fresh chervil leaves.

Fresh for...
August
19th

Ginger & Carrot with Lime

Ingredients

1 tablespoon sunflower oil
1 tablespoon, finely grated fresh ginger, about 20g
1 garlic clove, crushed
2 small onions, sliced
900g carrots, sliced
900ml vegetable stock
1 lime, juice of
150ml milk
150ml double cream

For the garnish:
very thin slices of lime
lime juice

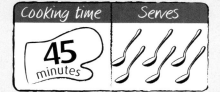

Cooking time	Serves
45 minutes	6

- Heat the oil in a saucepan, add the ginger, garlic and onion, then cover and cook gently for 10 minutes, without browning.
- Add the carrots and the stock, then cover, bring to the boil and simmer for 20 minutes until the vegetables are tender.
- Blend until smooth.
- Stir in the lime juice little by little to taste, then add the milk and cream. Season to taste.
- This soup is delicious served hot or chilled. Garnish with thin slices of lime and a sprinkle of lime juice.

Fresh for...
August
20th

Iced Cucumber, Yoghurt & Mint

Ingredients

1 teaspoon salt
1 large cucumber, peeled, deseeded and cut into small dice
275ml plain yoghurt
275ml tomato juice
1 small garlic clove, finely chopped
570ml chicken stock
a small bunch fresh mint, finely chopped
275ml single cream
Tabasco or chilli powder, to taste

To garnish:
6 small sprigs of fresh mint

Time	Serves
50 minutes	6
+ chilling time	

- Sprinkle the salt on the cucumber and leave to drain for 30 minutes. Wash the cucumber and squeeze out any excess moisture in a clean towel.
- Mix together the yoghurt, tomato juice, garlic, stock and mint and infuse for 30 minutes. Strain through a fine sieve.
- Stir the cucumber into the yoghurt mixture along with the cream and Tabasco or chilli powder, then season to taste.
- Chill well and serve garnished with sprigs of mint.

Avocado & Cucumber

Fresh for...
August
21st

Ingredients

15g butter
1 small onion, finely chopped
3 large ripe avocados, peeled and stoned
1 teaspoon lemon juice
900ml vegetable stock
150g cucumber, chopped
75ml milk
50ml single cream

To garnish:
1 tablespoon each of:
cucumber, avocado and tomato, diced into fine cubes

Cooking time	Serves
15 minutes	6
+ chilling time	

- Melt the butter in a saucepan, add the onion, then cover and cook gently for 5 minutes, until soft, without browning.
- Mash the avocado to a pulp, then add the lemon juice and stir into the onion.
- Add the stock and cucumber, then simmer for 5 minutes. Blend until smooth with the milk and cream.
- Season to taste, then chill well.
- Serve garnished with the diced cucumber, avocado and tomato.

Fresh for...
August
22nd

Butternut Squash, Apricot & Ginger

Ingredients

a knob of butter
1 small onion, diced
1 teaspoon fresh root ginger, grated
1 small butternut squash, diced
350ml vegetable stock
50g dried apricots, diced
4 tablespoons double cream

Cooking time	Serves
40 minutes	4

- Melt the butter in a saucepan, add the onion and ginger, then cook gently for 5–10 minutes.
- Add the butternut squash, stock and apricots. Season to taste.
- Bring to the boil, then simmer gently for 25–30 minutes.
- Blend until smooth.
- Stir in the cream, then reheat gently and serve.

Vichyssoise

Fresh for...
August
23rd

Ingredients

50g butter
450g leeks, finely sliced
225g potatoes, peeled and thinly sliced
570ml water
275ml milk
75ml single cream

To garnish:
150ml natural yoghurt

Cooking time	Serves
35 minutes	6
+ chilling time	

- Melt the butter in a saucepan, add the leeks and potatoes, then cover and cook gently for 10 minutes, without browning.
- Add the water, cover, bring to the boil and simmer for a further 20 minutes until the vegetables are tender.
- Blend until smooth.
- Stir in the milk and cream and season to taste.
- Chill well, then serve garnished with a swirl of yoghurt.

Fresh for...
August
24th

Avocado Gazpacho

Ingredients

570ml soured cream
275ml milk
570ml tomato juice
570ml passata
4 tablespoons lemon juice
2 tablespoons extra virgin olive oil
2 garlic cloves, very finely chopped
2 bay leaves
2 cucumbers, peeled, deseeded and finely chopped
2 tomatoes, skinned, deseeded and finely diced
Tabasco, to taste
3 avocados, peeled and stoned
2 tablespoons lemon juice

For the garnish:
1 tablespoon sunflower oil
3 rashers thin unsmoked streaky bacon, finely sliced

Cooking time	Serves
10 minutes + chilling time	4

- Combine the soured cream, milk, tomato juice, passata, lemon juice, oil and garlic. Add the bay leaves, cucumber and tomatoes, then add the Tabasco and seasoning to taste. Chill well.
- For the garnish: heat the oil in a frying pan, add the bacon, then fry until crispy. Drain on kitchen paper.
- Just before serving the soup, mash the avocados with the lemon juice. Remove the bay leaves from the soup, then stir in the mashed avocados.
- Season to taste, then serve in chilled bowls, garnished with the crispy bacon.

Fresh for... August 25th

Barolo & Blackberry

Ingredients

700g blackberries
5 tablespoons sugar
450ml Barolo wine, or any other full-bodied red wine
1 cinnamon stick
2 strips orange zest

To garnish:
vanilla ice cream

Cooking time	Serves
10 minutes	

- Place all the ingredients in a saucepan and bring to the boil.
- Simmer very gently for 8 minutes.
- Serve warm or chilled, garnished with vanilla ice cream.

Fresh for...
August
26th

Spicy Tomato, Aubergine & Apricot

Ingredients

3 aubergines (675g)
6 tablespoons olive oil
1 teaspoon cumin seeds
1 medium onion, finely chopped
2 garlic cloves, finely chopped
1 red chilli, deseeded and finely chopped
110g dried apricots, finely chopped
2.5cm piece of ginger, peeled and finely chopped
450ml tomato passata
half a lemon, juice of
1.5 litres vegetable stock
1 tablespoon fresh coriander leaves, chopped

Cooking time: 1:10 hour & minutes
Serves: 4

- Preheat the oven to 200°C/400°F/gas mark 6.
- Cut the aubergines in half, brush with 3 tablespoons of oil, then bake for 30 minutes until soft. Remove from the oven and chop roughly.
- Heat the remaining oil in a saucepan. Add the cumin, onion, garlic and chilli, then cook gently for 2–3 minutes, without browning.
- Add the apricots, ginger, passata, lemon juice, aubergines and half the stock. Bring to the boil, then simmer for 20 minutes.
- Blend until smooth, then add the remaining stock and season to taste. Stir in the coriander and serve.

Truly Tomato

Fresh for...
August
27th

Ingredients

1 tablespoon olive oil
25g butter
1 carrot, peeled and diced
1 small onion, finely diced
half a red pepper, deseeded and diced
1 stick celery, diced
600g tinned tomatoes (1.5 tins)
500ml vegetable stock
half an eating apple, peeled and diced
50ml double cream

Cooking time	Serves
35 minutes	4

- Heat the oil and butter in a saucepan. Add the carrot, onion, pepper and celery, then cook for 10–15 minutes until well softened.
- Add the tomatoes and stock before bringing to the boil. Cover and simmer for 10–15 minutes.
- Add the apple, then cover and simmer for a further 5 minutes.
- Blend until completely smooth.
- Reheat gently, add the cream, then season to taste.

Fresh for...
August
28th

Chilled Melon & Ginger Soup

Ingredients

2 small, full-flavoured melons (halved, seeds removed and flesh removed from the skin)
6 pieces of ginger preserved in syrup, sliced
290ml Greek yoghurt
2 tablespoons sugar
290ml single cream

To garnish:
150ml double cream
a few fresh mint leaves

Time	Serves
10 minutes + chilling time	4

- Blend the melon flesh, ginger slices, Greek yoghurt and sugar until very smooth.
- Empty into a bowl, then stir in the single cream.
- Chill well.
- To serve, ladle into bowls, then garnish with a swirl of double cream and a sprinkling of freshly chopped mint.

Thai Coconut & Corn

Fresh for...
August
29th

Ingredients

2 tablespoons vegetable oil
3 medium onions, finely sliced
2 garlic cloves, crushed
1–2 tablespoons fresh root ginger, peeled and freshly grated
1–2 teaspoons turmeric
425ml coconut milk
1 litre vegetable stock
340g sweetcorn kernels (preferably fresh)
1 red pepper, deseeded and finely diced
1 stick lemongrass, bruised
3 tablespoons fresh coriander leaves, chopped
2 tablespoons Thai fish sauce
2 tablespoons maple syrup
lime juice, to taste

Cooking time	Serves
35 minutes	4

- Heat the oil in a saucepan, add the onions, then cook gently for 15 minutes until soft and lightly browned. If they begin to stick, simply add a few drops of water.
- Stir in the garlic, ginger and turmeric, then cook for 1 minute.
- Add the coconut milk, stock, sweetcorn, red pepper and lemongrass. Cover, bring to the boil and simmer gently for 10 minutes until the corn is tender.
- Remove from the heat, discard the lemongrass, then add the coriander.
- Mix the fish sauce, maple syrup and lime juice together in a bowl, then add a little to the soup and taste, continuing to add little by little until a balanced flavour is achieved.

Fresh for...
August
30th

Potato, Leek & Lavender

Ingredients

50g butter
450g leeks, washed well and finely sliced
675g potatoes, peeled and roughly chopped
1.5 litres vegetable stock
425ml whole milk
flowers from 3 lavender heads
2 tablespoons crème fraîche

To garnish:
12 lavender flowers on their stalks, 5cm long

Cooking time	Serves
40 minutes + chilling time	4

- Melt the butter in a saucepan, add the leeks, then cover and cook gently for 5 minutes, without browning.
- Add the potatoes, stock, milk and lavender flowers. Cover, bring to the boil, then simmer gently for 20–25 minutes or until the vegetables are tender.
- Blend until smooth.
- Stir in the crème fraîche, then season to taste. Thin the soup a little with water if required.
- Serve chilled, garnished with the lavender flowers.

Runner Bean & Braised Ham Broth

Fresh for...
August
31st

Ingredients

850ml ham stock
100g ham, shredded
250g runner beans, sliced
100g baby carrots, cut into batons
1 leek, finely sliced
1 tablespoon fresh chives, chopped
1 tablespoon fresh parsley, chopped

Cooking time	Serves
15 minutes	4

- Place the stock in a saucepan and bring to the boil.
- Add the ham and all the vegetables, then cover and cook rapidly for 5–7 minutes or until the vegetables are crisp but tender.
- Add the chopped herbs, season to taste, then serve.

Fresh for...
September
1st

Carrot, Apricot & Sesame Seeds

Ingredients

225g dried apricots, soaked overnight in 1.2 litres water
1 medium onion, finely chopped
3 medium carrots, thinly sliced
1 cinnamon stick
1 tablespoon clear honey
1 bay leaf
570ml chicken stock
150ml Greek yoghurt

To garnish:
2 tablespoons sesame seeds, toasted
1 tablespoon honey

Cooking time	Serves
55 minutes	4

+ overnight soaking, chilling

- Drain the apricots, reserving 570ml of the soaking liquor.
- Place the apricots, apricot soaking liquor, onion, carrots, cinnamon, honey, bay leaf and stock in a saucepan, then season to taste. Cover, then simmer gently for 50 minutes, adding more water if necessary.
- Take out the cinnamon stick and bay leaf and skim off any fat.
- Blend with the yoghurt until smooth. Season to taste, then chill well.
- To toast the sesame seeds, heat a dry pan, and when very hot add the sesame seeds. Shake over a moderate heat until the seeds begin to brown, then cool.
- Serve the soup garnished with a drizzle of honey and a sprinkling of toasted sesame seeds.

Red Lentil, Cumin & Coriander

Fresh for...
September 2nd

Ingredients

2 tablespoons extra virgin olive oil
1 medium onion, finely chopped
1 level teaspoon ground coriander
1 level teaspoon ground turmeric
1 level teaspoon ground cumin
pinch of ground cloves
350g red lentils, washed
1.2 litres vegetable stock
1 x 400g tin chopped tomatoes
20g fresh coriander leaves

To garnish:
1 tablespoon extra virgin olive oil
1 large fresh green chilli, chopped
2 tablespoons fresh coriander leaves

Cooking time	Serves
50 minutes	4

- Heat the oil in a saucepan, add the onion, then cover and cook gently for 5 minutes, without browning. Add the dried spices, then cook, stirring frequently, for a further 5 minutes.
- Add the lentils and stock, cover, then bring to the boil. Simmer gently for 20 minutes until the lentils are tender.
- Add the tomatoes, then simmer for 10 minutes. Blend with the fresh coriander leaves until smooth. Season to taste.
- For the garnish: heat the oil in a frying pan, then fry the green chilli for 2 minutes.
- Serve the soup garnished with the chilli and fresh coriander leaves.

Fresh for...
September
3rd

Clam Chowder

Ingredients

3 medium potatoes (about 700g), peeled and quartered
1.35kg baby clams in their shells
175g unsmoked streaky bacon, finely chopped
1 tablespoon sunflower oil
1 medium onion, finely chopped
3 sticks celery, finely chopped
2 teaspoons fresh thyme, chopped
1 level tablespoon dried dill
half a teaspoon ground white pepper
25g plain flour
570ml fish stock
150ml dry white wine
3 bay leaves
275ml double cream

To garnish:
18 clams in their shells (reserved from main quantity)
2 tablespoons finely chopped fresh flat-leaf parsley

Cooking time	Serves
1:10 hour & minutes	4

- Simmer the potatoes in plenty of salted water until tender. Cool, then slice and set aside.
- Wash the clams at least 6 times in plenty of cold water to remove any grit. Place in a large, covered saucepan over a high heat. Cook until the clams are just open, shaking the pan frequently.* Cool, then remove all but 18 clams from their shells, setting those aside for the garnish. Also reserve the pan juices.
- Fry the bacon in the oil in a saucepan until crispy, then add the onion and celery. Cover and cook gently for 8 minutes. Add the thyme and dill, season with pepper, then cook for 2 minutes. Stir in the flour, then cook very gently, stirring constantly, for 5 minutes.
- Place the clam juices, fish stock, white wine and bay leaves in a separate saucepan, then bring to the boil and simmer gently for 5 minutes.
- Gradually stir the broth into the bacon and onion pan, cover, then simmer gently for 10 minutes, stirring frequently. Add the potatoes, roughly mashing one-quarter of them against the side of the pan, then add the clams.
- Gently reheat the chowder, stir in the cream and garnish with the reserved clams and finely chopped parsley.

* As with all cooked shellfish, discard any that do not open during the cooking process as they may not be fresh.

Fresh for...
September
4th

Simple Red Lentil Soup

Ingredients

2 medium onions, finely chopped
250g carrots, finely chopped
110g red lentils
1.7 litres ham or vegetable stock
freshly ground black pepper

Cooking time	Serves
35 minutes	4

- Place all the soup ingredients in a saucepan, cover, then simmer for 30 minutes, or until the vegetables and lentils are tender.
- Blend until smooth.
- Reheat gently, then serve.

Fresh for...
September
5th

Kedgeree Soup

Ingredients

550g undyed smoked haddock fillets
1 bay leaf
750ml water
75g butter
1 tablespoon olive oil
1 medium onion, finely diced
2 teaspoons curry powder
200g Basmati rice
2 eggs, hard-boiled
1 tablespoon fresh coriander, finely chopped
2 tablespoons fresh flat-leaf parsley, finely chopped
2 lemons (juice of 1, the other cut into wedges)

Cooking time	Serves
30 minutes	4

- Place the haddock in a saucepan, add the bay leaf, cover with the water, then bring to the boil. Cover and simmer for 5 minutes until just cooked.
- Drain the cooking liquid into a bowl, then set aside, discarding the bay leaf.
- Wrap the haddock in kitchen foil to keep warm.
- Melt 50g butter and the olive oil in the same pan you cooked the haddock in, fry the onion until soft, then add the curry powder. Cook for 1 minute.
- Add the rice to the onion, stir well, then add the cooking liquid set aside earlier. Cover, then simmer gently for 10–15 minutes.
- Meanwhile, skin, then flake the haddock into large chunks. Peel the eggs and cut into wedges.
- When the rice is cooked, gently stir in the haddock, coriander, half the parsley, juice of 1 lemon and the remaining butter, then fork through to combine.
- Sprinkle over the remaining parsley and serve with the lemon wedges.

Minestra

Fresh for...
September 6th

Ingredients

2 tablespoons olive oil
1 small onion, diced
1 clove garlic, crushed
1 medium carrot, sliced
1 stick celery, diced
1 small potato, diced
1 x 400g tin chopped tomatoes
1 tablespoon tomato purée
600ml vegetable stock
4–5 sprigs of thyme
1 bay leaf
30g macaroni
200g tinned baked beans

Cooking time	Serves
40 minutes	4

- Heat the oil in a saucepan, add the onion and garlic, then cook gently for a few minutes.
- Add the carrot, celery and potato, then cook gently for 5 minutes.
- Add the tomatoes, tomato purée, stock, sprigs of thyme and bay leaf, then bring to the boil. Cover and simmer for 20 minutes or until the vegetables are almost tender.
- Add the macaroni and baked beans, then simmer for a further 10 minutes until the pasta is just cooked.
- Season to taste, then serve.

Fresh for...
September
7th

Mussel, Fennel & Saffron

Ingredients

200ml dry white wine
1kg fresh mussels*
25g butter
2 tablespoons olive oil
1 medium carrot, peeled and diced
1 leek, diced
half a medium fennel bulb, diced
2 cloves garlic, crushed
500ml fish stock
4 medium vine tomatoes, chopped
a sprig of thyme
good pinch of saffron
200ml double cream
1 tablespoon parsley, chopped

Cooking time	Serves
40 minutes	4

- Heat the wine in a pan, add the mussels*, cover with a tight-fitting lid, then cook for 5–7 minutes, shaking occasionally until the mussels open.
- Drain into a colander set over a bowl (to catch the mussel liquor). Let the mussels cool slightly, set aside one-quarter, then remove the remaining three-quarters from their shells.
- Heat the butter and oil in a saucepan, add the carrot, leek, fennel and garlic, then cover and cook for 5–10 minutes, until softened.
- Gently pour the mussel liquor into a jug, leaving behind any sediment, then make up to 750ml using the fish stock.
- Add the stock, tomatoes, thyme and saffron to the pan, stir, then cover and simmer gently for 20 minutes.
- Remove the thyme, blend until smooth, then pass through a sieve.
- Rinse out the pan, return it to the heat, then add the cream and mussels before reheating.
- Serve, ensuring you have a good portion of mussels in each bowl, then garnish with the reserved mussels in their shells and parsley.

* As with all mussels, tap sharply with a knife before cooking and discard any that do not close as they may not be fresh.

Fresh for... September 8th

Beetroot, Lemon & Chive

Ingredients

2 tablespoons olive oil
1 carrot, peeled and chopped
1 onion, finely chopped
500g raw beetroot, peeled and chopped
1 clove garlic, crushed
750ml beef stock
1 teaspoon sugar
1 medium potato, peeled and chopped
1 tablespoon fresh chives, chopped
half a lemon, juice of

Cooking time	Serves
50 minutes	4

- Heat the oil in a saucepan, add the carrot, onion, beetroot and garlic, then cook gently for 10 minutes, until softened.
- Add the stock, sugar and potato, then cover and simmer for 40 minutes or until the vegetables are tender.
- Blend until smooth, then stir in the chives. Season to taste, then add the lemon juice and more sugar if necessary (this will depend on how earthy in flavour you like your beetroot).
- Reheat, then serve.

Fresh for...
September
9th

Bolognese Soup

Ingredients

2 tablespoons olive oil
1 small onion, finely chopped
2 cloves garlic, crushed
1 small carrot, peeled and diced
1 stick celery, diced
100g pancetta
150g beef mince
150g pork mince
200ml red wine
1 x 400g tin chopped tomatoes
2 teaspoons dried oregano
400ml beef stock
4 tablespoons tomato purée
2 tablespoons fresh basil, shredded

Cooking time	Serves
2 hours	4

- Heat the oil in a saucepan, add the onion, garlic, carrot and celery, then cook gently until soft and browned.
- Place the pancetta in a large frying pan, then fry until it starts to brown and the fat starts to run.
- Add the beef and pork mince to the frying pan, then brown thoroughly. Add the wine, reduce a little, then transfer to the saucepan of vegetables.
- Add the tomatoes, oregano, stock and tomato purée to the saucepan, cover, then simmer gently for 1½ hours.
- Add the shredded basil, then season to taste. Add a little more stock or water if necessary.
- Reheat gently and then serve.

Fresh for...
September
10th

Wilted Spinach & Stilton

Ingredients

50g butter
2 leeks, sliced
1 medium potato, diced
700ml vegetable stock
500g spinach leaves, washed and drained
100g Stilton cheese, crumbled
50g crème fraîche

Cooking time	Serves
35 minutes	

- Melt the butter in a saucepan, add the leeks, then cook gently for 5 minutes, until softened.
- Add the potato, cook for 2–3 minutes, then add the stock.
- Bring to the boil, cover, then simmer gently for 15–20 minutes until the potato is tender.
- Meanwhile, place the spinach leaves in a separate saucepan of boiling water, then cook gently until just wilted. Drain.
- Add the crumbled Stilton to the leek and potato mix, then stir until melted. Add the drained spinach, then blend until smooth.
- Reheat gently, stir in the crème fraîche. Season to taste, then serve.

Fresh for... September 11th

Mussels, White Wine & Garlic

Ingredients

2kg mussels, cleaned
5 tablespoons olive oil
3 cloves garlic, finely chopped
370ml white wine
4 shallots, finely sliced
1 red chilli, finely chopped
120ml double cream
1 small bunch flat-leaf parsley, finely chopped

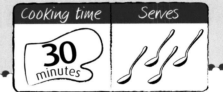

Cooking time: 30 minutes

Serves: 4

- Clean the mussels thoroughly under cold running water, scrubbing well to get rid of any barnacles and removing the mussel beards. (Discard any open ones that do not close when tapped sharply.) Change the water several times.
- Heat 2 tablespoons of oil in a saucepan, add half the garlic and all the mussels, then cover and shake vigorously to coat the mussels with the oil. Add the wine, then cover and cook for 2–3 minutes until the shells open.
- Pour the mussels and cooking juices into a large bowl to cool.
- Remove three-quarters of the mussels from their shells, discarding any that have not opened. Reserve and set aside the cooking juices.
- Return the pan to the heat, add the remaining oil and garlic, the shallots and chilli, then cook for 5 minutes, until golden.
- Add the reserved cooking juices, cream and half the parsley, then reduce slightly to thicken.
- Add the cooked mussels, then reheat for 5 minutes, stirring frequently. Season to taste, then add the remaining parsley and serve.

Fresh for...
September
12th

Trout & Watercress

Ingredients

1 whole trout, filleted
565ml fish stock
50g butter
2 medium onions, finely chopped
2 medium potatoes, finely chopped
2 cloves garlic, crushed
1 litre vegetable stock
250g watercress, hard stalks trimmed

Cooking time	Serves
45 minutes	

- Poach the trout fillets in the fish stock for 5–10 minutes until cooked. Remove the fish from the stock, cool, discard the skin and bones, then flake the fish into a bowl and set aside.
- Melt the butter in a saucepan, add the onions, potato and garlic, then cover and cook gently for 10 minutes, without browning.
- Add the vegetable stock, then bring to the boil. Add the watercress, bring back to the boil, then simmer gently for 5 minutes.
- Blend until smooth.
- Season to taste, then reheat gently for 2 minutes.
- Divide the flaked trout across the serving bowls, pour over the soup and serve.

Fresh for...
September
13th

Tomato, Fennel & Feta

Ingredients

1 tablespoon olive oil
1 fennel bulb, finely sliced
1 small potato, diced
1 tablespoon tomato purée
1 small onion, diced
1 clove garlic, finely chopped
1 teaspoon caster sugar
2 tablespoons white wine vinegar
300g tomatoes, chopped
1 tablespoon sun-dried tomato paste
450ml water
50g feta cheese, diced

Cooking time	Serves
1:05 hour & minutes	4

- Heat the oil in a saucepan, add part of the fennel (only 40g at this stage), followed by all of the potato, tomato purée, onion and garlic. Cook gently for 8–10 minutes until the vegetables are soft and without too much colour.
- Add the sugar and white wine vinegar, then reduce by half.
- Once reduced, add the chopped tomatoes and sun-dried tomato paste, then cook for a further 5 minutes.
- Add the water, cover, then cook gently for a further 30 minutes.
- Blend until smooth, then add the feta cheese and remaining fennel. Season to taste, then cook gently for a further 10 minutes and serve.

Fresh for...
September
14th

Mediterranean Vegetable & Tomato

Ingredients

1 tablespoon olive oil
1 small onion, finely chopped
1 clove garlic, crushed
half a red pepper, diced
half a yellow pepper, diced
2 courgettes, diced
1 teaspoon sweet smoked paprika
1 teaspoon fresh rosemary, finely chopped
1 teaspoon balsamic vinegar
1 x 400g tin chopped tomatoes
1 litre vegetable stock
1 tablespoon sun-dried tomato paste
1 teaspoon fresh parsley, finely chopped

Cooking time	Serves
30 minutes	4

- Heat the oil in a saucepan, add the onion and garlic, then cook gently for 5 minutes, without browning.
- Add the peppers, courgettes, paprika and rosemary, then cook for 3 minutes, stirring all the while.
- Add the balsamic vinegar, simmer for 2 minutes, then add the chopped tomatoes and stock.
- Bring to the boil, then cover and simmer for 15 minutes or until the vegetables are tender.
- Stir in the sun-dried tomato paste and parsley, then season to taste and serve.

Fresh for...
September
15th

Spicy Chicken, Pea & Apricot

Ingredients

1 tablespoon olive oil
1 small onion, finely chopped
1 clove garlic, crushed
750ml chicken stock
1 teaspoon Harissa paste
50g rice
75g cooked chicken, diced
100g fresh peas
50g dried apricots, diced
1 sprig of fresh coriander, chopped

Cooking time	Serves
35 minutes	4

- Heat the oil in a saucepan, add the onion and garlic, then cook gently for 5 minutes, without browning.
- Add the stock and Harissa, bring to the boil, then reduce to a simmer.
- Add the rice, cooked chicken, peas and apricots, then simmer for 15–20 minutes, or until the rice is cooked.
- Season to taste, garnish with fresh coriander, then serve.

Fresh for...
September
16th

Cauliflower & Vintage Cheddar

Ingredients

25g butter
1 small onion, finely chopped
1 medium potato, diced
1 medium cauliflower, broken into small florets
500ml vegetable stock
150ml milk
100g vintage Cheddar, grated

Cooking time	Serves
35 minutes	

- Melt the butter in a saucepan, add the onion and potato, then cook gently for 5 minutes, without browning.
- Add the cauliflower and stock, bring to the boil, then cover and simmer for 20 minutes until the vegetables are tender.
- Blend until smooth.
- On a gentle heat, add the milk and Cheddar cheese, stirring continuously until the cheese has melted – but don't let it boil.
- Season to taste and then serve.

Fresh for...
September
17th

Duck & Pomegranate

Ingredients

2 duck legs
2 teaspoons dried mushrooms
1 pomegranate
1 litre chicken stock
2 tablespoons Tamari soy sauce
2 teaspoons pomegranate molasses
3 spring onions, sliced

Cooking time	Serves
1 hour	4

- Preheat the oven to 200°C/400°F/gas mark 6.
- Season the duck legs, then roast on a rack for 40 minutes. Allow to cool slightly but, while still warm, remove the meat, skin and bones (discarding the skin and bones), then shred the meat with two forks.
- Meanwhile, soak the dried mushrooms in a cup of freshly boiled water for 30 minutes.
- Halve the pomegranate, juicing one half and removing the seeds from the other half. (To remove the seeds, hold the pomegranate cut-side down over a board and bang the skin; the seeds will fall away from the pith.)
- Heat the stock in a saucepan, add the meat, mushrooms and their water, pomegranate juice, Tamari and the molasses. Bring to the boil and simmer gently for 5 minutes.
- Add the pomegranate seeds and spring onions, then season to taste. Heat for a further 2 minutes and serve.

Spicy Mussels

Fresh for...
September
18th

Ingredients

160g fresh mussels
1 small onion, diced
1 tablespoon vegetable oil
25g unsalted butter
1 teaspoon curry powder
1 tablespoon plain flour
610ml fish stock
4 tablespoons double cream
40g coconut cream
1 teaspoon fresh coriander, chopped
1 tablespoon lime juice

Cooking time	Serves
30 minutes	4

- Clean the mussels thoroughly under cold running water, scrubbing well to get rid of any barnacles and removing the mussel beards. (Discard any that are open or that have cracked shells.) Change the water several times.
- Place the mussels in a saucepan with half the chopped onion and a little water (approximately 1cm), then steam for 5 minutes until the mussels are open.
- Remove the mussels from the liquid and set to one side to cool, reserving the liquid for later. When cool, remove the mussels from their shells and set aside.
- Heat the oil and butter in a pan, then add the remaining onion and curry powder. Cook for 2 minutes to release the flavours, taking care not to burn the ingredients.
- Add the flour, then stir well. Add the fish stock and cooking liquid, stirring all the time, then cook gently for 10 minutes until thickened.
- Add the double cream and coconut cream, then simmer for 2 minutes. Blend until smooth.
- Heat gently, add the mussels, coriander and lime juice, and season to taste. Reheat gently for a further 3 minutes, then serve.

Fresh for...
September
19th

Turnip, Honey & Roasted Garlic

Ingredients

25g butter
1 medium onion, finely diced
3 medium carrots, diced
2 medium potatoes, diced
300g turnips, diced
1 stick celery, sliced
750ml chicken stock
6 cloves garlic, roasted in skin until soft
4 teaspoons honey

Cooking time: 1:20 hour & minutes

Serves: 4

- Melt the butter in a saucepan, add the onion, then cover and cook gently for 10 minutes, without browning.
- Add the carrots, potatoes, turnips, celery and stock to the pan. Bring to the boil, cover, then simmer gently for 1 hour, stirring occasionally.
- Remove from the heat, blend half the soup until smooth, then return it to the pan.
- Squeeze the roasted garlic cloves from their skins, mash to a paste, then add to the soup along with the honey. Season to taste, then reheat gently for 2–3 minutes and serve.

Fresh for...
September
20th

Red Lentil & Chickpea Dhal

Ingredients

225g red lentils, rinsed well
3 tablespoons groundnut oil
1 large onion, finely sliced
1 large green chilli, deseeded and finely chopped
1 large red chilli, deseeded and finely chopped
15g ginger, peeled and finely chopped
1 clove garlic, crushed
1 teaspoon ground turmeric
1 teaspoon ground coriander
1 teaspoon ground cumin
half a teaspoon freshly ground black pepper
275ml chicken stock
2 large tomatoes, chopped
100ml coconut cream
1 dessertspoon salt
1 dessertspoon tamarind purée
15g fresh coriander, chopped

Cooking time	Serves
50 minutes	

- Put the lentils in a saucepan, then add enough water to cover them by 4cm. Bring to the boil and simmer fairly rapidly for 10 minutes, stirring occasionally and skimming off any scum from the surface. Remove from the heat, cover tightly, then set aside.
- Meanwhile, heat the oil in another saucepan, add the onion and cook for 15–20 minutes until golden brown.
- Reduce the heat, then stir in the green and red chillies, ginger and garlic.
- Cover, then cook gently for 3 minutes. Stir in the turmeric, coriander, cumin and black pepper, then cook gently for a further 2 minutes, stirring frequently.
- Add the remaining ingredients except the coriander and stir well. Increase the heat and bring almost (but not quite) to the boil. Remove from the heat, then blend until not quite smooth.
- Reheat the soup, stirring, until almost at boiling point. Remove from the heat, stir in the chopped coriander, then serve.

Fresh for...
September
21st

Butter Bean, Haricot Bean & Sage

Ingredients

150g dried butter beans
60g dried haricot beans
25g butter
half a medium onion, finely chopped
1 clove garlic, crushed
1.2 litres vegetable stock
1 heaped teaspoon tomato purée
150g tinned chopped tomatoes
1 teaspoon Demerara sugar
1 tablespoon fresh sage, finely chopped
150ml milk
1 tablespoon double cream

Cooking time	Serves
1:10 hour & minutes	4
+ oaking time	

- Soak the butter beans in 200ml of water for 1 hour. At the same time, soak the haricot beans in 75ml water for 1 hour, and then drain.
- Melt the butter in a saucepan, add the onion and garlic, then cover and cook gently for 10 minutes, without browning.
- Add the stock, tomato purée, drained butter beans and tomatoes, then cover and simmer gently until the butter beans are tender.
- Blend until smooth, then add the haricot beans, sugar, sage and salt to taste. Add more water if necessary to achieve the desired consistency.
- Simmer for 45 minutes, until the haricot beans are tender. Stir in the milk and cream, then serve.

Scotch Broth

Fresh for... September 22nd

Ingredients

1.35kg scrag end of mutton (or, if unavailable, stewing lamb)
3.6 litres water
1 teaspoon salt
2 tablespoons pearl barley, washed well
1 medium onion, finely chopped
1 leek, sliced
1 carrot, roughly chopped
1 turnip, peeled and roughly chopped
1 stick celery, roughly chopped
1 tablespoon fresh flat-leaf parsley, finely chopped

Cooking time: 3:15 hours & minutes

Serves: 6

- Place the meat in a saucepan with the water and salt. Cover, bring to the boil and simmer gently for 2 hours.
- Add the washed pearl barley and vegetables, then cover and simmer gently for a further 1 hour.
- Strain, returning the broth to a clean saucepan.
- Cut the meat into small pieces, removing any fragments of bone, and return the meat and vegetables to the broth.
- Reheat gently, stir in the parsley, season to taste and serve.

Fresh for...
September
23rd

Sweet Potato & Avocado

Ingredients

350g sweet potatoes, peeled and diced
1 small onion, finely chopped
1 litre water
2 medium ripe avocados, peeled and stoned
half a lemon, grated rind & juice of
1 small orange, grated rind & juice of
half a teaspoon ground mace
pinch of salt

To garnish:
half an avocado, finely diced
rind of 1 orange and 1 lemon

Cooking time	Serves
20 minutes + chilling time	4

- Place the potatoes, onion and water in a saucepan, add salt and simmer for 15 minutes.
- Blend, together with the avocado flesh, until smooth.
- Stir in the lemon and orange rind and juice, along with the ground mace and salt.
- Serve well chilled, garnished with the diced avocado and orange and lemon rind.

Fresh for...
September
24th

Leek & Orange Vichyssoise

Ingredients

15g butter
1 small onion, finely chopped
300g leek, finely sliced
900ml vegetable stock
1 teaspoon lemon juice
juice of 2 large oranges
75ml milk
50ml single cream

To garnish:
150ml crème fraîche
2 tablespoons fresh chives, chopped

Cooking time: 30 minutes + chilling time

Serves

- Melt the butter in a saucepan, add the onion, then cover and cook gently for 10 minutes, until soft, without browning. Add the leek, then cook for a further 5 minutes.
- Add the vegetable stock, lemon and orange juice and simmer until the vegetables are tender.
- Blend, together with the milk and cream, until smooth, then season to taste.
- Serve chilled, garnished with a swirl of crème fraîche and a sprinkling of chopped chives.

Fresh for...
September
25th

Mussels, Tomato & Red Pepper

Ingredients

1.35kg mussels
150ml red wine
700g ripe tomatoes, skinned
1 small red pepper, halved and deseeded
75g butter
2 large garlic cloves, finely chopped
1 heaped teaspoon paprika
40g plain flour
450ml fish stock
150ml double cream

Cooking time	Serves
50 minutes	6

- Wash the mussels thoroughly, scraping off any barnacles and discarding any open or cracked shells. Place in a large saucepan with the wine, then cover and cook gently for 5–10 minutes, shaking occasionally until the mussels open. Strain well, reserving the cooking liquid and discarding any mussels that have not opened.

- Set aside 18 mussels for garnishing and remove the remaining mussels from their shells.

- Blend the skinned tomatoes and red pepper until smooth and set aside. Melt the butter in a saucepan, add the garlic and paprika, then remove from the heat and stir in the flour. Gradually stir in the stock, then add the puréed tomatoes and pepper and the cooking liquid. Return to the boil, stirring until the soup thickens. Cover, then simmer very gently for 30 minutes.

- Add the cream to the soup and stir, then add the cooked mussels. Serve the soup garnished with the reserved mussels.

Fresh for...
September
26th

Chicken Mulligatawny

Ingredients

75g butter
1 small chicken, cut into pieces
2 medium onions, finely chopped
1 tablespoon mild Madras curry powder
1 garlic clove, finely chopped
1 tablespoon plain flour
1.8 litres cold water
225g lean ham, cut into fine strips
4 cloves
large pinch of mace
a sprig of thyme
a sprig of basil
a sprig of marjoram
1 lemon, juice of
1 tablespoon soured cream

Cooking time	Serves
2 hours	4

- Melt the butter in a saucepan, add the chicken pieces and brown all over. Remove from the pan and set aside.
- Add the onion to the pan, and cook gently for 5–10 minutes until transparent and soft. Add the curry powder and garlic, then cook for a further 2–3 minutes.
- Add the flour, then cook for a further minute, stirring well. Gradually stir in the water and add the browned chicken pieces.
- Add the ham, cloves, mace, herbs, lemon juice and seasoning, bring to the boil, then simmer gently for 1–1½ hours until the chicken is tender.
- Remove the chicken pieces from the pan, then strip off all the meat (discarding the skin and bones). Return the meat to the pan, remove the herbs and cloves, then season to taste. Just before serving, swirl in the soured cream.

Fresh for...
September
27th

Jamaican Sweet Potato & Redcurrant

Ingredients

25g butter
1 tablespoon sunflower oil
675g onions, finely sliced
2 medium sweet potatoes, diced
900g redcurrants, stalks removed
850ml chicken stock
1–2 teaspoons curry powder
6 juniper berries
275ml coconut milk
honey or maple syrup, to taste (optional)

To garnish:
4 sprigs of redcurrants (on their stalks)
icing sugar

Cooking time	Serves
30 minutes + chilling time	

- Heat the butter and oil in a saucepan, add the onions, then cook for 10 minutes until golden, stirring frequently.
- Add the sweet potatoes, redcurrants, stock, curry powder and juniper berries, then cover and cook gently for 15 minutes or until the sweet potatoes are soft.
- Blend until smooth, then add the coconut milk, adding a little water to thin, if necessary.
- Season to taste, adding honey or maple syrup to taste if desired. Pass through a sieve and then chill.
- Serve chilled, garnished with redcurrant sprigs and a sprinkling of icing sugar.

Fresh for...
September
28th

Cajun Chicken Gumbo

Ingredients

3 tablespoons olive oil
1 small onion, finely chopped
2 large cloves garlic, crushed
50g fresh root ginger, finely grated
1 medium red chilli, finely chopped (with seeds)
2 chicken breasts, diced
50g butter
50g plain flour
400ml milk
2 oranges, juice of 2 and zest of 1
2 teaspoons Dijon mustard
1 level teaspoon peanut butter
2 tablespoons soy sauce
2 tablespoons fresh flat-leaf parsley, chopped

Cooking time	Serves
35 minutes	4

- Heat the oil in a saucepan, add the onion, garlic, ginger and chilli, then cook gently for 2 minutes, stirring frequently. Add the diced chicken, then cook for 10 minutes.
- Add the butter and flour, then cook very gently for a further 10 minutes, until the mixture has a nutty colour and aroma.
- Remove from the heat, then gradually whisk in the milk.
- Return to the heat and bring to the boil. Add the orange juice and zest, mustard, peanut butter, soy sauce and parsley.
- Season to taste, simmer gently for 10 minutes, then serve.

Fresh for...
September
29th

Moules Marinière

Ingredients

1.3kg fresh mussels, in their shells
1 tablespoon extra virgin olive oil
3 large shallots, chopped
1 large garlic clove, finely chopped
1 bay leaf
a sprig of fresh thyme
450ml dry white wine
275ml single cream
a large handful finely chopped fresh flat-leaf parsley

Cooking time	Serves
20 minutes	4

- Scrub the mussels under running water and remove any barnacles.* Wash very thoroughly 2 or 3 times in plenty of cold water. Drain well.
- Heat the oil in a saucepan, add the shallots, garlic, bay leaf and thyme, then cover and cook gently for 10 minutes until soft, but without browning.
- Add the mussels and wine, then cover and place over a high heat. Shake the pan vigorously for about 3–5 minutes until the mussels have opened. Remove from the heat and discard any mussels that are still closed.
- Add the cream and parsley to the pan and season to taste. Toss the mussels to coat, then serve immediately.

* Discard any that do not close when tapped sharply with a knife as these may not be fresh.

Beef Borscht

Fresh for...
September
30th

Ingredients

500g braising steak, cut into 2cm cubes
1 litre beef stock
1 tablespoon olive oil
1 green pepper, diced
2 medium carrots, diced
2 cloves garlic, sliced
1 large onion, chopped
2 medium potatoes, diced
200g tinned chopped tomatoes
200g shredded red cabbage
250g cooked beetroot, cut into large dice
2 teaspoons lemon juice
2 teaspoons brown sugar
2 tablespoons fresh dill, chopped
2 tablespoons fresh parsley, chopped

Cooking time: 2 hours
Serves

- Place the beef and stock in a saucepan, bring to the boil, then cover and simmer gently for 1 hour and 15 minutes.
- After an hour of cooking time, heat the oil in a separate saucepan, add the green pepper, carrots, garlic and onion, then cover and cook for 15 minutes until soft. Add to the beef and stock.
- Add the potatoes, tomatoes and cabbage to the beef and stock, then cook for a further 20 minutes.
- Add the cooked beetroot, lemon juice, sugar and herbs. Season to taste, then cook for a further 5 minutes.
- Remove from the heat, leave to stand for 3 minutes, then serve.

Fresh for...
October
1st

Cauliflower & Chive

Ingredients

25g butter
1 tablespoon olive oil
1 medium onion, finely chopped
1 medium potato, diced
1 medium cauliflower, outer leaves removed, cut into small florets
650ml vegetable stock
4 tablespoons Greek yoghurt
1 tablespoon chives, chopped

Cooking time	Serves
35 minutes	4

- Heat the butter and olive oil in a saucepan, add the onion and potato, then cover and cook gently for 10 minutes, until soft.
- Add the cauliflower florets and the stock, bring to the boil, then cover and simmer for 15–20 minutes, until the cauliflower is tender.
- Blend until velvety smooth, then reheat gently, stirring in the Greek yoghurt and chives.
- Season to taste, and then serve.

Fresh for...
October
2nd

Puy Lentil & Smoky Bacon

Ingredients

2 tablespoons olive oil
12 rashers smoked streaky bacon, chopped
1 medium onion, finely chopped
1 medium carrot, diced
1 clove garlic, crushed
850ml chicken stock
120g Puy lentils, rinsed
1 x 400g tin chopped tomatoes
1 bay leaf
1 tablespoon tomato purée
5–6 sprigs of fresh thyme
1 tablespoon fresh parsley, chopped

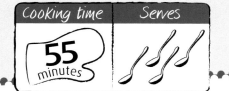

Cooking time	Serves
55 minutes	4

- Heat the oil in a saucepan, fry the bacon for a few minutes until lightly browned.
- Add the onion, carrot and garlic, then cook for 5–10 minutes, until softened.
- Add the stock, lentils, tomatoes, bay leaf, tomato purée and thyme sprigs, bring to the boil, then cover and simmer for 40 minutes until the vegetables and lentils are tender.
- Remove the thyme sprigs and bay leaf, then stir in the parsley. Season to taste, then serve.

Fresh for...
October
3rd

Sausage, Bacon & Tomato

Ingredients

12 rashers smoked streaky bacon
2 tablespoons olive oil
1 small onion, finely diced
2 x 400g tins chopped tomatoes
pinch of dried oregano
1 tablespoon fresh basil, chopped
pinch of sugar
4 tomatoes, halved
12 chipolata sausages
4 eggs

Cooking time: 50 minutes

Serves: 4

- Chop 4 rashers of bacon. Heat the oil in a saucepan, then fry the chopped bacon and onion until softened.
- Add the tinned tomatoes, herbs and sugar, then simmer gently for 20 minutes.
- Meanwhile, preheat the grill on a medium setting, season the tomato halves and grill with the sausages and remaining bacon rashers.
- When the tinned tomatoes and herbs are cooked, fry the eggs in a frying pan.
- Pour the tomato soup into serving bowls, then garnish with three sausages, two rashers of bacon and top with a fried egg. Serve with crusty bread.

Fresh for...
October
4th

Easy Cauliflower Cheesy

Ingredients

50g butter
1 small onion, finely diced
1 medium potato, peeled and diced
1 small cauliflower, cut into florets
700ml vegetable stock
100ml milk
100–150g cheese, finely grated

Cooking time	Serves
35 minutes	

- Melt the butter in a saucepan, add the onion, then cook for 10 minutes, until soft.
- Add the potato and cauliflower, stir, then add the stock.
- Bring to the boil, cover, then simmer for 20 minutes.
- Blend until completely smooth.
- Reheat gently, adding the milk and cheese, then stir until the cheese has melted.

Fresh for...
October
5th

Butternut Squash & Goat's Cheese

Ingredients

2 tablespoons olive oil
150g onion, diced
1 teaspoon garlic purée
1 teaspoon dried sage
800g butternut squash, peeled and cubed
600ml vegetable stock
100g soft, mild goat's cheese, crumbled

Cooking time	Serves
50 minutes	4

- Heat the oil in a large saucepan, add the onion, then cook for 10 minutes, until soft.
- Add the garlic purée, sage and butternut squash, then cook gently for 10 minutes, stirring occasionally.
- Add the stock, bring back to the boil, then cover and simmer for 20 minutes or until the squash is tender.
- Stir in the goat's cheese until melted.
- Blend until smooth, reheat gently, then season to taste and serve.

Fresh for...
October
6th

Roast Pumpkin & Bramley Apple

Ingredients

1 large pumpkin
2 tablespoons olive oil
25g butter
1 small onion, finely chopped
670ml chicken stock
1 small Bramley apple, peeled and finely diced

Cooking time	Serves
1 hour	

- Preheat oven to 230°C/450°F/gas mark 8.
- Cut the pumpkin into quarters, scoop out and discard the seeds.
- Brush the flesh with olive oil, then place in a roasting tin. Bake for 25 minutes until the flesh is soft, then allow to cool. Once cooled, scoop the flesh out of the skin.
- Melt the butter in a pan, add the onion, cover, then cook for 10 minutes, without browning.
- Add the stock and pumpkin flesh, then cover and simmer gently for 15 minutes.
- Add the apple, cover, then simmer for a further 5 minutes, until tender.
- Blend a third of the soup, return to the pan, season to taste and stir. Reheat for 2 minutes, and then serve.

Fresh for...
October
7th

Sweet Potato, Butternut Squash & Chilli

Ingredients

25g butter
1 clove garlic, crushed
225g sweet potato, diced
1 small butternut squash, diced
half a teaspoon sweet smoked paprika
half a red chilli, finely diced
750ml vegetable stock
2 teaspoons wholegrain mustard
1 tablespoon Parmesan cheese, finely grated
125ml double cream

Cooking time	Serves
35 minutes	

- Melt the butter in a saucepan, add the garlic, sweet potato and butternut squash, then cover and cook for 10 minutes.
- Add the smoked paprika and red chilli, then cook for 1 minute.
- Add the stock and bring to the boil, then cover and simmer for 15–20 minutes, until the vegetables are tender.
- Allow to cool a little, then stir in the mustard and Parmesan. Blend until smooth.
- Add the cream, season to taste, then reheat gently for 2 minutes and serve.

Cream of Celeriac & Truffle

Fresh for...
October
8th

Ingredients

25g butter
1 tablespoon olive oil
1 medium celeriac, finely diced
1 large potato, finely diced
1 small onion, finely chopped
850ml vegetable stock
a few sprigs of fresh thyme
3 tablespoons double cream
half a teaspoon truffle oil

Cooking time	Serves
50 minutes	

- Melt the butter and olive oil in a saucepan, add the celeriac, potato and onion. Cover, then cook gently for 10 minutes, until the vegetables begin to soften.
- Add the stock and thyme, cover, then simmer for 20–30 minutes, until the vegetables are tender.
- Blend until smooth.
- Return to the pan, add the cream and truffle oil then season to taste.
- Reheat gently for a further 5 minutes and serve.

Fresh for...
October
9th

Chicken Broth

Ingredients

4 medium potatoes, diced
2 medium carrots, diced
half a swede, diced
1 medium onion, finely chopped
2 chicken breasts, cut into slices
845ml chicken stock
75g pearl barley

Cooking time	Serves
45 minutes	4

- Cook the potatoes in a pan of water for 10 minutes, drain and set aside.
- In a fresh pan put the carrots, swede, onion, chicken, stock and pearl barley.
- Bring to the boil and simmer for 15 minutes.
- Add the cooked potatoes, season to taste, cook for a further 20 minutes, then serve.

Fresh for...
October
10th

Creamy Baked Garlic & Onion

Ingredients

3 large onions, cut into 1cm slices
1 head garlic, cloves separated and peeled
565ml chicken stock
1 teaspoon dried thyme
25g butter
220ml double cream
1 tablespoon fresh parsley, chopped

Cooking time	Serves
1:35 hour & minutes	

- Preheat oven to 180°C/350°F/gas mark 4.
- Place the onions and garlic in an ovenproof dish, add 425ml chicken stock, sprinkle with thyme, season, then dot with the butter.
- Cover tightly with foil, then bake for 1½ hours, stirring once or twice during cooking.
- Remove the dish from the oven, cool slightly, then add the remaining stock.
- Blend until smooth.
- Add the cream and parsley, season to taste. Reheat gently on the hob for 5 minutes and serve.

Fresh for…
October
11th

Lentil & Bacon

Ingredients

25g butter
1 garlic clove, finely chopped
1 medium onion, peeled and thinly diced
175g red lentils, rinsed well
50g split peas, rinsed well
2 tablespoons tomato purée
1.5 litres ham stock
110g streaky bacon, finely chopped
175g carrots, peeled and finely diced
1 tablespoon parsley, finely chopped

Cooking time	Serves
50 minutes	

- Melt the butter in a saucepan, add the garlic and onion and cook gently for 2–3 minutes, without browning.
- Add the lentils, split peas and tomato purée, then cook for a further 2–3 minutes, stirring constantly to prevent sticking.
- Add the stock, bring to the boil, then simmer for 20–25 minutes, until the lentils and split peas are soft.
- Blend until smooth.
- Add the bacon, carrot and parsley, then simmer for a further 12–15 minutes until the carrots are tender, and then serve.

Celeriac & Bacon

Fresh for...
October
12th

Ingredients

10 rashers streaky bacon
25g butter
1 medium leek, diced
300g celeriac, diced
1 large potato, diced
750ml water
a squeeze of fresh lemon juice
1 bay leaf
50ml double cream

Cooking time	Serves
55 minutes	4

- Roughly chop 5 rashers of bacon. Heat the butter in a saucepan, add the chopped bacon and leeks, then cook for 5–10 minutes, until softened.
- Add the celeriac, potato, water, lemon juice and bay leaf, bring to the boil, then simmer for 20–25 minutes, until the vegetables are tender.
- Meanwhile, fry the remaining bacon rashers until crispy. Drain on kitchen paper and set aside for garnishing.
- Remove the bay leaf, then blend the soup until smooth, reheat gently, then add the cream.
- Serve with the crispy bacon rashers crumbled on top of the soup.

Fresh for...
October
13th

Tuscan Bean & Pancetta

Ingredients

110g pancetta, cubed
1 tablespoon olive oil
1 medium onion, chopped
1 x 410g tin mixed beans
1 x 400g tin chopped tomatoes
1 clove garlic, crushed
600ml vegetable stock
1 teaspoon dried mixed herbs
pinch of chilli powder
1 tablespoon fresh basil, finely chopped

Cooking time	Serves
35 minutes	

- Fry the pancetta in a frying pan until golden brown, then drain on kitchen paper.
- Meanwhile, heat the oil in a saucepan, add the onion and cover and cook gently for 10 minutes, until soft, without browning.
- Add the remaining ingredients (except the pancetta) to the pan, bring to the boil, then cover and simmer for 10 minutes.
- Add the pancetta, then cover and simmer for a further 10 minutes.
- Season to taste, then serve.

Butternut Squash & Parmesan

Fresh for... October 14th

Ingredients

25g butter
1 tablespoon olive oil
1 large butternut squash, peeled, deseeded and diced
1 medium onion, chopped
2 cloves garlic, crushed
650ml vegetable stock
1 bay leaf
1 tablespoon lemon juice
30–40g Parmesan cheese, grated

Cooking time	Serves
40 minutes	4

- Heat the butter and oil in a saucepan, add the onion and butternut squash, then cook gently for 10 minutes, stirring occasionally.
- Add the garlic, then cook for a further 5 minutes.
- Add the stock and bay leaf, then bring to the boil and simmer for 15–20 minutes.
- Blend until smooth, add the lemon juice, season to taste, then add the Parmesan.
- Reheat gently for 3 minutes, then serve.

Fresh for...
October
15th

Smoked Haddock & Horseradish

Ingredients

25g butter
2 small leeks, sliced
1 medium potato, peeled and chopped
1 bay leaf
300ml milk
300ml fish stock
300g undyed smoked haddock fillets, skinned and diced
100ml single cream
1 tablespoon fresh chives, snipped
1 tablespoon horseradish sauce (or to taste)

Cooking time	Serves
30 minutes	

- Melt the butter in a saucepan, add the leeks, then cover and cook gently for 10 minutes, until softened.
- Add the potatoes, bay leaf, milk and stock, then cover and simmer gently for a further 10 minutes.
- Add the smoked haddock, then simmer for 5 minutes until the haddock is cooked.
- Remove the bay leaf, blend until smooth, then reheat gently for 3 minutes.
- Add the cream, chives and horseradish to taste, stir and then serve.

Fresh for... October 16th

Parsnip & Orange

Ingredients

1.2 litres chicken stock
8 medium parsnips, peeled and roughly chopped
4 oranges, juice of

To garnish:
1 orange, peel cut into fine shreds, and orange segments

Cooking time	Serves
35 minutes	

- Pour the stock into a saucepan and bring to the boil. Add the parsnips, then cover. Simmer gently for 20 minutes, until tender.
- Place the shreds of orange peel in a small bowl, cover with boiling water, then leave to stand for 1 minute. Drain, then refresh under cold water.
- Blend the parsnips and stock until smooth, add the orange juice and season to taste.
- Reheat gently for 3 minutes, then serve garnished with the orange segments and shreds of peel.

Fresh for...
October
17th

Cream of Celeriac

Ingredients

25g butter
400g celeriac, peeled and roughly chopped
125g potatoes, peeled and roughly chopped
1 garlic clove, crushed
570ml vegetable stock
1 tablespoon fresh lemon juice
275ml milk

Cooking time	Serves
40 minutes	6

- Melt the butter in a saucepan, add the celeriac, potatoes and garlic, then cook gently for 5 minutes, without browning.
- Add the stock and lemon juice, then bring to the boil. Simmer gently for 25–30 minutes, until the vegetables are tender.
- Blend the soup with the milk, until smooth.
- Season to taste, then reheat gently for 3 minutes and serve.

Fresh for...
October
18th

Simple Parsnip & Apple

Ingredients

50g butter
5 parsnips, peeled and cut into chunks
1 large Bramley apple, peeled and cut into chunks
1 litre vegetable stock
600ml milk

Cooking time: 40 minutes
Serves: 4

- Melt the butter in a saucepan, add the parsnips and apple, then cook gently for 5–10 minutes.
- Add the stock, then cover and simmer for a further 20 minutes, or until the parsnips are cooked.
- Remove from the heat and allow to cool for a few minutes, then add the milk.
- Blend until smooth.
- Season to taste, reheat gently for 5 minutes, then serve.

Fresh for...
October
19th

Pear & Apple

Ingredients

50g butter
3 pears, peeled, cored and roughly chopped
1 red apple (we use Russet but any red apple can be used), peeled, cored and roughly chopped
1 teaspoon turmeric
1.25 litres chicken or vegetable stock
3 tablespoons single cream
2 egg yolks

Cooking time	Serves
40 minutes	6

- Melt the butter in a saucepan, add the pears, apple and turmeric, then cook very gently for 10 minutes.
- Add the stock, bring to the boil, then simmer for 20 minutes. Remove from the heat.
- Blend until smooth. Beat the cream and egg yolks together in a bowl, add a ladleful of soup, stir, then pour into the pan.
- Cook gently for a further 10 minutes, until the mixture thickens, stirring continuously. Season to taste, then serve.

Apple, Cider & Honey Roasted Parsnip

Fresh for... October 20th

Ingredients

250g parsnip, peeled and diced
1 tablespoon honey
2 tablespoons olive oil
1 onion, diced
100g Bramley apples, peeled and diced
500ml vegetable stock
100ml dry cider (or apple juice)
2 tablespoons double cream

Cooking time	Serves
50 minutes	

- Preheat your oven to 180°C/350°F/gas mark 4.
- Coat the parsnips in the honey and 1 tablespoon of oil, then spread on a baking tray. Roast in the oven for 15–20 minutes, until golden brown. Set aside.
- Heat the remaining oil in a saucepan, add the onion, then cover and cook gently for 5–10 minutes, until soft.
- Add the apples, roasted parsnips, stock and cider to the pan, season to taste, then simmer gently for 15–20 minutes, until the apples are cooked.
- Add the cream and stir. Blend until smooth, then serve.

Fresh for...
October
21st

Malaysian Chicken Laksa

Ingredients

1 tablespoon rapeseed or vegetable oil
1 teaspoon grated galangal (or fresh root ginger)
1 clove garlic, crushed
1 red chilli, deseeded and chopped
1 onion, finely chopped
1 teaspoon ground coriander
pinch of ground turmeric
1 teaspoon lemongrass, finely chopped
4 spring onions, sliced
100g chicken breast, cut into fine strips
2 teaspoons fish sauce
500ml water
200ml coconut milk
1 teaspoon–1 tablespoon lime juice, to taste
25g Thai fragrant rice (or basmati)
1 tablespoon fresh coriander, chopped
1 teaspoon fresh mint, chopped

Cooking time	Serves
30 minutes	4

- Heat the oil in a saucepan, add the galangal, garlic, chilli and onion, then cook gently for 5–10 minutes, or until the onion is soft.
- Add the dry spices and salt, then cook for a further 2–3 minutes.
- Add the lemongrass, spring onion and chicken, then fry for 5 minutes.
- Add the fish sauce, water, coconut milk and lime juice, and then cook for a further 5 minutes.
- Add the rice, then cook gently for 5–10 minutes, or until the rice is cooked through.
- Season to taste, add the fresh herbs, then reheat gently and serve.

Fresh for...
October
22nd

Beetroot & Roasted Parsnip

Ingredients

1 tablespoon olive oil
1 large parsnip, diced
knob of butter
1 medium onion, diced
1 clove garlic, crushed
4 cooked beetroots, diced
350ml vegetable stock
2 tablespoons double cream

Cooking time	Serves
55 minutes	

- Preheat the oven to 200°C/400°F/gas mark 6.
- Coat the parsnips in the olive oil, spread evenly on a baking tray, then bake in the oven for 20–30 minutes, until cooked through and golden. Set aside.
- Melt the butter in a saucepan, add the onion and garlic, then cook gently for 5 minutes.
- Add the roasted parsnips, beetroot and stock, then season to taste. Bring to the boil, and then simmer gently for 15 minutes.
- Blend until smooth.
- Stir in the cream, reheat gently, and then serve.

Fresh for...
October
23rd

Lebanese Lentil & Chickpea

Ingredients

1 tablespoon olive oil
1 medium onion, chopped
1 clove garlic, crushed
2 teaspoons ground cumin
2 pinches of cinnamon
2 teaspoons ground coriander
1 teaspoon Harrisa paste
50g red pepper, diced
1 teaspoon tomato purée
1 tomato, skin removed and diced
70g cooked chickpeas
70g red lentils
1 medium potato, diced
500ml vegetable stock
1 tablespoon lemon juice
1 tablespoon fresh coriander, chopped

Cooking time	Serves
40 minutes	

- Heat the olive oil in a saucepan, add the onion, then cook gently for 5–10 minutes, until soft.
- Add the garlic, cook for a few minutes, and then add the dry spices and Harrisa paste. Season to taste, then cook for 2–3 minutes.
- Add the pepper, cook for a further 2–3 minutes, and then add the tomato purée, tomato, chickpeas, lentils, potato, stock and lemon juice.
- Simmer for 20 minutes, or until the potato and lentils are soft, then serve garnished with the fresh coriander.

Cream of Fennel

Fresh for...
October
24th

Ingredients

50g butter
2 medium onions, finely chopped
1 garlic clove, finely chopped
2 heads of fennel, finely sliced
900ml chicken stock
half an orange, finely grated rind of
110ml double cream

Cooking time	Serves
1:15 hour & minutes	

- Melt the butter in a saucepan, add the onion and garlic, then cover and cook gently for 10 minutes, without browning.
- Add the fennel, then cover and cook gently for 30 minutes, stirring occasionally.
- Add the stock and orange rind. Cover, bring to the boil, then simmer gently for 30 minutes, until the vegetables are tender.
- Blend until smooth, then pass through a sieve.
- Stir in the cream and season to taste. Reheat gently for 3 minutes, then serve.

Fresh for...
October
25th

Chicken Stew With Matzo Balls

Ingredients

half a plump chicken
1 medium turnip, peeled and halved
1 small parsnip, peeled and halved
2 garlic cloves, whole
1 *bouquet garni*
1.7 litres light chicken stock
1 medium swede, peeled and chopped
3 medium carrots, chopped
3 medium leeks, chopped
2 medium onions, chopped
4 sticks celery, chopped

For the matzo balls:
fat from the soup
110g matzo meal (or crackers, crushed finely)
grated onion, to taste (optional)
1 egg
2 tablespoons of the soup

Cooking time: 2:15 hours & minutes
Serves: 4

- Place the chicken in a large saucepan, add the turnip, parsnip, garlic cloves, *bouquet garni* and cover with the stock. Bring to the boil. Skim off any scum, then cover and simmer very gently for 1 hour until there is a layer of fat on the surface. With a large spoon, transfer most of the fat to a bowl and set aside (this will be used to make the matzo balls). Add the remaining vegetables, cover and simmer for another hour until the vegetables are tender. Add salt to taste.
- To make the matzo balls: mix all the ingredients together, adding a little more matzo meal if the mixture is too sticky, or a little more soup if too dry, until the right consistency is achieved. Allow to stand for a few minutes, then roll into small balls (with floured hands) and set aside.
- Remove the turnip, parsnip and garlic from the soup, squeezing any juices back into the soup, and discard. Remove the bones from the chicken, and return to the heat.
- Reheat the soup until very hot, then add the matzo balls. Simmer for 3–5 minutes, until the matzo balls turn whitish and bob to the surface, then serve.

Onion Panade

Fresh for... October 26th

Ingredients

50g butter
4 large onions, thinly sliced
250g stale sourdough bread, thinly sliced
75g Parmesan cheese, grated
75g Gruyère cheese, grated
lightly salted boiling water
2 tablespoons Cognac
shavings of butter

Cooking time	Serves
2:05 hours & minutes	6

- Preheat the oven to 180°C/350°F/Gas Mark 4.
- Melt the butter in a saucepan, add the onions, then cover and cook gently, stirring occasionally, for 1 hour, removing the lid after 40 minutes. After an hour, they should be caramelising lightly. Turn up the heat a little and cook for a further 10 minutes, stirring occasionally, until a rich caramel colour.
- Spread the slices of bread thickly with the caramelised onions, reserving a layer of plain bread for the top. In a separate bowl mix the two grated cheeses together.
- In a large ovenproof dish, put a layer of bread over the base. Cover with a thick layer of cheese and repeat the process, pressing down each layer gently and avoiding empty spaces. Continue layering until the dish is three-quarters full, then put a final layer of plain bread on top and sprinkle with cheese.
- Slowly pour salted boiling water down the side of the dish, allowing the bread to swell and the mass to rise, until just floating. Bake in the preheated oven for 20 minutes.
- Remove the dish from the oven, add a little more boiling water and a little more cheese. Add the Cognac, top with a few shavings of butter and bake for 30 minutes for a rich golden crust. Allow to cool a little before serving.

Fresh for...
October
27th

Leftover Game & Chestnut

Ingredients

450g chestnuts, fresh, peeled (or tinned)
1 tablespoon olive oil
1 medium carrot, roughly diced
1 onion, thinly sliced
1 stick celery, sliced
1 medium potato, peeled and roughly diced
scraps of cooked game meat
1.5 litres game or chicken stock
1 bay leaf
a sprig of fresh thyme

Cooking time	Serves
1 hour	

- This is an ideal way of using up the carcass and scraps from a roasted pheasant, partridge or grouse.
- To peel the chestnuts: plunge into a pan of boiling water, simmer for 15 minutes, drain, then peel.
- Meanwhile, heat the oil in a saucepan, add the carrots, onion, celery and potatoes, then cover and cook gently for 5 minutes, without browning.
- Add the chestnuts and any leftover cooked game, then add the stock, bay leaf and thyme. Cover, then simmer gently for 40 minutes until the chestnuts and vegetables are very tender.
- Season to taste, and then serve.

Simply Pumpkin

Fresh for...
October
28th

Ingredients

25g butter
1 medium onion, finely chopped
200g potatoes, peeled and chopped
900g pumpkin, diced
250g carrots, diced
1.2 litres vegetable stock
150ml milk
Demerara sugar, to taste
nutmeg, finely grated, to taste

Cooking time	Serves
35 minutes	

- Melt the butter in a saucepan, add the onion, then cover and cook gently for 5 minutes, without browning.
- Add the potato, 700g of pumpkin, carrots and stock. Cover, then bring to the boil and simmer gently for 20 minutes until the vegetables are tender.
- Blend until smooth, then stir in the milk.
- Meanwhile, place the remaining pumpkin in a separate saucepan of boiling salted water and cook for 2 minutes. Drain the pumpkin, then add to the blended soup. Add the sugar and nutmeg, then season to taste. Reheat gently and serve in a hollowed-out pumpkin.

Fresh for...
October
29th

Pumpkin & Crispy Chorizo

Ingredients

25g butter
1 medium onion, diced
1 red chilli, deseeded and chopped
2-3 fresh sage leaves
650g pumpkin flesh
650ml chicken stock
100g chorizo, diced
2 cloves garlic, diced
1 tablespoon olive oil

Cooking time	Serves
45 minutes	4

- Melt the butter in a saucepan, add the onion, chilli and sage, then cook for 10 minutes until well softened.
- Add the pumpkin and sweat for a couple of minutes. Pour in the stock, then cover and simmer for 20–25 minutes.
- Meanwhile, fry the chorizo and garlic in the olive oil until the chorizo is browned.
- Blend the soup, season to taste, then reheat gently, adding the chorizo and garlic, along with the oil from the chorizo pan.

Pumpkin & Pesto

Fresh for...
October
30th

Ingredients

1-2 tablespoons olive oil
1 medium onion, chopped
1 clove garlic, crushed
600g pumpkin flesh
half a teaspoon ground cinnamon
half a teaspoon ground cumin
1 bay leaf
650ml chicken or vegetable stock
2 tablespoons single cream

To garnish:
1-2 tablespoons fresh pesto, mixed with olive oil to drizzle over the soup

Cooking time	Serves
40 minutes	4

- Preheat the oven to 200°C/400°F/gas mark 6.
- Meanwhile, heat the oil in a saucepan, add the onion and garlic, then cook gently for 10 minutes, until softened.
- Add the pumpkin flesh, spices and bay leaf, then cook for a further 5 minutes.
- Add the stock, bring to the boil, then cover and simmer for 20 minutes, or until the pumpkin is tender.
- Remove the bay leaf, then blend until smooth.
- Reheat gently, adding the cream. Season to taste, and then garnish with a drizzle of pesto.

Fresh for...
October
31st

Pumpkin & Carrot

Ingredients

25g butter
1 medium onion, finely chopped
1 medium pumpkin, chopped
2 large carrots, chopped
670ml vegetable stock
125ml milk
nutmeg, freshly grated, to taste

Cooking time	Serves
45 minutes	

- Melt the butter in a saucepan, add the onion, then cover and cook gently for 5 minutes, without browning.
- Add the pumpkin, carrots and stock, then bring to the boil. Cover and simmer gently for 20 minutes, until the vegetables are tender.
- Add the milk and nutmeg then blend until smooth.
- Season to taste, reheat gently for 3 minutes, and then serve in a hollowed-out pumpkin.

Beetroot, Raspberry & Champagne

Fresh for...
November
1st

Ingredients

3 beetroots, cooked
1 small red onion, finely chopped
90g fresh raspberries
1 tablespoon caster sugar
1 teaspoon red wine vinegar
565ml vegetable stock
2 tablespoons champagne or sparkling wine

Cooking time	Serves
45 minutes	

- Place the beetroot, red onion, raspberries and sugar in a saucepan, then heat gently for 5–10 minutes, until the raspberries and the beetroot start to colour the other ingredients.
- Add the red wine vinegar, bring to the boil, then reduce the liquid by half.
- Add the vegetable stock and bring to the boil. Cover and simmer for 30 minutes or until the beetroot starts to break down.
- Blend until smooth.
- Add the champagne, season to taste, and then serve.

Fresh for...
November
2nd

Spicy Sweet Potato, Butternut Squash & Chickpea

Ingredients

1 tablespoon olive oil
1 medium onion, finely chopped
2 garlic cloves, crushed
1 teaspoon cumin seeds, roasted lightly and ground
1 teaspoon coriander seeds, roasted lightly and ground
2 tablespoons sesame seeds, lightly roasted
1cm fresh root ginger, peeled and finely grated
1 green chilli, deseeded and chopped
1 lime, zest and juice
1 teaspoon runny honey
340g sweet potato, peeled and diced into 2cm cubes
340g butternut squash, peeled and diced into 2cm cubes
1.2 litres vegetable stock
1 x 410g tin chickpeas, drained
handful of fresh coriander leaves, chopped

Cooking time	Serves
45 minutes	3

- Heat the oil in a saucepan, add the onion and garlic, then cover and cook for 10 minutes, without browning.
- Add the spices, sesame seeds, ginger, chilli, lime zest and honey, then stir for 30 seconds.
- Add the sweet potato, butternut squash, half the lime juice and stock. Cover, bring to the boil, then simmer for 10 minutes, or until the vegetables are almost tender.
- Add the chickpeas and season to taste. Simmer for 10 minutes, then add the remaining lime juice to taste. Blend until very smooth.
- Reheat gently, then stir in the coriander just before serving.

Fresh for...
November
3rd

Spicy Vegetable & Peanut

Ingredients

2 medium onions, finely chopped
110g crunchy peanut butter
1 x 400g tin chopped tomatoes
900ml vegetable stock
175g potatoes, peeled and chopped
75g pimentos, drained weight
175g carrots, chopped
75ml single cream
cayenne pepper, to taste
paprika, to taste

Cooking time: 45 minutes
Serves

- Place the onions, peanut butter and 1 tablespoon of water in a saucepan, then cover and cook for 5 minutes.
- Add the tomatoes, vegetable stock, potatoes, pimentos and carrots.
- Cover, bring to the boil, then simmer gently for 30 minutes, until the vegetables are tender.
- Stir in the cream, cayenne pepper and paprika to taste. Reheat gently for 3 minutes, and then serve.

Fresh for...
November
4th

Bangers & Beans

Ingredients

1 tablespoon olive oil
6 sausages, each cut into 6 pieces
1 small red onion, finely chopped
1 teaspoon sweet smoked paprika
2 tablespoons red wine
1 medium potato, diced
1 x 410g tin haricot beans
2 carrots, diced
1 litre beef stock
565ml tomato passata
1 teaspoon oregano
Worcestershire sauce, to taste
1 tablespoon fresh parsley, chopped

Cooking time: 1:35 hour & minutes
Serves

- Heat the oil in a saucepan, add the sausage pieces and fry for 10 minutes, until all sides are browned. Remove from the pan and set aside.
- Add the red onion to the pan and cook gently for 5 minutes.
- Add the paprika and red wine, then cook for a further 45 minutes.
- Add the potato, haricot beans, carrots, stock, passata and oregano.
- Bring to the boil, add the browned sausages, then cover and simmer gently for 30 minutes, until the vegetables are tender.
- Add the Worcestershire sauce, season to taste, and then serve garnished with chopped parsley.

Bangers, Mash & Savoy Cabbage

Fresh for...
November
5th

Ingredients

50g butter
1 onion, diced
500g floury potatoes (e.g. Maris Piper), diced
600ml chicken stock
200g savoy cabbage, cored and finely shredded
24 cocktail sausages
100g cream cheese

To garnish:
4 tablespoons fresh pesto

Cooking time: 45 minutes
Serves: 4

- Melt half the butter in a saucepan, add the onion and potatoes, then cover and cook for 10 minutes, without browning.
- Add the stock, then simmer for a further 20 minutes, until the potatoes are soft.
- Meanwhile, heat the remaining butter in a separate saucepan, add the cabbage and 2 tablespoons of water, cover and cook for 5–10 minutes, or until just tender. Season to taste.
- Fry the sausages until cooked and golden brown.
- Add the cream cheese to the soup, then blend until smooth.
- Reheat the soup, season to taste, then serve topped with the cabbage, sausages and a drizzle of pesto.

Fresh for...
November
6th

Lentils & Thyme with Roasted Vegetables

Ingredients

25g butter
1 medium onion, finely chopped
1 garlic clove, crushed
175g carrots, chopped
90g potatoes, peeled and chopped
110g red lentils, washed
900ml vegetable stock
2 teaspoons chopped fresh thyme
60g Puy lentils, washed

To garnish:
25g aubergine, cut into 4cm strips
25g courgette, cut into 4cm strips
25g red pepper, cut into 4cm strips
25g yellow pepper, cut into 4cm strips
2 tablespoons extra virgin olive oil
4 anchovy fillets, finely chopped

Cooking time: 1:15 hours & minutes
Serves: 6

- Preheat the oven to 200°C/400°F/gas mark 6.
- Melt half the butter in a saucepan, add three-quarters of the onion and the garlic, then cover and cook gently for 10 minutes, until soft, without browning.
- Add the carrots, half the potatoes, the red lentils, vegetable stock and thyme. Cover, bring to the boil and simmer for 15 minutes until the vegetables are tender. Blend until smooth.
- Melt the remaining butter in a separate pan, add the remaining onion and potatoes and cook gently for 3 minutes, stirring occasionally. Add to the blended soup, along with the Puy lentils, then season to taste. Cover and simmer gently for 20 minutes.
- For the garnish, toss the vegetables in the oil, place in an ovenproof dish, then roast in the oven for 20 minutes until brown at the edges. Allow to cool, then mix gently with the anchovies.
- Reheat the soup, then serve garnished with the roasted vegetables.

Simply Swede

Fresh for...
November
7th

Ingredients

1 swede, diced
1 tablespoon honey
3 tablespoons olive oil
1 small onion, diced
1 teaspoon thyme, chopped
5 tablespoons double cream
715ml chicken stock
1 teaspoon pumpkin oil

Cooking time: 1:10 hours & minutes

Serves

- Preheat the oven to 170°C/325°F/gas mark 3.
- Toss the swede in the honey and 2 tablespoons of olive oil, season to taste, then roast in the oven for 1 hour.
- Heat the remaining olive oil in a pan, add the onion and thyme, then cook gently for 5 minutes, until soft and brown.
- Add the roasted swede, cream and chicken stock and bring to the boil.
- Blend until smooth.
- Season to taste, add the pumpkin oil, and serve.

Fresh for...
November 8th

Swede, Turnip & Parsnip

Ingredients

25g butter
1 medium onion, finely chopped
2 medium carrots, roughly chopped
225g swede, peeled and roughly chopped
175g turnips, peeled and roughly chopped
150g parsnips, peeled and roughly chopped
725ml vegetable stock
nutmeg, freshly grated
100ml double cream

Cooking time: 35 minutes
Serves: 4

- Melt the butter in a saucepan, add the onion, carrot, swede, turnip and parsnip, then cover and cook gently for 10 minutes, without browning.
- Add the vegetable stock and nutmeg, then season to taste.
- Cover, bring to the boil and simmer gently for 15–20 minutes, or until the vegetables are tender.
- Blend until smooth, then add the cream.
- Season to taste, reheat gently, then serve.

Lamb & a Ragout of Roots

Fresh for...
November
9th

Ingredients

2 tablespoons olive oil
2 medium leeks, finely sliced
375g lamb neck fillet, cut into 1cm cubes
quarter swede, scrubbed, unpeeled and cut into 2.5cm cubes
1 parsnip, scrubbed, unpeeled and cut into 2.5cm cubes
375g pumpkin, peeled, deseeded and cut into 2.5cm cubes
175g potato, scrubbed, unpeeled and cut into 2.5cm cubes
half a savoy cabbage, shredded
1 carrot, scrubbed, unpeeled and sliced
1.75 litres vegetable stock
110g red lentils
2 tablespoons fresh parsley, chopped
1 tablespoon fresh marjoram, chopped
1 teaspoon fresh thyme, chopped

Cooking time	Serves
55 minutes	3

- Heat the oil in a saucepan, add the leeks, then cook gently for 2–3 minutes, without browning.
- Add the lamb and remaining vegetables, stir well, then cook for a further 5 minutes.
- Add the stock, bring to the boil, then turn down to a simmer.
- Add the lentils and herbs, then cook slowly, uncovered, for 35–40 minutes, adding more stock if required.
- Season to taste, and then serve.

Fresh for...
November
10th

Creamy Parsnip, Leek & Lemon

Ingredients

25g butter
450g parsnips, peeled and sliced
3 leeks, sliced
1 litre vegetable stock
half a lemon, grated rind and juice of
1 bay leaf
150ml single cream

- Melt the butter in a saucepan, add the parsnips and leeks, then cover and cook gently for 5 minutes, without browning.
- Add the vegetable stock, grated lemon rind and bay leaf. Bring to the boil, then simmer gently for 15 minutes, until the vegetables are tender.
- Remove the bay leaf, add the lemon juice, then blend until smooth.
- Add the cream, season to taste. Reheat gently and serve.

Goulash Soup

Fresh for...
November
11th

Ingredients

2 tablespoons plain flour
500g braising steak, cut into small cubes
3 tablespoons olive oil
500ml beef stock
1 large onion, finely chopped
2 cloves garlic, crushed
1 teaspoon caraway seeds
2 tablespoons paprika
1 x 400g tin chopped tomatoes
100g new potatoes, cubed
a few drops of Tabasco
1 tablespoon fresh parsley, chopped
3 tablespoons soured cream

Cooking time: 2:25 hours & minutes

Serves: 4

- Season the flour, then coat the braising steak well.
- Heat a little of the oil in a frying pan, then fry the steak in batches until nicely browned, setting aside each batch when browned. Add a few tablespoons of the stock, then stir to collect the pan juices.
- Heat the remaining oil in a saucepan, add the onion, then cook gently for 5 minutes, until softened and golden. Add the garlic, caraway seeds and paprika, then cook for a further 2 minutes.
- Add the steak and tomatoes to the saucepan, stir, then add the remaining stock. Bring to a simmer, cover, then simmer gently for 1 hour, stirring occasionally.
- Add the new potatoes and simmer gently for a further 1 hour, until the potatoes are cooked and the beef is very tender.
- Season and add Tabasco to taste, then stir in the chopped parsley and a dollop of soured cream. Reheat gently, then serve.

Fresh for...

November

12th

Root Vegetable & Red Lentil

Ingredients

2 tablespoons olive oil

2 medium leeks, sliced

2 medium carrots, diced

half a medium swede, diced

2 medium potatoes, diced

2 parsnips, diced

100g red lentils, rinsed and drained

750ml vegetable stock

50ml milk

Cooking time	Serves
45 minutes	4

- Heat the oil in a large saucepan, add the leeks, then cook gently for 5–10 minutes until softened.
- Add the rest of the vegetables and lentils, stir for a few minutes, then add the stock.
- Bring to the boil, cover and simmer for 30 minutes or until all the vegetables are tender.
- Blend until smooth, then reheat gently, adding the milk.
- Season to taste, and serve. This soup tastes great with a dash of Worcestershire sauce.

Sausage & Stout

Fresh for...
November
13th

Ingredients

16 cocktail sausages
2 tablespoons olive oil
3 medium onions, finely sliced
2 tablespoons plain flour
300ml dark stout
500ml beef stock
1 tablespoon fresh thyme, finely chopped
2 small carrots, diced small
1 medium potato, diced small
2 teaspoons Dijon mustard
2 teaspoons Worcestershire sauce
1 tablespoon redcurrant jelly
1 tablespoon fresh parsley, finely chopped

Cooking time: 40 minutes
Serves: 4

- Fry the sausages for 8–10 minutes until browned, then set aside.
- In the same pan, heat the oil, then fry the onions until well browned. Add the flour and stout, stirring continuously until you have a thick sauce.
- Transfer to a saucepan, then add the stock and thyme. Cover, then simmer for 15 minutes.
- Meanwhile, in a separate pan, simmer the carrots and potato until almost cooked through.
- Strain the carrots and potato, then add these to the stock pan, along with the mustard, Worcestershire sauce and redcurrant jelly. Simmer for a further 5 minutes, season to taste, then serve sprinkled with fresh parsley.

Fresh for...
November
14th

Caramelised Root Vegetable

Ingredients

1 medium potato, diced
2 medium carrots, diced
1 small swede, diced
1 turnip, diced
1 leek, sliced
1 parsnip, diced
426ml vegetable stock
25g butter
1 tablespoon honey

Cooking time: 40 minutes

Serves: 4

- Place half of the potato, carrots and swede into a saucepan, followed by all of the turnip, leek, parsnip and vegetable stock.
- Bring to the boil, then cover and simmer for 20 minutes. Blend until smooth, then set aside.
- Melt the butter in a pan (use the same one as before if you've blended in a bowl – anything to save washing up!), add the remaining potato, carrot and swede, then gently cook until lightly browned.
- Add the honey and allow to caramelise on a medium heat for 7 minutes.
- Add the blended soup, season to taste, then stir well and serve.

Honey-Glazed Chantenay Carrot

Fresh for...
November
15th

Ingredients

400g Chantenay carrots, top and tailed
50g butter
1 medium potato, diced
1 medium onion, diced
3 tablespoons Acacia honey
700ml vegetable stock

Cooking time	Serves
1:05 hour & minutes	4

- Place the carrots in a saucepan of water, then boil for 20 minutes until *al dente*.
- Meanwhile, melt half of the butter in a separate pan, add the potato and onion, cover and cook gently for 10 minutes without browning.
- Drain the carrots, return them to the pan, melt the remaining butter over the top, then add the honey.
- Heat, stirring frequently, until the liquid is reduced and lightly coloured.
- Add the stock to the carrot pan, stirring well, then add the cooked potato and onion.
- Bring to the boil, then cover and simmer for 20 minutes.
- Blend until smooth.
- Return to the pan and season to taste. Heat gently for 2 minutes, then serve.

Fresh for...
November
16th

Oxtail

Ingredients

3 tablespoons plain flour
700g oxtail, cut into pieces (your butcher will do this for you)
3–4 tablespoons olive oil
2 medium carrots, peeled and chopped
2 onions, finely chopped
2 sticks celery, diced
300ml red wine
850ml beef stock
1 bay leaf
1 tablespoon fresh thyme, chopped
1 tablespoon fresh parsley, chopped

Cooking time	Serves
3:25 hours & minutes	4

- Season the flour with salt and pepper, then lightly coat the oxtail pieces.
- Heat half the oil in a frying pan, then fry the oxtail in batches until browned. Transfer to a casserole dish.
- Preheat your oven to 150°C/300°F/gas mark 2.
- Fry the carrots, onions and celery in the remaining oil until brown, then pour in any remaining seasoned flour to soak up the juices. Scrape the pan to gather up any of the crispy bits at the bottom.
- Add the wine to the pan, stir, then reduce a little. Add the stock, bay leaf and thyme, stir, then bring to a simmer.
- Transfer to the casserole dish, stir well, then place in the oven to cook very gently for 2–3 hours.
- Remove the bay leaf and discard. Remove the oxtail pieces and fork out the meat, shredding a little if you need to.
- Return the meat to the mixture, blend, then reheat gently. Stir in the parsley, and then serve.

Fresh for...
November
17th

Celeriac, Coconut & Chilli

Ingredients

2 tablespoons groundnut oil
900g celeriac, peeled and roughly chopped
1.75 litres chicken or vegetable stock
1 lime, juice of
2.5cm fresh ginger, grated
1 teaspoon lemon thyme, freshly chopped
1 green chilli, deseeded and chopped
small bunch fresh coriander, leaves and stalks separated
75g creamed coconut

To garnish:
4 spring onions, chopped

Cooking time: 50 minutes
Serves: 4

- Heat the oil in a saucepan, add the celeriac, then cover and cook gently for 10 minutes, without browning.
- Add the stock, lime juice, ginger, lemon thyme, chopped chilli and coriander stems. Bring to the boil, then cover and simmer for 30 minutes until the vegetables are tender.
- Remove from the heat and add the creamed coconut. Blend until smooth.
- Season to taste, then reheat gently, stirring in most of the chopped coriander leaves. Serve garnished with the remaining coriander and spring onions.

Fresh for...
November
18th

Wild Mushroom

Ingredients

75g dried cep mushrooms
300ml warm water
50g butter
2 medium onions, finely chopped
2 garlic cloves, crushed
225g chestnut mushrooms, sliced
2 dessertspoons plain flour
900ml vegetable stock
150ml dry white wine
2 dessertspoons finely chopped fresh flat-leaf parsley
225ml double cream

- Soak the cep mushrooms in the warm water for 20 minutes. Drain, reserving the soaking liquor.
- Melt the butter in a saucepan, add the onions and garlic, then cover and cook gently for 10 minutes, without browning.
- Add the chestnut mushrooms and soaked ceps and cook for a further 2 minutes.
- Stir in the flour and cook for 2 minutes. Gradually add the stock, the reserved soaking liquor and the white wine.
- Cover, bring to the boil, then simmer gently for 20 minutes until the vegetables are tender.
- Add the parsley, then blend until smooth. Stir in the cream and reheat gently. Season to taste, and then serve.

Chicken, Pea & Vermicelli

Fresh for...
November
19th

Ingredients

1 chicken, cut into 8 pieces, (and giblets if included) or chicken bones
3 litres water
2 tablespoons mixed fresh herbs, chopped
1 small leek, chopped
1 small swede, chopped
4 sticks celery, halved
1 large onion, coarsely chopped
450g carrots, chopped

To garnish:
110g fresh green peas, shelled (if unavailable, frozen peas)
110g egg vermicelli

Cooking time: 2:40 hours & minutes + overnight chilling

Serves: 4

- For the stock: put the chicken in a large saucepan with the water. Cover, bring to the boil, then simmer very gently for 5 minutes, carefully skimming off any scum. Add the chopped herbs and all the vegetables except the carrots. Simmer very gently for 1½ hours, skimming from time to time.
- Remove the chicken and separate the meat from the bone, reserving it for the soup. Cover and simmer for a further 30 minutes. Discard the vegetables. Cool the stock and chill overnight. Remove the solid fat which will have formed on the surface.
- Transfer the stock to a saucepan, cover, bring to the boil, then add the carrots. Season to taste, then simmer for 10–15 minutes, or until the carrots are tender. Meanwhile, cut the chicken into bite-sized pieces.
- Add the peas and egg vermicelli, then cook for 5 minutes. Return the chicken pieces to the soup, then serve.

Fresh for...
November
20th

Pea & Bacon

Ingredients

1 tablespoon olive oil
6 rashers bacon, diced
a knob of butter
1 leek, diced
1 small onion, diced
470ml vegetable stock
1 carrot, grated
1 celery stick, diced
115g yellow split peas
grate of fresh nutmeg (or pinch of ground nutmeg)
100g peas (fresh or frozen)

Cooking time	Serves
1 hour	4

- Heat the olive oil in a frying pan, add the bacon, then fry until crispy. Set aside on kitchen paper.
- Meanwhile, melt the butter in a saucepan, add the leeks and onion, then cook gently for 10 minutes.
- Add the stock, carrot, celery, yellow split peas and nutmeg.
- Bring to the boil, then simmer for a further 20 minutes.
- Blend until smooth.
- Add the bacon and peas, then simmer gently for 15 minutes.
- Cook gently for 5 minutes, then serve.

Vegetable Balti

Fresh for...
November
21st

Ingredients

1 tablespoon olive oil
1 small onion, diced
2 cloves garlic, crushed
1 teaspoon ground coriander
half a teaspoon ground ginger
half a teaspoon ground cumin
half a teaspoon smoked paprika
half a teaspoon garam masala
1 green chilli, deseeded & chopped
1 cardamom pod
1 x 400g tin chopped tomatoes
70g long-grain rice
280ml vegetable stock
half a turnip, diced
2 carrots, diced
80g cauliflower florets (approx 3)

Cooking time: 30 minutes
Serves: 4

- Heat the olive oil in a saucepan, add the onion, then cook gently for 5 minutes.
- Add the garlic, spices, chilli and cardamom pod, then cook for a further 5 minutes.
- Add half the tomatoes and half the rice along with the stock, then bring to the boil and simmer gently for 20 minutes, stirring occasionally.
- Blend until smooth.
- Add the remaining tomatoes and rice, along with the turnip and carrot, then simmer for 10 minutes, stirring occasionally.
- Add the cauliflower, cook for a further 10 minutes, adding more stock or water, if necessary. Serve.

Fresh for…
November 22nd

Roasted Sweet Potato

Ingredients

3–4 sweet potatoes, peeled and diced
1 medium onion, peeled and cut into 8 wedges
2 tablespoons olive oil
1 teaspoon ground cumin
750ml hot vegetable stock
4 tablespoons natural yoghurt

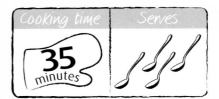

Cooking time: 35 minutes

Serves

- Preheat the oven to 200°C/400°F/gas mark 6.
- Place the sweet potato and onion in a roasting tin, drizzle with the olive oil, then sprinkle over the cumin. Season a little, then toss together to coat evenly.
- Roast for 25–30 minutes or until the vegetables are tender and have taken on some colour.
- Blend the roasted vegetables with the hot stock until completely smooth.
- Reheat gently in a saucepan, season to taste, then serve with a dollop of natural yoghurt on top.

Butternut Squash, Chilli & Ginger

Fresh for...
November
23rd

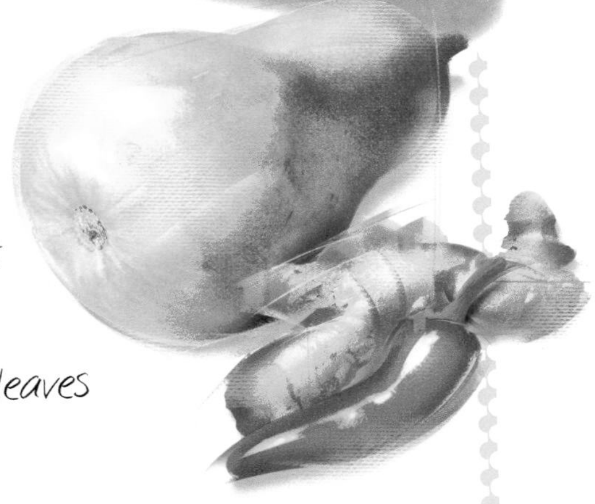

Ingredients

1 tablespoon olive oil
50g butter
1 large butternut squash, peeled, deseeded and diced
2 onions, diced
2 cloves garlic, crushed
1 red chilli, finely diced
2cm root ginger, peeled and chopped
900ml hot vegetable stock
50g sachet creamed coconut

To garnish:
fresh coriander leaves

Cooking time: 35 minutes
Serves: 6

- Heat the oil and butter in a saucepan, add the butternut squash, onion and garlic, then cover and cook gently for 5 minutes.
- Add the chilli and ginger, then cook for a further 5 minutes.
- Add the hot stock, bring to the boil, then cover and simmer for 15–20 minutes until the butternut squash is soft.
- Blend until smooth.
- Reheat gently before adding the coconut cream. Season to taste, then serve garnished with a few coriander leaves.

Fresh for...
November
24th

Chicken, Vegetable & Pearl Barley

Ingredients

1.5 litres chicken stock
1 small onion, chopped
3 medium potatoes, peeled and diced
1 clove garlic, crushed
1 tablespoon flour
1 small carrot, peeled and chopped
50g pearl barley
1 small leek, chopped
50g peas
100g cooked chicken, cut into small cubes
50ml double cream
1 tablespoon fresh parsley, finely chopped

Cooking time	Serves
1:10 hour & minutes	4

- Place the chicken stock, onion, one third of the potatoes and garlic in a large pan, bring to the boil, then cover and simmer for 20 minutes until the vegetables are tender.
- Mix the flour with a little water to make a paste, then add to the soup and stir until thickened.
- Blend until smooth before adding the carrots, remaining potatoes and the pearl barley. Cook for 25 minutes.
- Add the leeks and cook for 10 minutes.
- Add the peas and chicken before cooking for a further 5–10 minutes.
- Stir in the cream and parsley, then serve.

Fresh for...
November
25th

Indian Spiced Vegetable

Ingredients

150g celeriac, peeled and diced
1 carrot, peeled and diced
1 parsnip, peeled and diced
1 sweet potato, peeled and diced
4 tablespoons olive oil
1 teaspoon ground coriander
1 teaspoon cumin seeds
half a teaspoon chilli powder
half a teaspoon black onion seeds (optional)
1 small onion, finely chopped
1 clove garlic, crushed
1 celery stick, diced
850ml vegetable stock

Cooking time: 50 minutes

Serves

- Preheat your oven to 190°C/375°F/gas mark 5.
- Place the celeriac, carrot, parsnip and sweet potato in a roasting tin and drizzle them with 2 tablespoons of olive oil.
- Sprinkle over all the spices and salt and pepper, then stir to coat all the vegetables.
- Roast for 40 minutes, turning occasionally.
- After about 25 minutes, heat the remaining olive oil in a pan, add the onion, garlic and celery, then cover and cook gently for 15 minutes.
- Add the roasted vegetables and stock, bring to a simmer, then cover and cook for 10 minutes.
- Blend until completely smooth. Reheat gently, then serve.

Fresh for...
November
26th

Purple Sprouting Broccoli & Leek

Ingredients

50g butter
2 medium potatoes, diced
3 leeks, finely sliced
845ml vegetable stock
200g purple sprouting broccoli
200ml milk

Cooking time	Serves
45 minutes	4

- Melt half the butter in a saucepan, add the potatoes and 2 of the leeks. Cover and cook for 10 minutes, without browning.
- Add the stock, bring to the boil, then cover and simmer for 15 minutes.
- Add the broccoli and cook for a further 8–10 minutes, or until tender.
- Blend until smooth.
- Add the milk, season to taste, then reheat gently.
- Meanwhile, melt the remaining butter in a frying pan and fry the remaining leek, until lightly caramelised.
- Ladle the soup into bowls, sprinkle the crispy leek over the top, and serve.

Fresh for...
November
27th

Caerphilly, Leek & Wild Garlic

Ingredients

25g butter
2 leeks, finely sliced
2 small floury potatoes (e.g. Maris Piper), diced
400ml vegetable stock
ground nutmeg, pinch of
90g Caerphilly cheese (or Wensleydale)
3 tablespoons white wine
30g crème fraîche
half a tablespoon wild garlic (or fresh chives), chopped
1 tablespoon fresh parsley, chopped

Cooking time	Serves
25 minutes	4

- Melt the butter in a saucepan, add the leeks, then cook gently for 5–10 minutes, or until soft.
- Add the potato, stock and nutmeg, bring to the boil, then simmer gently for 10 minutes.
- Blend until smooth, then add the cheese, white wine and crème fraîche. Season to taste, then stir over a gentle heat until the cheese has melted.
- Add the wild garlic and parsley, stir, then serve.

Fresh for...
November
28th

Chicken, Black Bean & Chipotle Chilli

Ingredients

1 tablespoon olive oil
1 onion, diced
1 clove garlic, crushed
1 fresh red chilli, deseeded and chopped
1 green pepper, deseeded and diced
1 chicken breast, cut into small strips
1–2 teaspoons Chipotle chilli paste (or another red chilli)
1 teaspoon tomato purée
1 x 400g tin chopped tomatoes
100g cooked black turtle beans
400ml chicken stock
1 tablespoon fresh coriander, chopped

Cooking time: 40 minutes
Serves

- Heat the olive oil in a saucepan, add the onion, then cook gently for 10 minutes, until soft.
- Add the garlic, red chilli and green pepper, then cook for a few minutes.
- Add the chicken, cook for a few minutes until browned, and then add the Chipotle chilli paste and tomato purée, stir and cook for a minute.
- Add the tomatoes, black turtle beans and stock, season to taste, and then simmer for 20 minutes.
- Garnish with coriander, and serve.

Fresh for...
November
29th

Spiced Beef & Red Pepper

Ingredients

1 tablespoon olive oil
1 small onion, diced
2 teaspoons smoked paprika
1 clove garlic, crushed
half a teaspoon caraway seeds
210g plum tomatoes, chopped
1 tablespoon tomato purée
1 potato, diced
1 red pepper, deseeded & diced
400ml beef stock
200g cooked beef, diced
2 tablespoons soured cream

Cooking time: 50 minutes
Serves: 4

- Heat the oil in a saucepan, add the onion, paprika and garlic, then cook for 5–10 minutes.
- Add the caraway seeds, plum tomatoes, tomato purée, potatoes, red pepper and stock, bring to the boil, and then simmer gently for 20 minutes.
- Add the beef, season to taste, and then cook for a further 15 minutes.
- Stir in the soured cream, reheat for 5 minutes, and then serve.

Fresh for...
November
30th

Chicken & Chorizo Gumbo

Ingredients

1–2 tablespoons olive oil
1 small onion, diced
3 celery sticks, diced
50g chorizo sausage, diced
half a red pepper, deseeded and diced
half a green pepper, deseeded and diced
1 clove garlic, crushed
1 teaspoon sweet smoked paprika
3–4 pinches of cayenne pepper
100g chicken, cut into small strips
50ml Bourbon (or whisky)
1 potato, diced
1 sweet potato, diced
500ml chicken stock
1 bay leaf
half a teaspoon thyme, chopped

Cooking time: 40 minutes
Serves

- Heat the olive oil in a saucepan, add the onion, celery, chorizo and red and green peppers then fry for 5–10 minutes, or until the onion is soft.
- Add the garlic, paprika and cayenne pepper, cook for a few minutes, then add the chicken, and season to taste. Cook for a further 3 minutes.
- Add the Bourbon, then cook for 5 minutes.
- Add the potato, sweet potato, stock, bay leaf and thyme, bring to the boil, simmer for 20 minutes, and then serve.

Steak & Ale

Fresh for...

December 1ST

Ingredients

4 tablespoons olive oil
2 large onions, finely diced
2 cloves garlic, crushed
200g button mushrooms, whole
1kg braising steak, cut into 4cm cubes
2 tablespoons flour
600ml ruby or pale ale
2 bay leaves
4–5 sprigs of thyme

Cooking time: 2:30 hours & minutes

Serves: 6

- Heat 1–2 tablespoons of olive oil in a saucepan, add the onions, then cook gently for 10 minutes, until the onions have softened and taken on some colour.
- Add the garlic and mushrooms, then cook for 5 minutes. Transfer to a dish, then set aside. Reheat the saucepan, add the remaining olive oil, then brown the beef in batches.
- Once all the beef is browned, return it to the pan, sprinkle over the flour, then stir and cook for 2 minutes.
- Add the onions, mushrooms and ale, scraping the base of the pan to retain all the flour and juices. Add the bay leaves and thyme and bring back to a simmer. Cover, then simmer gently for 1½ hours.
- Stir, then cook for a further 30 minutes, either partially covered or without the lid, depending on the consistency you prefer.
- Remove the thyme and bay leaves, season to taste, then serve.

Fresh for...
December 2nd

Celeriac, Smoked Bacon & English Mustard

Ingredients

1 tablespoon olive oil
6 rashers smoked bacon, diced
25g butter
1 medium onion, diced
2 small leeks, diced
160g celeriac, diced
400ml chicken or vegetable stock
1 teaspoon English mustard
1 teaspoon lemon juice
5 tablespoons double cream

Cooking time: 55 minutes
Serves

- Heat the olive oil in a frying pan, add the bacon, and then fry until crispy. Set aside on kitchen paper.
- Meanwhile, melt the butter in a saucepan, add the onion and leeks, then cook gently for 10 minutes.
- Add the celeriac, stock and mustard, then season to taste. Bring to the boil, then simmer gently for 25–30 minutes.
- Blend until smooth.
- Add the crispy bacon, cook for 5 minutes
- Stir in the lemon juice and cream, cook for a further 5 minutes, and then serve.

Roasted Chestnut & Truffle Oil

Fresh for...
December
3rd

Ingredients

50g butter
2 sticks celery, chopped
1 large onion, finely chopped
2 cloves garlic, chopped
1 medium potato, peeled and diced
300g chestnuts, roasted and shelled
2 bay leaves
3 juniper berries, crushed (optional)
850ml chicken stock
100ml single cream
1 dessertspoon truffle oil

Cooking time	Serves
40 minutes	4

- Melt the butter in a saucepan, add the celery, onion and garlic, then cook for 10 minutes until softened.
- Add the potato, chestnuts, bay leaves and juniper berries, then stir.
- Pour over the stock, bring to the boil, then cover and simmer for 15–20 minutes until the potatoes are cooked. Remove the bay leaves, then blend until smooth.
- Add the cream, season to taste, then add the truffle oil, again to taste, and any additional stock if necessary.
- Reheat gently for a few minutes and then serve.

Fresh for...
December
4th

Pheasant & Roasted Shallot

Ingredients

8 shallots, peeled
2 tablespoons olive oil
25g butter
3 pheasant breasts
2 tablespoons dry sherry
1 large potato, diced
2 medium carrots, diced
565ml chicken stock
2 tablespoons fresh thyme, chopped
1 tablespoon parsley, finely chopped

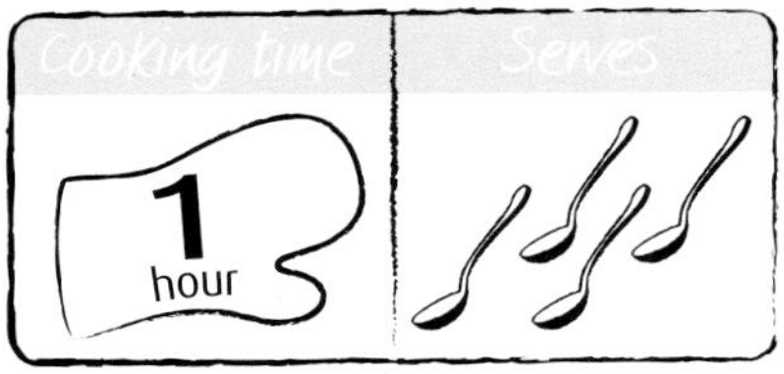

- Preheat the oven to 190°C/375°F/gas mark 5.
- Toss the shallots in 1 tablespoon of the olive oil, then roast in the oven for 20 minutes, until soft and caramelised.
- Heat the butter and remaining olive oil in a saucepan, then seal the pheasant breasts on both sides.
- Add the sherry, bring to the boil, then simmer for 2 minutes. Add the potato and carrots, then stir for 1 minute.
- Add the stock, thyme and shallots, bring to the boil and simmer for a further 30 minutes. Remove the pheasant breasts and set aside to cool.
- Blend until smooth.
- Once the pheasant breasts are cooled, shred the meat using 2 forks.
- Season the soup to taste, add the meat and parsley, then reheat gently for 5 minutes and serve.

Mushroom, Stilton & White Wine

Fresh for...
December
5th

Ingredients

50g butter
1 large onion, finely chopped
1 clove garlic, crushed
400g closed cup mushrooms, sliced
700ml vegetable stock
1 bay leaf
100g Stilton cheese, crumbled
1 tablespoon fresh parsley, chopped
200ml white wine
3 tablespoons double cream

Cooking time: 40 minutes
Serves

- Melt half the butter in a saucepan, add the onion and garlic, then cover and cook gently for 10 minutes until soft, without browning.
- Add two-thirds (275g) of the mushrooms, all of the stock and the bay leaf, then bring to the boil. Cover and simmer for 20 minutes, stirring occasionally.
- Remove from the heat, add the cheese and half the parsley, then stir until melted.
- Remove the bay leaf and blend until smooth.
- Meanwhile, melt the remaining butter in a frying pan, fry the remaining mushrooms for 5 minutes until lightly coloured, then add the remaining parsley and set aside.
- Add the wine and cream to the soup, then season to taste.
- Reheat gently for 5 minutes. Add the fried mushrooms and serve.

Fresh for...
December
6th

Venison, Bramley Apple & Blackberry

Ingredients

15g butter
60g venison meat, cut into strips
1 small red onion, diced
1 small carrot, diced
1 leek, sliced
1 small potato, diced
1 small Bramley apple, diced
1 stick celery, diced
2 tablespoons red wine
1 tablespoon red wine vinegar
25g brown sugar
15g plain flour
80g fresh blackberries
1 litre beef stock

Cooking time: 50 minutes

Serves

- Melt the butter in a saucepan, add the venison, then cook until lightly browned. Remove and set aside.
- Add the red onion, carrot, leek, potato, apple and celery to the pan, then cook for 10 minutes, until they start to brown.
- Add the red wine and red wine vinegar, bring to the boil, then reduce the liquid by half.
- Reduce the heat to simmer, add the sugar and flour and stir well.
- Add half the blackberries and all the beef stock, then bring to the boil. Cover and simmer for 20 minutes.
- Add the cooked venison and remaining blackberries, simmer gently for 5 minutes and then serve.

Roasted Parsnip & Parmesan

Fresh for...
December
7th

Ingredients

450g parsnips, cut into lengths
50g freshly grated Parmesan cheese
2 tablespoons extra virgin olive oil
15g butter
1 medium onion, finely chopped
1 tablespoon plain flour
1.35 litres light chicken stock
4 tablespoons double cream

Cooking time: 1:25 hours & minutes
Serves: 4

- Preheat the oven to 200°C/400°F/gas mark 6.
- Place the parsnips in a saucepan of water, bring to the boil, then simmer for 3 minutes. Drain well, then toss in half the Parmesan.
- Pour the olive oil into a roasting tin, then heat in the oven for 3–4 minutes.
- Arrange the parsnips in the roasting tin, add the butter, then bake for 45 minutes, basting frequently.
- Drain the excess oil into a saucepan, add the onion, then cook gently for 10 minutes until soft, without browning.
- Stir in the flour and cook for 1 minute. Add the stock to the pan, stirring constantly, and bring to the boil. Add the roasted parsnips. Cover and simmer for 10 minutes.
- Blend the soup with the remaining Parmesan. Stir in the cream, then season to taste. Reheat gently, then serve.

Fresh for...

December

8th

Venison Sausage Cassoulet

Ingredients

1 tablespoon goose fat or olive oil
4 venison sausages
100g bacon lardons
2 cloves garlic, crushed
1 small onion, finely diced
1 stick celery, finely chopped
200g tinned chopped tomatoes
1 bay leaf
1 teaspoon fresh thyme, chopped
1 teaspoon fresh rosemary, chopped
500ml beef stock
1 x 410g tin haricot beans
1 tablespoon tomato purée
1 tablespoon fresh parsley

Cooking time: 1:15 hour & minutes

Serves: 4

- Heat the goose fat or olive oil in a saucepan, add the sausages, then cook for 10 minutes, turning frequently until browned. Remove from the pan and set aside.
- Add the bacon to the pan and fry until browned, adding a little oil if required.
- Add the garlic, onion and celery, then cook gently for 5 minutes.
- Add the tomatoes, bay leaf, thyme, rosemary and stock to the pan, then bring to the boil.
- Cut each sausage into 5, then add to the pan. Add the haricot beans, then simmer gently for 30–40 minutes, stirring occasionally.
- Add the tomato purée, then season to taste.
- Reheat gently for 5 minutes, garnish with fresh parsley then serve.

Fresh for...

December 9th

Brussel Sprout & Chestnut

Ingredients

25g butter
1 medium onion, finely chopped
250g potatoes, peeled and chopped
1kg brussel sprouts, quartered
50–110g chestnuts, roasted and shelled
900ml vegetable stock
freshly grated nutmeg
150ml milk
75ml single cream

Cooking time: 30 minutes

Serves: 4

- Melt the butter in a saucepan, add the onion, then cover and cook gently for 5 minutes, without browning.
- Add the potatoes, three-quarters of the brussel sprouts, chestnuts and stock. Cover, bring to the boil then simmer gently for about 10 minutes until the brussels are tender. Blend until smooth.
- Stir in the remaining sprouts and add nutmeg to taste. Cover, bring to the boil, then simmer gently for 5–10 minutes until the sprouts and chestnuts are tender.
- Stir in the milk and cream, and season to taste.
- Reheat gently for 5 minutes and then serve.

Fresh for...
December
10th

Hot Fruit Soup

Ingredients

25g butter
2 lemons, finely pared rind and juice of
2 oranges, finely pared rind and juice of
2 cinnamon sticks
10 cloves
10 apricots, halved and stoned
3 pears, peeled, cored and sliced
4 peaches, peeled, halved, stoned and sliced
4 tablespoons brandy
4 tablespoons port
1 apple, peeled, halved, cored and sliced
150g white seedless grapes
1 small pineapple, skin removed and cut into small pieces
175g cherries, stoned

Cooking time: 25 minutes
Serves

- Melt the butter in a saucepan, then stir in the pared rind of the lemons and oranges.
- Add the cinnamon sticks and cloves, then cook gently for 2 minutes.
- Add the apricots, pears and peaches, then cook for a further 2 minutes.
- Add the brandy and ignite with a match. When the flames have subsided, add the port, apple, grapes, pineapple, cherries, lemon and orange juice. Cover, then simmer very gently for 10 minutes.
- Remove the rind, cinnamon sticks and cloves, then serve with ice cream.

Fresh for...
December
11th

Spicy Turnip & Lentil Dhal

Ingredients

2 tablespoons olive oil
2 small onions, finely chopped
2 cloves garlic, crushed
1 teaspoon turmeric
half a teaspoon chilli powder
half a teaspoon ground ginger
120g red lentils, washed
750ml hot water
2 small turnips, finely diced
1 medium carrot, finely diced
3 large tomatoes, skinned and chopped
1 teaspoon garam masala
2 tablespoons fresh coriander, chopped
25g butter
1 teaspoon ground cumin

Cooking time: 40 minutes
Serves: 4

- Heat the oil in a saucepan, add half the onions, then cook for 5 minutes until softened.
- Add the garlic, turmeric, chilli and ginger, then cook for 2–3 minutes.
- Add the red lentils and hot water, then bring to the boil. Add the turnips, carrot and tomatoes, then cover and simmer for 20 minutes, or until the vegetables and lentils are tender.
- Add the garam masala and stir well. Blend half the soup until smooth.
- Return to the pan with the unblended soup, reheat gently, then stir in the coriander.
- Meanwhile, heat the butter in a separate pan, add the remaining onions and ground cumin, then cook for 5 minutes until the onions are coloured, sweet and soft. Stir the onion and cumin mix into the soup and then serve.

Fresh for...
December
12th

Brown Ale, Lentil & Mushroom

Ingredients

2 tablespoons extra virgin olive oil
1 medium onion, finely chopped
2 garlic cloves, crushed
2 tablespoons tomato purée
50g brown lentils, washed in plenty of cold water
110g flat mushrooms, finely sliced
110g chestnut mushrooms, finely sliced
275ml brown ale
850ml vegetable stock
15g dried cep or porcini mushrooms, soaked in 200ml warm water for 20 minutes, drained (reserve the soaking liquor) and roughly chopped
Worcestershire sauce, dash of (optional)

Cooking time: 1 hour
Serves: 4

- Heat the oil in a saucepan, add the onion, then cook for 5–10 minutes until beginning to brown.
- Reduce the heat, add the garlic, then cook gently for 2 minutes.
- Stir in the tomato purée and lentils, then the flat and chestnut mushrooms. Cook for 5 minutes.
- Stir in the brown ale and stock. Cover, bring to the boil, then simmer gently for 30 minutes.
- Add both the reconstituted cep and their soaking liquor to the pan, bring back to the boil and simmer for a further 10 minutes. Add Worcestershire sauce to taste.
- Season to taste and then serve.

Far East Hot Pepper & Turkey

Fresh for... December 13th

Ingredients

- 3 tablespoons olive oil
- 1 small red onion, finely sliced
- 25g fresh root ginger, peeled and finely sliced
- 1 red pepper, deseeded and finely sliced
- 1 yellow pepper, deseeded and finely sliced
- 3 garlic cloves, crushed
- 4 turkey breasts, cut into 3cm dice
- 2–3 teaspoons thick, hot chilli sauce
- 2 teaspoons Chinese five-spice seasoning
- 2 teaspoons garam masala
- 1 tablespoon tomato purée
- 250g fresh beansprouts
- 225ml chicken stock
- 2 teaspoons cornflour
- 100ml mango juice
- 1 bunch fresh coriander
- 1 lime, zest of

Cooking time: 45 minutes

Serves: 4

- Heat the oil in a saucepan, then fry the red onion, ginger and red and yellow peppers gently for 5 minutes, without browning. Turn the heat down, add the garlic and continue to cook gently for 5 minutes.
- Move the vegetables to one side, then add the diced turkey to the bottom of the pan. Turn up the heat and stir the meat quickly to brown, adding a little more oil if necessary.
- Stir in the chilli sauce, Chinese five-spice seasoning, garam masala, tomato purée and half the beansprouts. Cover, then cook gently for 5 minutes, stirring occasionally. Add a third of the stock, then mix well.
- Mix the cornflour to a smooth paste with a little stock, then stir into the soup. Add the remaining stock and mango juice, then season to taste.
- Bring to the boil and simmer gently for 5 minutes or until the turkey is cooked. Sit the rest of the beansprouts on top of the soup, along with a handful of roughly torn coriander leaves and the lime zest.
- Cover, remove from the heat and allow to rest for 5 minutes to infuse the lime and coriander. Serve in deep Chinese bowls.

Fresh for...
December
14th

Lobster & Leek

Ingredients

2 cooked lobsters (700g each)
1.5 litres water
1 bay leaf
pinch of salt
50g butter
2 small onions, finely chopped
1 large leek, chopped
1 medium carrot, chopped
4 medium potatoes, peeled and chopped
275ml milk
1 glass dry white wine
half a lemon, juice of
10ml single cream

Cooking time: 1:35 hour & minutes
Serves: 6

- Thoroughly clean the lobster shells. Remove all the meat and cut it into small pieces. Put all the shells in a saucepan with the water, bay leaf and salt. Bring to the boil and simmer for 45 minutes, skimming from time to time. Strain well, reserving the cooking liquor, and then set aside.

- Melt the butter in a saucepan, add the onion, then cover and cook gently for 5 minutes, without browning.

- Add the leek, carrots and potatoes, then cook for 10 minutes until soft.

- Add 1.2 litres of the reserved cooking liquor to the vegetables, cover, then simmer for a further 20 minutes until the vegetables are tender.

- Add the milk, blend until smooth, then stir in the lobster meat, white wine and lemon juice.

- Season to taste, then reheat gently. Stir in the cream just before serving.

Fresh for...
December 15th

Winter Greens & Stilton

Ingredients

28g butter
1 large leek, diced
2 small floury potatoes, e.g. Maris Piper, diced
250ml vegetable stock
50g winter greens (or savoy cabbage), shredded
60g Stilton cheese, crumbled
50ml white port or medium sherry
190ml milk
40ml double cream

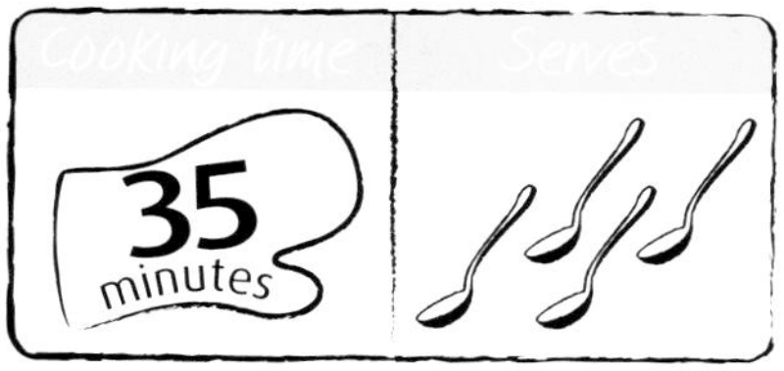

- Heat the butter in a saucepan, add the leeks, then cook gently for 10 minutes until soft, without browning.
- Add the potato and stock, and simmer for 15 minutes or until the potatoes are soft.
- Blend until smooth.
- Add the winter greens, Stilton, white port, milk and cream, then season to taste.
- Cook gently for 5 minutes until the greens have softened, then serve.

Fresh for...
December
16th

Maple Roasted Carrot & Goat's Cheese

Ingredients

25g butter
1 small onion, diced
1 small clove garlic, crushed
200g carrots, diced
500ml vegetable stock
80g soft goat's cheese, cubed
1 tablespoon fresh parsley, chopped

For the maple roasted carrots:
200g carrots, diced
1 tablespoon maple syrup
1 teaspoon olive oil

Cooking time	Serves
40 minutes	

- Preheat the oven to 180°C/350°F/gas mark 4.
- Place all the maple roasted carrot ingredients in a roasting tin, stir to coat evenly, and then bake for 20 minutes, or until cooked through and browned. Set aside for garnishing.
- Meanwhile, heat the butter in a saucepan, add the onion and garlic, then cook gently for 10 minutes, until soft.
- Add the carrots and stock, then season to taste and simmer gently for 20 minutes.
- Add the goat's cheese, then blend until smooth.
- Reheat gently, and serve garnished with the roasted carrots and parsley.

Red Cabbage, Apple & Ginger

Fresh for...
December
17th

Ingredients

1 tablespoon olive oil
1 small onion, diced
half a red pepper, deseeded and diced
1 clove garlic, crushed
2.5cm fresh root ginger, grated
375ml vegetable stock
half a lemon, juice of, to taste
half a small red cabbage, finely shredded
2 carrots, cut into matchsticks
50g plum tomatoes, chopped
2 apples, peeled and finely diced

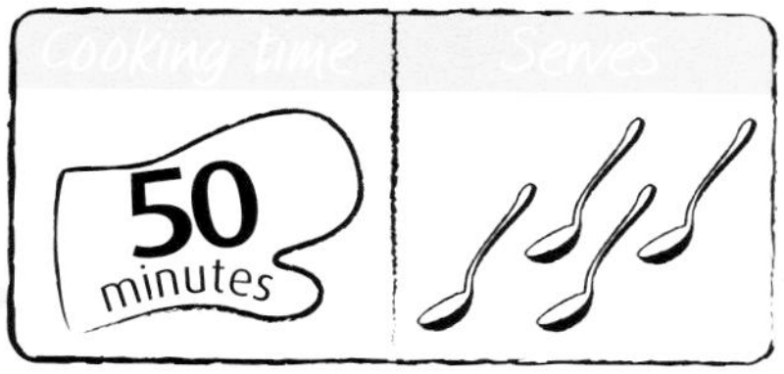

- Heat the oil in a saucepan, add the onion, red pepper, garlic and ginger, then cook gently for 10 minutes.
- Add the stock, lemon juice, red cabbage, carrot and tomatoes. Bring to the boil, cover, and then simmer gently for 30 minutes, or until the vegetables are softened.
- Add the apple, season to taste, then simmer for a further 5 minutes.
- Serve.

Fresh for...
December 18th

Venison, Mushroom & Red Wine

Ingredients

40g butter
2 medium onions finely chopped
1 garlic clove, crushed
125g chestnut mushrooms, sliced
200g venison, cut into small strips
1 dessertspoon plain flour
2 tablespoons tomato purée
1 dessertspoon chopped fresh tarragon
1 litre game or beef stock
110ml red wine

To garnish:
1 tablespoon olive oil
3 rashers unsmoked streaky bacon, chopped

Cooking time: 1:10 hour & minutes
Serves: 4

- Melt the butter in a saucepan, add the onion and garlic, then cover and cook gently for 5 minutes, without browning.
- Add the mushrooms and venison and stir to seal the meat for 2 minutes. Stir in the flour, tomato purée and tarragon, then add the stock and red wine.
- Cover, bring to the boil, then simmer gently for 45 minutes until the meat is tender. Season to taste.
- Meanwhile, heat the oil for the garnish in a separate pan, then fry the bacon until crispy. Drain on kitchen paper.
- Serve the soup garnished with the crispy bacon.

Brussel Sprout & Gammon

Fresh for...
December 19th

Ingredients

50g butter
1 clove garlic, crushed
1 small onion, finely chopped
300g brussel sprouts, finely sliced (reserving 8 whole sprouts)
100g chestnuts, roasted, shelled and chopped
400ml vegetable stock
200g gammon, cooked and shredded
400ml water
6 tablespoons single cream

Cooking time: 35 minutes
Serves

- Melt the butter in a saucepan, add the garlic and onion, then cook gently for 5 minutes, until softened.
- Add the sprouts and chestnuts, then cook for a further 5 minutes, without browning.
- Add the stock and 150g of the gammon, then boil rapidly, uncovered, for 5–10 minutes, until the stock has reduced by half and the sprouts are just tender.
- Blend until smooth, adding a little of the water if necessary.
- Add the remaining water and cream, season to taste, then reheat gently for 5 minutes.
- Meanwhile, cut the remaining sprouts into quarters, then cook in boiling water for 5–10 minutes until *al dente*.
- Place the remaining gammon in the middle of the serving bowl, ladle over the soup, garnish with the sprouts and serve.

Fresh for...
December
20th

Parsnip, Apple & Chestnut

Ingredients

50g butter
3 parsnips, diced
1 medium potato, diced
1 small onion, finely chopped
1.2 litres vegetable stock
1 medium Braeburn apple, peeled and diced
1 teaspoon fresh rosemary, finely chopped
3 tablespoons single cream
75g chestnuts, roasted, shelled and finely sliced

Cooking time	Serves
50 minutes	4

- Melt half the butter in a saucepan, add the parsnips, potato and onion, then cover and cook gently for 10 minutes, until soft.
- Add the stock, apple and rosemary, cover, then simmer for a further 20 minutes or until the vegetables are tender.
- Blend until smooth.
- Return to the pan, add the cream, season to taste, then reheat gently for 5 minutes.
- Meanwhile, melt the remaining butter in a pan, add the roasted chestnuts, season to taste, then fry for 3–4 minutes until they are lightly coloured, ensuring the butter does not burn.
- Spoon the chestnuts into the centre of the serving bowl, ladle the soup over and serve.

Christmas Dinner Soup

Fresh for...

December 21st

Ingredients

200g ready-made stuffing
15g dried cranberries
25g butter
1 leek, finely sliced
1 stick celery, finely chopped
1 small onion, finely chopped
750ml chicken stock
1 bay leaf
a few sprigs of fresh thyme
100ml single cream
200g cooked turkey, diced

Cooking time: 1:15 hour & minutes

Serves

- Preheat the oven to 190°C/375°F/gas mark 5.
- Roll the stuffing into balls, then cook in the oven for approximately 20 minutes, until golden brown. Remove, then set aside.
- Soak the dried cranberries in a cup of boiling water for 15 minutes, then drain and set aside.
- Melt the butter in a saucepan, add the leek, celery and onion, then cook for 5–10 minutes, until soft.
- Add the stock, bay leaf and thyme, then cover and simmer for 20 minutes, or until the vegetables are tender.
- Remove the herbs, then blend until smooth. Add the cream, turkey and cranberries, then season to taste. Reheat gently for 10 minutes, stirring occasionally.
- Place the stuffing balls in the centre of the serving bowl, ladle the soup over and serve.

Fresh for…

December 22nd

Spicy Parsnip & Pear

Ingredients

3 tablespoons olive oil
1 medium onion, diced
1 clove garlic, crushed
1 teaspoon garam masala
1 teaspoon ground cumin
1 teaspoon ground coriander
1cm piece ginger, chopped
3 large parsnips, chopped
800ml vegetable stock
1 pear, peeled and diced
100ml single cream

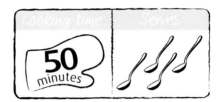

Cooking time: 50 minutes

Serves

- Heat the oil in a saucepan, add the onion and garlic, then cover and cook gently for 10 minutes until soft.
- Add the garam masala, cumin, coriander and ginger, stir well, then cook for 2 minutes.
- Add the parsnips and stock, bring to the boil, then cover and simmer for a further 30 minutes until the vegetables are tender.
- Add the pear, then blend until smooth.
- Reheat gently, adding the cream and stirring well, then serve.

Mushroom & Roasted Chestnut

Fresh for...
December
23rd

Ingredients

750ml vegetable stock
1 stick celery, chopped
1 small onion, diced
1 small carrot, diced
1 bay leaf
3 tablespoons olive oil
400g mixed mushrooms, sliced (we use portabello, girolle, shiitake and chestnut)
150g chestnuts, roasted, shelled and sliced
1 tablespoon soy sauce
1 tablespoon fresh parsley, chopped

Cooking time: 35 minutes
Serves

- Add the stock, celery, onion, carrot and bay leaf to a saucepan, bring to the boil, then cover and simmer for 20 minutes.
- Meanwhile, heat the oil in a frying pan, add the mushrooms, then fry until browned. Add the chestnuts, fry for a few minutes. Set 6 tablespoons of the chestnut and mushroom mix aside for garnishing.
- Add the remaining fried mushrooms and chestnuts to the stock saucepan, then simmer for a further 10 minutes.
- Remove the bay leaf then blend until smooth. Reheat gently, adding the soy sauce.
- Put a spoonful of the set-aside mushrooms and chestnuts in each serving bowl, ladle the soup over the top, sprinkle with parsley, then serve.

Fresh for...
December 24th

White Christmas

White Onion, Stilton & Sherry

Ingredients

2 tablespoons olive oil
1 medium onion, sliced
1 small onion, diced
1 large potato, diced
600ml vegetable stock
1 tablespoon fresh thyme, finely chopped
100g Stilton cheese, diced
2 tablespoons flour
150ml milk
2 tablespoons sweet sherry (or dessert wine)
50ml double cream
1 tablespoon fresh parsley, finely chopped

Cooking time: 45 minutes

Serves: 4

- Heat half the oil in a frying pan, then fry the sliced onion for 10 minutes until soft and translucent. Remove from the pan and set aside.
- Heat the rest of the oil in a saucepan, add the diced onion, then cook for 5–10 minutes, until soft.
- Add the potato, stock and thyme to the saucepan, bring to the boil, then cover and simmer for a further 10–15 minutes until the potatoes are tender.
- Remove from the heat and stir in the Stilton until melted. Blend until completely smooth.
- Mix the flour with a little water and stir to form a paste. Add to the soup, along with the fried sliced onions, milk and sherry.
- Reheat gently for a further 5–10 minutes, stirring frequently.
- Stir in the double cream, season to taste, stir in the parsley and then serve.

Golden Saffron Soup

Fresh for...

December 25th

Ingredients

good pinch of saffron
3 medium onions, finely chopped (reserve the skins and tie together with cook's string)
25g butter
1 tablespoon olive oil
3 medium potatoes, peeled and chopped
1 clove garlic, chopped
650ml chicken stock
150ml single cream
1 tablespoon lemon juice (or to taste)

Cooking time	Serves
45 minutes	4

- Soak the saffron in 50ml boiling water, then set aside.
- Wash the brown onion skins (they will add flavour and colour to the soup).
- Heat the butter and oil in a saucepan, add the onions and onion skins, then cook for 10 minutes.
- Add the potato and garlic, then cook for a further 5–10 minutes so that the onions take on a golden colour.
- Add the stock and soaked saffron, then cover and simmer for 15 minutes until the potatoes are cooked.
- Remove the onion skins and discard, then blend the soup until smooth.
- Reheat gently, stir in the cream, season to taste, add the lemon juice to taste, and then serve.

Fresh for...

December 26th

Christmas Wrapping

Turkey & all the Trimmings

Ingredients

2 tablespoons olive oil
2 small carrots, diced
half a small swede, diced
2 small parsnips, diced
1 small onion, diced
1 tablespoon fresh thyme, chopped
850ml turkey stock
100g turkey meat
1 tablespoon fresh parsley, chopped

Trimmings to garnish:
8 stuffing balls
8 cocktail sausages
8 rolled-up rashers of bacon

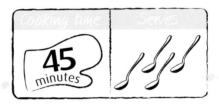

Cooking time: 45 minutes
Serves: 4

- Heat the oil in a saucepan, then cook all the vegetables for 10 minutes, without browning.
- Add the thyme and stock, then cover and simmer for 20 minutes.
- Add the turkey and cook for a further 10 minutes.
- Meanwhile, heat the stuffing balls, sausages and rolled-up bacon rashers until they are piping hot.
- Blend the soup, then reheat gently. Add the parsley and season to taste.
- Pour the soup into bowls, then serve with the trimmings on top.

Leftover Soup

Fresh for... December 27th

Ingredients

8 shallots, whole
2 tablespoons olive oil
2 parsnips, cut into eighths
2 carrots, cut into eighths
1 teaspoon fresh rosemary, finely chopped
25g butter
2 medium potatoes, diced
1 small onion, finely chopped
1 clove garlic, crushed
half a small swede, diced
725ml turkey or chicken stock
1 teaspoon fresh thyme, finely chopped
1 bay leaf
100g brussel sprouts, whole

Cooking time: 50 minutes | Serves: 4

- Preheat the oven to 190°C/375°F/gas mark 5.
- Plunge the shallots into boiling water for 2–3 minutes, then soak in cold water to allow the skins to slip off easily.
- Heat the oil in a roasting pan, add the parsnips, carrots and whole shallots, toss in the oil and sprinkle with the rosemary.
- Roast for 20 minutes until cooked and lightly caramelised.
- Meanwhile heat the butter in a saucepan. Add the potatoes, onion, garlic and swede.
- Cover, then cook gently for 10 minutes, without browning.
- Add the stock, thyme and bay leaf, then cover and simmer for 15 minutes.
- Add the sprouts, then cook for a further 10 minutes, until tender.
- Blend until smooth.
- Return the blended soup to the pan, add the roasted parsnip, carrots and shallots and season to taste. Reheat gently for 5 minutes, then serve.

Fresh for...

December 28th

Turkey & Cranberry

Ingredients

4 tablespoons olive oil
225g each of parsnips, carrots and potatoes, cut into evenly sized pieces
125g shallots, finely chopped
110g fresh cranberries or 150g dried cranberries
1 orange, grated rind and juice of
850ml hot turkey or chicken stock
1 sprig of fresh rosemary
1 sprig of fresh thyme
125g brussel sprouts, trimmed and roughly chopped
leftover turkey meat (approximately 250g)
2 tablespoons fresh flat-leaf parsley, finely chopped

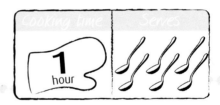

Cooking time: 1 hour

Serves

- Heat the oil in a saucepan, add the parsnips, carrots, potatoes and shallots, then cook gently for 10 minutes, stirring frequently, until evenly browned.
- Separately, cook the cranberries with the orange rind and juice until they burst. If using dried cranberries, soak them in the orange rind and juice for at least 30 minutes.
- Add the hot stock, rosemary and thyme to the root vegetables. Next, add the sprouts and half the cranberries. Cook for a further 10 minutes.
- Remove the sprigs of herbs, then blend until smooth.
- Remove the turkey meat from the bone and shred. Add to the soup with the remaining cranberries and parsley, then season to taste.
- Reheat gently for 5 minutes, then serve.

Maple Roast Parsnip

Fresh for...
December
29th

Ingredients

2 tablespoons olive oil
4 medium parsnips, cut into lengths
2 tablespoons maple syrup
25g butter
1 medium onion, finely chopped
1 clove garlic, crushed
1 tablespoon plain flour
1 litre chicken stock
4 tablespoons double cream

Cooking time: 1:15 hour & minutes
Serves

- Preheat the oven to 190°C/375°F/gas mark 5.
- Place the olive oil in a roasting dish, then heat in the oven for 5–10 minutes.
- Steam the parsnips for 6 minutes or until soft.
- Toss the steamed parsnips into the roasting dish, then bake in the oven for 15 minutes until starting to colour. Add the maple syrup, then roast for a further 10–15 minutes until sticky and caramelised.
- Remove the roasting dish from the oven and allow to cool.
- Meanwhile, melt the butter in a pan, add the onion and garlic, then cook gently for 10 minutes, until soft. Add the flour, then cook for a further minute.
- Add the stock and roasted parsnips, bring to the boil, cover and simmer for 10 minutes.
- Blend until smooth. Stir in the cream, then season to taste.
- Reheat gently for a further 2 minutes, then serve.

Fresh for...
December
30th

Ham & Piccalilli

Ingredients

1 tablespoon olive oil
1 small onion, diced
pinch of Demerara sugar
1 clove garlic, crushed
half a teaspoon ground turmeric
1 heaped teaspoon English mustard
325ml chicken or ham stock
100g cauliflower florets, diced (approx 4 florets)
1 medium potato
2 teaspoons white wine vinegar
1 teaspoon chilli sauce

To garnish:
2 cauliflower florets, diced
1 small onion, diced
1 carrot, diced
half a green pepper, deseeded and diced
half a red pepper, deseeded and diced
50g ham, diced

Cooking time: 55 minutes
Serves

- Heat the olive oil in a saucepan, add the onion, sugar, garlic, turmeric and mustard, then cook gently for 5–10 minutes until the onions are softened.
- Add the stock, cauliflower, potato, white wine vinegar and chilli sauce. Bring to the boil, then simmer for 20 minutes.
- Blend until smooth.
- Place all the vegetables for the garnish in a separate pan, and then bring to the boil and simmer gently for 10 minutes. Drain then add to the blended soup saucepan.
- Add the ham to the saucepan, then season to taste. Simmer for a further 10 minutes, and then serve.

Fresh for...

December 31st

Hot & Sour Chicken

Ingredients

1 litre chicken stock
2–3 red chillies, deseeded and finely sliced
1 stick lemongrass (inner part only), finely sliced
1 clove garlic, finely sliced
2cm piece fresh root ginger, cut into fine strips
1 teaspoon sugar
1 lime, juice of
3 tablespoons fish sauce
150g baby chestnut mushrooms, quartered
2 chicken breasts
4 spring onions, finely sliced
20g fresh coriander, chopped

Cooking time: 25 minutes

Serves

- Heat the stock in a saucepan with the chillies, lemongrass, garlic, ginger, sugar, lime juice and fish sauce and bring to the boil.
- Add the mushrooms and simmer for 3–4 minutes.
- Meanwhile, place the chicken breasts in a sheet of cling film and beat with a rolling pin until thin (like an escalope). Season the chicken before dry-frying it for 3–4 minutes on each side or until cooked through.
- Slice the cooked chicken thinly, then divide it evenly among the serving bowls. Do the same with the spring onions and coriander.
- Pour the soup over the chicken, spring onions and coriander, and then serve.

Chicken Stock

2kg chicken bones, cut into small pieces
6 litres water
3 small carrots, roughly chopped
1 medium onion, roughly chopped
1 large leek, roughly chopped
3 sticks celery, roughly chopped
8 peppercorns, crushed

Cooking time	Makes
8:30 hours & minutes	4–5 litres

- Place the bones in a large saucepan, add the water, then bring to the boil. Simmer for 20 minutes, skimming off any excess fat.
- Add the vegetables and peppercorns, then bring back to the boil. Simmer for 8 hours, skimming any excess fat frequently.
- Sieve the stock into a clean container, then seal until required.
- Discard the vegetables and bones.

Vegetable Stock

4 small carrots, roughly chopped
3 sticks celery, roughly chopped
2 medium leeks, roughly chopped
6 litres water
2 teaspoons peppercorns
1 bay leaf
2 cloves garlic, roughly chopped

Cooking time	Makes
3 hours	4 litres

- Place the vegetables in a large saucepan, cover with the water and bring to the boil. Simmer for 30 minutes.
- Add the peppercorns, bay leaf and garlic cloves, then bring back to the boil. Simmer for 2½ hours, skimming frequently.
- Sieve the stock into a clean container and seal until required.
- Discard the vegetables.

Fish Stock

75g butter
2 medium onions, roughly chopped
6 peppercorns, crushed
25g fresh parsley, roughly chopped
1 lemon, juice of
2kg fish bones (sole, turbot or whiting), washed
5 litres water
1 bay leaf

Cooking time	Makes
45 minutes	5–6 litres

- Melt the butter in a large saucepan, add the onions, peppercorns, parsley and lemon juice, then cook for 15 minutes without browning.
- Add the fish bones and cover and cook for a further 5 minutes; try to avoid browning.
- Add the water and bay leaf, then bring to the boil and simmer for 20 minutes.
- Remove from the heat and skim off any excess fat.
- Sieve the stock into a clean container and seal until required.
- Discard the vegetables and bones.

Ham Stock

1 medium ham hock or joint (900g)
5 litres water
1 onion, roughly chopped
2 carrots, roughly chopped
2 sticks celery, roughly chopped
12 peppercorns
1 bay leaf

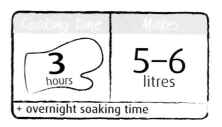

Cooking time	Makes
3 hours	5–6 litres
+ overnight soaking time	

- Place the ham in a large saucepan, cover with cold water, then soak overnight to remove any excess salt.
- Discard the soaking water. Pour 5 litres of water into the pan and bring to the boil, skimming off any excess fat.
- Add the vegetables, peppercorns and bay leaf, then simmer gently for 2½ to 3 hours until the ham is cooked through.
- Sieve the stock into a clean container, then seal until required.
- Discard the vegetables and reserve the ham for sandwiches.

Beef Stock

1kg beef bones, chopped into small pieces
500g veal bones (you can substitute the veal bones with beef bones, simply add the quantities together)
6 litres water
2 tablespoons olive oil
3 small carrots, roughly chopped
1 medium onion, roughly chopped
1 large leek, roughly chopped
3 sticks celery, roughly chopped
150g tomatoes, roughly chopped
8 peppercorns, crushed

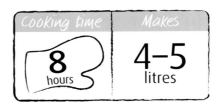

Cooking time	Makes
8 hours	4–5 litres

- Preheat the oven to 200°C/400°F/gas mark 6.
- Remove any excess fat from the bones and place the bones in a roasting tin. Cook in the oven for 50 minutes. Drain off any fat and transfer the bones to a large saucepan.
- Cover with the water, bring to the boil, then simmer for 20 minutes, skimming well to remove any excess fat.
- Meanwhile, heat the olive oil in another saucepan, then add the carrots, onion, leek and celery. Cook for 10 minutes until browned, but not burnt. Add to the pan containing the bones and water.
- Add the tomatoes and peppercorns to the bones and vegetables, bring to the boil and simmer for 6 hours, skimming frequently.
- Sieve the stock into a clean container and seal until required. Discard the vegetables and bones.